STUDIES IN PAUL

Theology for the Early Christian Mission

NILS ALSTRUP DAHL
Assisted by Paul Donahue

AUGSBURG PUBLISHING HOUSE
MINNEAPOLIS, MINNESOTA

STUDIES IN PAUL

Manufactured in the United States of America

CONTENTS

ACKNOWLEDGEMENTS

These essays appeared originally in the following
publications:

PAUL: A SKETCH in *Vestens Tenkere*, ed. by E. Skard and
A. H. Winsnes, Oslo: Aschehoug, 1962, I.

PAUL AND POSSESSIONS in *Kirke og Kultur* 52 (1947).

PAUL AND THE CHURCH AT CORINTH in *Christian History and Interpretation*,
ed. by W. Farmer et al. Cambridge University Press, 1967.

THE MISSIONARY THEOLOGY IN THE EPISTLE TO THE ROMANS in *Norsk
Tidsskrift for Misjon* 10 (1956)

THE DOCTRINE OF JUSTIFICATION in *Norsk teologisk tidsskrift*
65 (1964).

PROMISE AND FULFILLMENT and THE FUTURE OF ISRAEL in *Israel,
Kirken og verden*, ed. by M. Saebo. Oslo: Land og Kirke
(Gyldendal) 1972.

CONTRADICTIONS IN SCRIPTURE in *Svensk teologisk kvartalskrift*
45 (1969).

ABBREVIATIONS

BFCT	Beiträge zur Förderung christlicher Theologie
BHT	Beiträge zur historischen Theologie
CBQ	*Catholic Biblical Quarterly*
CTM	*Concordia Theological Monthly*
DTT	*Dansk teologisk tidsskrift*
FRLANT	Forschungen zur Religion und Literatur des Alten und Neuen Testaments
HNT	Handbuch zum Neuen Testament
HTR	*Harvard Theological Review*
IDBSup	Supplementary volume to *IDB*
JAC	Jahrbuch für Antike und Christentum
JBL	*Journal of Biblical Literature*
Judaica	*Judaica: Beiträge zum Verständnis...*
KD	*Kerygma und Dogma*
KJV	*King James Version*
MGWJ	*Monatsschrift für Geschichte und Wissenschaft des Judentums*
MNTC	Moffatt NT Commentary
NEB	*New English Bible*
NorTT	*Norsk Teologisk Tidsskrift*
NovT	*Novum Testamentum*
NTS	*New Testament Studies*
RB	*Revue biblique*
RevQ	*Revue de Qumran*
RSV	*Revised Standard Version*
SBLDS	SBL Dissertation Series
SBLSBS	SBL Sources for Biblical Study
SBT	Studies in Biblical Theology
SD	Studies and Documents
SNTSMS	Society for New Testament Studies Monograph Series

SO	Symbolae osloenses
SPB	Studia postbiblica
ST	*Studia theologica*
STK	*Svensk teologisk kvartalskrift*
TDNT	G. Kittel and G. Friedrich (eds.), *Theological Dictionary of the New Testament*
TLZ	*Theologische Literaturzeitung*
TSK	*Theologische Studien und Kritiken*
UUÅ	Uppsala universitetsårsskrift
WMANT	**Wissenschaftliche Monographien zum Alten und Neuen Testament**
ZNW	*Zeitschrift für die neutestamentliche Wissenschaft*
ZTK	*Zeitschrift für Theologie und Kirche*

GENERAL BIBLIOGRAPHY

This bibliography includes works for which the footnotes will list only author and page number (except in those cases where the author has more than one book on this list). The bibliography also includes some general works on Paul, which are recommended to the attention of students, even though I have not frequently referred to them.

Bjerkelund, C., PARAKALŌ: *Form, Function und Sinn der parakalō-Sätze in den paulinischen Briefen*. Oslo: University Press, 1967.

Bornkamm, G., *Paul*, tr. D. M. G. Stalker. New York: Harper & Row, 1971.

Bultmann, R., *The Theology of the New Testament*, Vol. I-II. tr. K. Grobel. New York: Scribner, 1951-55.

Dahl, N. A., *The Crucified Messiah and other Essays*. Minneapolis: Augsburg, 1974.

---- , *Jesus in the Memory of the Early Church*. Minneapolis: Augsburg, 1976.

Davies, W. D., *Paul and Rabbinic Judaism*. London: SPCK (1948), 2nd.ed. 1958.

Farmer, W. R. *et al.*, ed., *Christian History and Interpretation: Studies presented to John Knox*. Cambridge University Press, 1967.

Fridrichsen, Anton, *The Apostle and his Message*. Uppsala: Almqvist and Wicksell, 1947. (Also in *UUÅ*, 1947, 3).

Hurd, J. C., *The Origin of I Corinthians*. New York: Seabury, 1965.

Käsemann, E., *New Testament Questions of Today*. Philadelphia: Fortress, 1969.

---- , *Perspectives on Paul*, tr. M. Kohl, Philadelphia: Fortress, 1971.

---- , *An die Römer* (HNT 8a), Tübingen: Mohr, 1973. (2.ed. 1974).

Knox, W. L., *St. Paul and the Church of the Gentiles*. Cambridge University Press, 1939.

Kümmel, W. G., *Introduction to the New Testament*. Rev. ed., tr. H. C. Kee, Nashville (New York, London): Abingdon, 1975.

Malherbe, A. J., *Social Aspects of Early Christianity*. Baton Rouge/ London: Louisiana State University Press, 1977.

Meeks, W. A., *The Writings of St. Paul*. New York: Norton, 1972.

Munck, J., *Paul and the Salvation of Mankind*. tr. F. Clarke, Richmond: John Knox Press, 1959.

Munck, J., *Christ and Israel*. tr. J. Nixon. Philadelphia:
        Fortress, 1967.

Ridderbos, H. N., *Paul, An Outline of His Theology*. tr. S. R. DeWitt.
        Grand Rapids, Mich.: Eerdmans, 1975.

Rigaux, B., *The Letters of St. Paul: Modern Studies*. tr. S. Yonick.
        Chicago: Franciscan Herald Press, 1968.

Roetzel, C. J., *The Letters of Paul*. Atlanta: John Knox, 1975.

Sanders, E. P., *Paul and Palestinian Judaism*. Philadelphia:
        Fortress, 1977.

Schoeps, H. J., *Paul: The Theology of the Apostle in the Light
        of Jewish Religious History*. tr. H. Knight. Philadelphia:
        Westminster, 1961.

Schubert, P., *The Form and Function of the Pauline Thanksgivings*.
        Berlin: Töpelmann, 1939.

Schweitzer, A., *Paul and His Interpreters*. tr. W. Montgomery,
        New York: Macmillan, 1951 (Ger.ed. 1911).

---- , *The Mysticism of Paul the Apostle*. tr. W. Montgomery,
        New York: Macmillan, 1955 (Ger.ed. 1930).

Stendahl, K., *Paul Among Jews and Gentiles*. Philadelphia: Fortress,
        1976.

PREFACE

The studies collected in this volume were originally
prepared for various occasions, but they are all byproducts of
regular courses on Pauline exegesis and theology which I have
taught at Oslo and at Yale. The earliest study is a semester-
opening lecture from 1947 (Chapter II). The latest was intended
for the festschrift presented to Ernst Käsemann on occasion of
his 70th birthday in 1976 (Chapter X). Some studies deal with
favorite topics of my own (Chapters V and VI). In other cases,
I was asked to write or to speak on a given theme (Chapters I
and VII-VIII). The volume includes more or less experimental
contributions to scholarly debate (Chapters III and IV) and the
preliminary results of a research project that may never be
brought to full completion (Chapter IX).

Due to the prehistory of the volume, the choice of topics
is somewhat arbitrary. The attentive reader will detect that
over the years I have gained new insights and even changed my
opinion on some points. As the subtitle, "Theology for the Early
Christian Mission," indicates, the volume represents a fairly
unified perspective on Paul. In preparing the studies for
publication, I found that diversity caused fewer problems than
repetition. Both the diversity and the repetition are representative
of my study of Paul. Never fully satisfied with the standard works,
or with what I have myself said on some earlier occasion, I have
again and again had to read and reread the text of his letters,
approaching them from various angles, with new and old questions
in mind. I assume that I will continue to do so, and hope that
my studies will induce the readers to do the same.

By and large, I have left the original substance and form
of the studies unaltered. I have, however, rewritten Chapter V,
"The Missionary Theology in the Epistle to the Romans." I have
also added appendixes to Chapters II and V and footnotes to
Chapters I, II and IV. In the other chapters, I have only

occasionally made some deletions or additions, mostly in the footnotes. The English translation is, at some points, an improvement, clarifying or modifying the original.

Only Chapter III has earlier been available in English. Chapters IV and X are here published for the first time. All the other chapters have been published in Norwegian; Chapter IX also in a German translation. Professor Terry Callan has translated that chapter from the German version, but his translation has been checked against the Norwegian original. For the chapters which have been translated directly from Norwegian, my wife prepared a first draft which has been thoroughly revised by Professor Paul Donahue. Only their devoted work has made the appearance of this volume possible. Paul Donahue has also volunteered to work as my assistant at every stage of the preparation of the whole manuscript. He has, in fact, acted as a co-editor of the whole volume. Jouette Bassler and Ben Fiore, both graduate students at Yale, have also rendered valuable help. I am very grateful to all these fellow workers.

My gratitude extends to a much wider circle of persons, who have invited me to give lectures or to write an article on Paul, or who have stimulated my thoughts by their own studies and by their reactions to mine. I would like to mention the members of the Commission on Theology of the Lutheran World Federation, who discussed the doctrine of justification in the period 1958-63, and the members of the Society of Biblical Literature Seminar on Paul who in 1970-75 dealt with the form and function of Paul's letters. Earlier versions of Chapters VII and IX were parts of the Nils W. Lund Memorial Lectures which I had the honor to give in 1968, at North Park Theological Seminary. I am indebted to scholars who have differed sharply among themselves, such as Rudolf Bultmann, Anton Fridrichsen, Johannes Munck and Paul Schubert in the past and Ernst Käsemann and Krister Stendahl in the present generation.

The scholarly dialog continues. I have profited greatly from communication with my own students, to whose contributions I have often drawn attention in the footnotes, which otherwise only refer to a somewhat arbitrary selection of current literature. Finally, I recall with gratitude the response of audiences who have listened to my lectures on Paul - colleagues, students, pastors, and others. It is my hope that this book might be of interest to an equally wide audience.

Nils A. Dahl
The Divinity School
Yale University

CHAPTER I

Paul: A Sketch

During his travels as an apostle of Jesus Christ, Paul
arrived in Athens, a city which remained a center for Greek
culture and philosophy despite its decline in political significance. Luke describes Paul's debate with Epicurean and Stoic
philosophers living in Athens in Acts 17. These Athenian
philosophers appear to have thought at first that Paul was simply
one of the many sophists and rhetors who wandered from city to
city preaching popular moral philosophy, or perhaps the cult of
some Eastern deity. But Paul resisted easy classification; the
novelty of his message appealed to the philosophers' curiosity.
Despite their interest, these Athenian philosophers did not accept
Paul as a colleague or consider him their equal.

Though he might occasionally allude to popular Greek
philosophy or quote a Greek poet, Paul was not a philosopher,
not even in the sense in which Philo, the famous Alexandrian Jew
who lived at the beginning of the first century, was a philosopher.
Philo tried to prove that the Law of Moses embodied true philosophy.
Paul deliberately rejected philosophical argumentation and
rhetorical polish as vehicles of his message. His sole intention
was to proclaim "the word of the cross," the folly of God which
put the wisdom of men to shame.[1] Paul did not attempt to solve

---

The Norwegian version of this survey article appeared in
a collection of essays on "Thinkers of the West," from Socrates and
Plato to Wittgenstein, Heidegger, Sartre and others. I have added
chapter and verse references and some footnotes to the English
translation, without changing the non-technical form of presentation.
For some important works on Paul, see the General Bibliography.

[1]See 1 Cor. 2:1-5. Paul's own words and my paraphrase
need some qualification. Paul's message does set him apart from

1

the problems of existence by careful reflection on the meaning
of data gathered by prior observation and investigation. Paul is
an apostle; he is the representative of the one who sent him. He
proclaims the message entrusted to him. For this reason, Paul
does not recognize the validity of a judgment based on his
personal performance as a speaker or as a thinker. He demands
that those who hear him acknowledge the legitimacy of his commission
and his faithfulness in carrying it out.

Does Paul warrant a place in the history of Western thought?
Does he belong among the philosophers? Historians have to answer
these legitimate questions with a resounding yes. They must
recognize the significant impact of Paul's thought on the development of Western culture. Paul was the first to use formal logic
to attempt to make clear the implications of faith in Jesus Christ.
He is not only a religious hero, not only a missionary and church
leader, but also a "thinker," the first Christian thinker whose
writings have survived. Paul was not like some modern missionaries
who both preach the word and carry on some quite separate scholarly
pursuit like linguistics or anthropology. Paul's life as an
apostle and his thought were integrally related to each other.
His thought determined his daily activity, and the problems he
encountered in his daily activity as a missionary provided the
material for his reflection.

The Life

Paul came to Greece in 50 or 51. We can date his arrival
as closely as that because we know that Paul lived in Corinth when
Gallio was Roman proconsul of Achaia (Acts 18). With this date
as a point of departure, we can use other information (e.g., Gal.
1) to construct a Pauline chronology. Paul's conversion must have
occurred early in the thirties, only a couple of years after
Christ's death. At this time Paul was still a young man; we have
nothing which would enable us to determine his age more exactly.
Paul was a native of Tarsus in Cilicia, one of the many free

---

the tradition of ancient philosophy and rhetoric. Yet, if rhetoric
is properly understood as the art of persuasion, Paul was himself
a skillful rhetorician, at least when he wrote his letters (cf.
2 Cor. 10:10). In fact, depreciation of empty rhetoric and
sophistry was itself part of philosophical and rhetorical tradition.
See e.g. H. D. Betz, *Der Apostel Paulus und die Sokratische Tradition*
(Tübingen: Mohr, 1972). On the level of Paul's literary and
rhetorical culture, see also Malherbe, 29-59.

Hellenistic cities which, in the centuries after Alexander, disseminated Greek culture in Asia. Since he was both a Jew and a Roman citizen, the cities of Jerusalem and Rome jointly enjoyed a special significance for him. Paul came from a family of Pharisees, of the tribe of Benjamin. He was named for the tribe's most illustrious member, Saul, King of Israel. As was the case with many Hellenistic Jews, the boy also had a Graeco-Roman name, the Latin Paulus. We can speculate that one of Paul's ancestors was taken prisoner of war when Pompey conquered Palestine in 63 B.C., that he was sold as a slave, and was eventually emancipated by a Roman citizen belonging to the Roman *gens* Paulus. Such a history would explain both Paul's Latin name and his Roman citizenship.[2]

We do not know how much Paul learned of Greek culture during his childhood in Tarsus. His letters show a certain familiarity with the terminology and rhetorical style current in contemporary popular philosophy. Paul was completely comfortable with the Greek language without feeling the constraint of the formal rules of literary style. Acts 22 says that as a young man Paul went to Jerusalem to study and there he became a disciple of the most famous rabbi of the period, Gamaliel.[3] As was customary, he also learned a trade, tentmaking. Later in life, the apostle boasts that he supports himself by working with his hands. His educational career suggests that Paul's family was economically secure.[4]

Although Jerusalem was unique among the cities of the Graeco-Roman world, it was very much a part of that world. A Roman military administration governed Palestine, which by then had felt for centuries the impact of Hellenistic culture. Many Palestinian cities adopted Greek constitutions and the Greek language. Even in Jerusalem, the architecture of public buildings differed from that of the rest of the Graeco-Roman world only in

---

[2]Jerome reports that Paul's forebears were from the town of Gischala in northern Galilee but either migrated, or were deported, to Tarsus when a Roman army invaded and plundered the province, and that Paul went with them (*On Illustrious Men*, 5; *Commentary on Philemon*, v. 23). That is probably no more than a conjecture.

[3]W.C. van Unnik has convincingly argued that the word *anatethrammenos* ("brought up") in Acts 22:3 implies that Paul came to Jerusalem as a boy. See his article "Tarsus and Jerusalem" (1962, reprinted in *Sparsa Collecta*, I, Leiden: Brill, 1973, 259-320). But the reliability of the biographical data in Acts remains disputed. In any case, Paul usually uses the Greek Bible (Septuagint), but his letters demonstrate that he had some training in rabbinical methods of studying the Scriptures. See Chapter IX, "Contradictions in Scripture," pp. 159-177.

[4]See Chapter II, "Paul and Possessions," pp. 35-36.

the absence of sculpture. The Jews who lived throughout the
Roman world were frequent pilgrims to Jerusalem, and were themselves a source of continuing Greek influence. Some Greek-
speaking Jews settled in Jerusalem and organized their own
synagogues in which to worship.

In the rabbinic schools, there was no time for the study
of Greek literature. The Law, rabbinic traditions and their
interpretation required all the student's time. Secular scholarship was the domain of others not called to the higher state of
study of the Law, among them distinguished women. But even the
scribal education which Paul received had itself taken shape
both under the influence of and in reaction against the dominant
Hellenistic culture, just as in our own time the national,
cultural and religious renewal in the third world presupposes
the profound impact of Western civilization.

Although many efforts have been made to distinguish the
Greek from the Jewish component of Paul's though, the task is
hopeless: no real separation is possible. Even in the world
of the young disciple of Gamaliel, the rabbinic academy at
Jerusalem, Jewish and Greek elements were inextricably commingled.
The dominating factor, however, which supplied the young Paul
with a sense of direction, was Jewish in origin: his zeal for
the Law. His service to the Law exceeded, at least in his own
estimation, that of his pious contemporaries: even years later
he could describe his conduct while a Jew as "blameless."[5]

Paul's zeal for the Law led him to take an active role
in persecuting those who confessed their faith in the crucified
Messiah, Jesus of Nazareth. Paul is likely to have believed
that if Israel repented and obeyed the Law, then God would
intervene on her behalf; he did not subscribe to the view that
armed revolt would bring Israel's vindication. As a Pharisee,
Paul found that the followers of the Nazarene weakened observance
of the Law and diminished Israel's hope of entering the age to
come. For the disciple of Gamaliel as for the apostle of Jesus
Christ, there was an irreconcilable tension between the Mosaic
Law and the crucified Messiah as ways to salvation.

When Paul set out for Damascus, he was not tortured by a
troubled conscience, as the young monk Luther was. Rather, his
enthusiasm remained undimmed. When Christ appeared to him, Paul
had not wearied of the attempt to fulfill the Law perfectly. His
view of the relation of the Mosaic Law to the crucified Messiah

---

[5]Phil. 3:6. See e.g. Stendahl, 80.

did not change when Christ called him to become his ambassador
to the Gentiles; Paul simply abandoned one side of the fray to
enter the lists on the other. He never doubted that God himself
had intervened in his life to reveal his Son to him: that
fundamental presupposition underlies all of his subsequent life
and thought. That event completely transformed Paul's values;
the observance of the Law which he had once esteemed so highly
he reckoned a complete loss, nothing more than refuse in
comparison to his life's new direction: "To know Christ Jesus,
my lord" (Phil. 3:4-11). Paul began to preach the faith he
had formerly sought to exterminate.

We know little about Paul's first years as a Christian.
After his baptism, he spent several years in Arabia, by which
we should probably understand the Nabataean kingdom south of
Damascus. Later he paid a short visit to Jerusalem, where he
met Peter. After a trip to his native Tarsus, he came to Antioch
in Syria, a city which had become an important center for Greek-
speaking Christians, non-Jews as well as Jews. From what we
know about Paul, we may speculate that he worked as a missionary
even during this first period. But his wide-ranging missionary
journeys, carried out systematically, according to plan, began
only after his stay in Antioch. At first Barnabas, who must have
played an important role as a mediator between Antioch's Greek-
speaking Christians and those in Jerusalem, and between Paul
and the Jerusalem apostles, accompanied Paul on his missionary
journeys.

Several years later, Paul went to Jerusalem once again
with Barnabas. There the Jerusalem church and its leaders
recognized the right of non-Jews to enjoy Christian fellowship
without circumcision and without keeping the Law of Moses.
Further, the agreement gave Paul the freedom to carry out his
special mission to the Gentiles. The years which followed the
Jerusalem Council (ca. 48-57) constitute the climactic period
of Paul's apostolate. Long and difficult journeys took Paul
around the Eastern littoral of the Mediterranean, into the inner
recesses of Asia Minor, to Macedonia and to Achaia. At Corinth,
the capital of Achaia, and at Ephesus, the capital of Roman Asia,
he stayed for long periods of time. During this period Paul
wrote letters to the Christian congregations in Thessalonica,
Galatia, Corinth and Rome, possibly also to Philippi.

At the end of this period the apostle wrote: "But now,
since I no longer have any room for work in these regions, . . ."
(Rom. 15:23). This sounds strange to us, knowing as we do how

incomplete the Christianization of the Eastern Mediterranean was.
Paul wanted to preach Christ where no one had heard of him. When
Paul--and others--had founded congregations in the central cities
of the Eastern Mediterranean, Paul thought his work was complete:
these central cities would represent the provinces, receiving
Christ when, as Paul hoped, he would soon come again. Paul
looked beyond the Greek to the Latin world: toward Rome, and
then onward to Spain. For a time, problems in several congregations and the collection for the Jerusalem church delayed him.
The collection was of great importance to Paul because he had
agreed with the Jerusalem apostles to complete it, and because
it symbolized for him the unity of Jew and Gentile within the
church. If the Gentiles gave willingly, and if the Jerusalem
church received their gift with gratitude, it would be a meaningful expression of mutual solidarity. Paul was vitally concerned
that the Jerusalem church acknowledge his congregations by
accepting the gift; therefore he himself went to Jerusalem to
deliver it, aware as he was of the potential dangers (Rom. 15:
26-32).

   During his work as a missionary, Paul's life had several
times been in danger; he had been arrested and punished more
than once. In Jerusalem, Paul was arrested and imprisoned; for
two years, he was a prisoner in Caesarea, the coastal capital
of Roman Palestine; then he went on to Rome, where his imprisonment continued for two years more. At this point, Acts concludes
its story of Paul. That Paul finally had his opportunity to
preach the Gospel in the capital of the Empire is more important
to the author of Acts than Paul's personal fate. Paul was
executed in Rome during the reign of the Emperor Nero. According
to Roman tradition, he was buried outside the city walls, where
a famous basilica which bears his name stands today. But just
as we are unsure of the date of his birth, so too the exact date
of his death remains unknown.

Letters

   Acts relates many episodes in Paul's life, although its
account is both incomplete and at some points inexact. In his
letters, Paul himself comes to life. His letters enable us to
know more about Paul than about all but a very few other figures
from antiquity. The form of Paul's letters is distinctly personal,
differing both from common, casual correspondence and from polished,

literary work. The style is richly varied, sometimes more like
ordinary letters, with greetings, compliments, information and
requests, and sometimes more like a sermon. The letters were in
fact written to be read aloud in the congregation. Paul writes
sometimes in the vivid, persuasive style used by popular Greek
philosophers, appealing to an imaginary conversation partner;
in other places, like a true rabbi, he uses quotations from
Scripture to prove his point. On occasion Paul's thoughts tumble
out with such intensity that they destroy the sentence structure,
but the prose can also rise to nearly poetic, hymnic heights.
Although we can detect certain fixed patterns which underlie his
letters, Paul varies the structure according to the situation.
We find sustained development of thematic sentences juxtaposed
with digressions; sometimes an idea is mentioned and then
abandoned, only to be taken up again at a later point.[6]

For Paul, the letter form was not simply a literary or
didactic device. His letters always address particular situations.
He feels a pastoral responsibility toward the congregations which
he has left behind when he has moved to a new mission territory,
as 1 Thessalonians shows. In Galatians, Paul sternly exhorts
the inexperienced Gentile Christians not to adopt the Jewish
rite of circumcision or other Jewish ceremonies. In 1 Corinthians,
Paul rebukes the congregation for failings which have been reported
to him orally, and answers questions which the congregation put
to him in writing. Paul thanks the Philippians for a financial
contribution to his work. Sections of Romans resemble a theological
treatise presenting Paul's version of true Christian faith, but
even this letter has a specific purpose: to prepare for his visit
to Rome. It is important to Paul that the Roman church support
his work in the West, and also that it pray that the Jerusalem
church accept the collection which Paul is about to deliver.

In some respects, the Pauline letters have an official
character. They represent a speech rather than a private conversation. The sender is not a private person, but an earthly
ambassador of the heavenly Lord, the Risen Christ. However, Paul
avoids when possible the use of his apostolic authority to enforce
a solution. He does not write to his congregation like an
oriental despot to his subjects; rather, the style recalls the
manner Hellenistic kings adopted when writing to a free city,
whose autonomy they acknowledged.[7] The congregations themselves

---

[6]See also Chapter V, "The Missionary Theology in the Letter
to the Romans."
[7]See Bjerkelund, 59-74.

enjoy a direct relationship with Christ; Paul therefore respects
their freedom and independence, which they have in Christ. As
a result, Paul's letters begin by acknowledging the bond of
faith and love which ties him to his congregations. He reminds
them of his own role, how he worked for their good, how he
continues to pray for them and to suffer on their behalf. Paul
works to establish a foundation for his request that his congregations live in a manner appropriate to the privileges which
they have received and that they amend their shortcomings. Only
voluntary, comprehending obedience is the obedience of genuine
faith. Consequently, Paul constantly appeals to the personal
judgment of his readers; for him, reflection is a constituent
element of the life in faith.

In his letters, Paul discusses a wide range of issues.
He solves particular problems by relating them to the broad
scope of what is essential in Christianity. If he exhorts his
readers to think more about others and less about themselves,
he may adduce as an example a hymn about Christ, who renounced
his divine glory for the sake of men (Phil. 2). While discussing
prophecy, speaking in tongues and other spiritual gifts, he stops
suddenly to eulogize love in one of the New Testament's most
eloquent passages, 1 Cor. 13. We observe frequently the transition
from the recipient's concrete situation to God's act in Christ
and to the universal scope of the gospel, with a subsequent return
to the original problem, now viewed in a transformed light.

Because Paul seeks to convince his readers, to deepen
their understanding rather than simply to compel their obedience,
he accepts the premises of those to whom he writes. When Paul
writes to the Christians at Rome, he makes clear his respect for
their standing in the faith and for their autonomy; he introduces
himself as a preacher of the common gospel, in order to continue
with his attempt to prove that this common gospel implies the
doctrine of justification by faith. When he writes to the
Corinthians, he accepts their slogan, "All things are lawful to
me," but he modifies and corrects this slogan by introducing the
need to consider the position of the weak brother, by emphasizing
that love requires that a Christian do nothing that might make
his brother stumble. In 1 Corinthians Paul also appears to
endorse the view that "it is well for a man not to touch a woman."
Yet Paul's motivation for this endorsement is very different from
that which prompted Corinthian ascetics to make that statement.
Paul makes clear that the advantage of celibacy is that it makes
possible an individual's complete devotion to Christ; he does

not share the Corinthian ascetics' contempt for the body and
for sexual love (1. Cor. 7-8).

On some occasions, Paul feels obliged to speak a plain,
emphatic "No!", as when he forbids the Galatians to undergo
circumcision (Gal. esp. 5:2ff.). But when possible, he attempts
to accomodate his readers' presuppositions and experience. The
same attitude characterized his missionary work as a whole;
Paul made himself the servant of all, a Jew to the Jews, a Gentile
to the Gentiles, a weak man to the weak: "I have become all
things to all men, that I might by all means save some" (1 Cor.
9:22). He will not let unessential forms become an obstacle
to his work; he refuses to compromise his loyalty to Christ.
We can understand how Paul's opponents could interpret his
flexibility as vacillation and inconsistency. To respond to such
accusations, Paul points to God's unfailing word and to his
covenant in Christ; Paul, in all that he does, simply acts as
the servant of his Risen Lord (see, e.g., 2 Cor. 1:15-22).

Paul varies expression and argumentation to suit both
his recipients and the particular situation which he confronts.
He never confines himself to purely theological speculation, but
always includes pastoral guidance and exhortation. It was by
design and not by accident that Paul wrote letters and not
theological or philosophical treatises. To recognize the variety
of his pastoral concerns should not obscure this thought's inner
unity, a unity which flows not from a thoroughgoing doctrinal
system, but from the centrality in Paul's thought of faith in
Jesus Christ.

Christ and the Law

Some regard Paul as the second founder of Christianity,
as the one who transformed the simple faith of Jesus into the
dogmatic religion of the institutional church. Among other
errors, this view widely exaggerates Paul's historical significance.
Between Jesus and Paul lies not only the preaching of the first
apostles, both prior to and independent of Paul, but also the
beginnings of Hellenistic Christianity and its establishment,
e.g., in the cities of Damascus, Antioch and Rome. It was at
Damascus that Paul became convinced of the truth of the faith
that he had formerly tried to eradicate; he spent the rest of
his life among Greek-speaking congregations. Paul's Christological
statements in kerygmatic summaries, confessions and hymns are not

innovative. That also applies to the sacraments: Paul depends on
previously existing traditions and uses language which has already
become standard. Some passages in the Pauline letters clearly
reflect currently existing hymnic, liturgical and catechetical
texts; in some cases, we may have more or less verbatim quotations.[8]

Paul did not give belief in Christ any new content, but
he did think through its meaning and consequences in a more
radical way than others. Paul used material of widely different
origin to construct and to elaborate his thought. One scholar
has said that in order to gather the comparative material to
illustrate one of Paul's sentences one must make a round trip
through the thought world of antiquity.[9] Still, most important
for the former Pharisee was to relate the new which had come
with Christ to the old which was revealed in Israel's Holy
Scriptures: the belief in the one God who had created the world,
who had spoken through the prophets, who had acted in history,
who had promised to send the Messiah to redeem Israel, and who
is going to raise the dead and mete out to each person the just
consequence of his deeds. Paul's thought not only has a single
center, Jesus Christ, but a definite framework, the saving
history depicted in the Old Testament and in later Jewish
eschatological literature.

The "new" which had come with Jesus was not a new religion
but rather a new creation. Christ is the new Adam, who came in
the fullness of time, and who died for our sins, "to deliver us
from this present evil age" (Gal. 1:4). This was God's great
deed of love, the fulfillment of his promises. When he raised
Jesus from the dead, God acted as Creator; similarly, God's
creative power is constantly at work among believers. For Paul,
Jesus' resurrection was not an isolated event, but the inaugur-
ation of the general resurrection which will take place at the
end of the world. Those who have been baptized into Christ have,
Paul says, already died with Christ and been buried with him, in
order that they might share his resurrection life. He maintains

---

[8]See e.g. Bultmann, I, 133-152; A. M. Hunter, *Paul and
His Predecessors* (London: SCM, 1961, 24-44, 65-78); E. Krentz,
"The Early Dark Ages of the Church," *CTM* 41 (1970), 68-85.

[9]The scholar is Vilhelm Grönbech, the Danish historian
of religion, whose early works made a great impact on Johannes
Pedersen, Sigmund Mowinckel, and Scandinavian biblical scholarship
in general. His book, *Paulus, Jesu Christi Apostel* (Copenhagen,
1940) is, in some respects, a splendid caricature but, unfortunately, not available to me at the moment.

that in the gospel the righteousness of God reveals itself as
the power of salvation to all who believe. By "righteousness
of God" Paul does not mean some passive attribute of deity,
but the character of God's acting toward men, when, as Judge,
he intervenes to vindicate himself and to bring salvation. Those
who believe are already justified, they have been acquitted by
the divine court, though they were once guilty. God's Holy
Spirit, whose power the congregation experiences in its religious
life, guarantees the coming glory which Christians will receive.

A pervading feature of Paul's letters is the tension
between "now" and "not yet." Believers are already acquitted,
but they must still submit to the final judgment. They have
received a share in Jesus' resurrection life, but they still
live in the mortal body. They are in Christ, but also in the
world, exposed to its anxieties and temptations. Christians
must struggle constantly, and always face the possibility of
failure. The present is for Paul nothing more than an interlude
between the saving work of Jesus' life, death and resurrection,
and the cosmic drama which unfolds when he comes again in glory.
The Christian lives at the same time in two ages; he lives both
in the old aeon of sin and death, and in the new aeon, which
has arrived with Christ, of righteousness and life. Paul shares
the Old Testament view of time as consisting of epochs with
special content rather than as being an undifferentiated linear
progression.[10]

The new order which had come with Christ was quite
different from the Messianic age to which Paul had looked forward.
The Messianic congregation, the saints, the chosen ones, by no
means enjoyed a preeminent position in the world. On the contrary,
in addition to the problems common to all people, they had also
to confront persecution and suffering for the sake of their faith.
To some extent, Paul can deal with this problem by using traditional Jewish reflection on the sufferings of the just: they are
the means God uses to discipline the faithful in this life so
that their reward in the next will be all the more glorious. But
for Paul, another factor is decisive: the situation of the

---

[10]It is too simplistic to contrast a biblical concept of
linear time with a Greek concept of cyclic time. One should,
however, not forget that Paul does not himself speak of the "two
aeons" in the way which has become customary among his interpreters
after Albert Schweitzer's epoch-making works on Paul. The terminology of the two ages is simply an auxillary construction which
can help the modern reader to become aware of the apocalyptic
context of Paul's theology.

Christian corresponds to that of Christ himself, who lacked every
aspect of worldly glory, who was in the end condemned as a
criminal and executed. The believers' sufferings unite them
with Christ; when they share his sufferings they also participate in his hidden glory. For Paul, the sufferings which he has
himself endured are a proof of the legitimacy of his apostolate.

Paul's greatest theological problem was the relationship
between Christ and the Law. When Paul accepted the gospel about
Christ as true, when he came to believe that through this gospel
God forgave sinners and judged the ungodly righteous, then he
had to reject the Law as providing the proper rules for the
relation of man to God. At the same time, Paul did not question
the identity of the God who saved men through Christ with the
God who had given the Law through Moses. Paul found the solution
to his problem in the figure of Abraham, who had received a
promise from God and who had trusted that God would keep his
promise (Gal. 3, Rom. 4). Somewhat simplified, the juridical-
theological reasoning runs as follows: the Law cannot be a
permanent condition added after the fact to the original promise,
for then it would make the promise void. The Law was therefore
a temporary measure of limited validity. The Law was binding
only until the coming of Christ, which fulfilled God's promise
to Abraham. While he lived, Jesus himself obeyed the Law; his
death marks its limits. The Risen Lord is no longer bound by
the constraints of the Law, nor are those who are "in him"
through baptism into his death. This new situation legitimizes
Christian freedom from the Law.[11]

Paul also provides an explanation for God's purpose in
establishing the Law as a temporary measure: without law, there
can be neither crime nor punishment. The Law served to inhibit
the proliferation of human sinfulness, but at the same time it
transformed sin into transgression: when men sinned, they now
violated the specific commands of a written code, and deserved
punishment. That was exactly God's intention when he gave the
Law. Not until man stood before God as a justly condemned trans-
gressor could God display the full extent of his grace by granting
completely unmerited pardon. Paul concludes that the Law's
specific requirements were intended for the old aeon, and thus
had only a limited validity for those who lived in the new aeon
as well as in the old. The Law's eternally valid content is God's
good and holy will. Paul does not denigrate the Law when he points
out that its imperatives "You shall . . . You shall not" were

_____

[11]See Chapter IX, "Contradictions in Scripture."

unable to effect the results which they commanded (Rom. 7). The
fault lies within man: God's righteous commands and prohibitions
produce transgression. Man cannot convert his good intentions,
formed by the Law, into action. All apparent lawfulness is only
an illusion, for fulfillment of the specific commands becomes
the ground for self-assertion, both before men and God. Such
pride is the very essence of lawlessness, for the central thrust
of the Law is complete self-surrender to God, grateful acknowledgment of his benefits, and love of neighbor as self.

Paul is convinced that the Law itself was his ally in
his struggle for Christian freedom from the Law. To apply the
Law's regulations to those who belong to Christ is to misread it.
The Law's essential requirement--a right relationship to God
and to other people--Christians meet when they live the new
life in Christ, guided by the Spirit of God. Christian freedom
from the Law does not mean that Christians are exempt from doing
God's will. Paul repeatedly stresses that Christians must
manifest their new life in their personal conduct. God's forgiving
love is liberating and transforming: the one who is loved can
love, and love fulfills the Law.

Paul's doctrine of the Law enabled him to interpret his
own life experience. His zeal for the Law had led him to persecute
the church of Christ. In Christ, God had granted him forgiveness
for this grave sin. But more, Paul's doctrine of the Law provided
a theological foundation for the ongoing Gentile mission and
added to its impetus. Paul had not forgotten his pride in being
a Jew and not a sinful Gentile. But when he had accepted Christ,
he had, as had Peter and the others, acknowledged that before
God the Jew had no advantage. Jews as well as Gentiles depended
absolutely on God's grace. Thus, it was entirely inappropriate
to introduce Jew-Gentile distinctions into Christian congregations,
and to treat Gentiles as second-class Christians (Gal. 2:15ff.).

That many Gentiles accepted the gospel of Christ while
most Jews rejected it posed another problem. Had God's promise
to Israel come to nothing? Paul answers with an emphatic no.
In the first place, God's promise did not extend to all of
Abraham's descendents, but only to those whom God had chosen.
God is sovereign, free to choose and to reject whom he will.
Secondly, some Jews do believe; Paul himself is an example. They
are at present the faithful remnant, the recipients of what God
has promised Israel. Thirdly, Israel's present rejection of
Christ does not bring God's saving purpose to an end. Ultimately,
all of Israel will be saved. Gentile acceptance of the Gospel

simply makes clear that both Jews and Gentiles are saved only
by God's mercy and grace; it is the indirect path God has
chosen which nevertheless leads to the salvation of Israel (Rom.
9-11). The salvation of Israel remains one of Paul's personal
goals as well; he hoped that his work and success among the
Gentiles would move Israel to healthy jealousy, a jealousy
which would move Israel to accept the gospel.

     Paul's hopes for Israel were not realized. Paul's view
of God's plan for Israel illustrates, however, a fundamental
conviction which pervades his thought: God does not act as
people expect, nor as they imagine they merit. God rejects the
strong and puts the wise to shame; he exalts the humble and turns
the persecutor into his apostle. He has made those who were not
his people, the Gentiles, his people, in order to bestow his
grace on those whom he had first chosen, Israel. Paul's faith
that the Crucified One is Lord determines this interpretation
of history. Paul's interpretation also corresponds to Jesus'
attitude toward outsiders, to his love for tax-collectors and
sinners.

     Most important for Paul is that men recognize that they
cannot attain the right relationship to God, to their fellow
men, or to themselves by their own efforts, by their privileged
position, or by their own wisdom. When a man seizes the opportunity which God gives him in Jesus Christ, the consequences
of that decision will transform his life. Paul does not need
to develop his doctrine of justification, the Law and Israel
in order to make this point to his Gentile readers. He can also
use language more familiar to Greeks.

Renewed Humanity

     Paul draws his anthropological vocabulary both from the
Old Testament and from general Greek usage; from the Old Testament
terms like "heart" and "flesh," and from Greek terms like "body,"
"mind" and "conscience."   He has no interest in specifying man's
essence or his constituent parts. Paul's different anthropological
terms refer to aspects of a human being rather than to discrete parts.
Man as subject knows, wills, acts and suffers; as object he
experiences the results of the knowing, willing and acting both
of himself and of others.

     Paul does not develop any doctrine of the immortality
of the soul; his hope for life after death rests on his conviction

that God has the power to raise the dead, and that Christ is
Lord even over death itself. Paul is not concerned with dividing
a man into a lower, animal nature and a higher, rational nature;
rather he is concerned with the position of the whole man before
God, his relation to the world and its powers, to other men and
to himself. Paul's use of the word "flesh" provides a good
example. Flesh is not merely something which a man has. Man
is flesh; here Paul follows common Old Testament usage. But
Paul also speaks of the flesh as a sphere of influence, a cosmic
principle or power: man is in the flesh and can live "after
the flesh." By "flesh" Paul does not simply mean the material
and the sensuous; he means the whole realm of purely human desire
and achievement, the world which takes into account lineage,
position, worldly accomplishments, learning, circumcision and
works of the Law, the world in which a man has grounds for boasting,
but in which he encounters unhappiness, hatred and strife.

     Paul considers men representatives of the social groups
to which they belong. He speaks of Greeks and barbarians, but
far more commonly of Jews and Gentiles or Jews and Greeks. The
Jews demand signs and Greeks seek wisdom. Both groups display
the same attitude toward Christ: the Crucified One is a stumbling
block to the Jews and folly to the Greeks, "but to those who are
called, both Jews and Greeks, Christ is the power of God and the
wisdom of God" (1 Cor. 1:24). But these distinctions are fundamentally unimportant, for with reference to both groups Paul
states: "There is no distinction; since all have sinned and
fall short of the glory of God" (Rom. 3:22-23). To reach this
conclusion, Paul argues, using Greek natural theology, that the
world itself makes possible knowledge of God and of fundamental
moral principles. He does not use natural theology to provide
a rational foundation for morality, but simply to show that there
is no decisive distinction between the religious situations of
Jews and of Gentiles. Even those without the Law had an avenue
to approach God, and therefore have no excuse for their failure
to do so; they have merited the punishment they will receive. The
Jews' possession of the Law has given them no real advantage, for
there are also Gentiles who have done what the Law requires.

     Responsibility and guilt are common to all men and the
gospel is valid for all--God is certainly not God only of the Jews.[12]
Paul never abandoned the exclusiveness of Jewish monotheism. God
is the one God, who alone possesses Divine Majesty, who does not

---

[12]See Chapter X "The One God of Jews and Gentiles."

share divine dignity with any of the so-called gods, in contrast
to Greek philosophical monotheism, where the divine source
manifests itself in a multiplicity of divine powers, whose
worship thereby becomes a worship of the divine source. For
Paul, there is only one path which leads to a right relationship
with God: faith in Jesus Christ. All, without distinction, are
free to follow this path. From his Jewish and Christian presuppositions Paul can draw conclusions which approach the universalistic
conceptions of his contemporaries without coinciding with them.

"There is neither Jew nor Greek, there is neither slave
nor free, there is neither male nor female; for you are all one
in Christ Jesus" (Gal. 3:28). This sentence does not imply that
all national, social and physiological distinctions have disappeared.
The Greek who becomes a Christian remains a Greek, unlike the
Greek proselyte to Judaism, who abandons his own community to
become part of another. Paul thinks that Christian Jews ought
to continue to live as Jews, as long as their adherence to
tradition does not disrupt the unity of the Christian community.
Paul unreflectively accepted the social standards of his environment, with the roles they assigned both to slaves and to women,
and he did not anticipate that his views would figure, on both
sides, in the struggles over slavery and over women's liberation.
But that does not mean that he did not anticipate substantial
social change. The life in Christ had to make its mark on life
in the world, on the relationship between Jew and Greek, husband
and wife, master and slave. The life in Christ unites those
who are different, and alters the relations between them, without
destroying the differences.

The relationship between unity and multiplicity had for
a long time occupied Greek thinkers; Paul sometimes appropriates
the Greek stylistic traditions associated with this speculation.
But it is characteristic that he prefers to use masculine terms
rather than neuter: *heis* (the One, i.e., God) and *hoi pantes*
(all the people), not *hen* (one) and *ta panta* (all things) or
even *hen ta panta* (all things are one). Paul often applies
cosmological language to the human situation and especially to
the relation of Christ to the church. The church displays her
multiplicity not only in the varieties of peoples whom she
congregates, but also in the variety of gifts and ministries
which the Spirit bestows on members of the church. We can look
at such spiritual gifts from either of two perspectives. The
Christian receives a spiritual gift to serve others; the service
he renders testifies to the presence of the gift. Paul uses the

image of the body and its members to illustrate this relationship, an image used in antiquity for civil societies and for the universe as a whole. Paul's fundamental conviction is that the church is the body of Christ, and that those who believe in his name become, through baptism, part of that body. Associated with this conviction is the view that every member of the church has a specific function and that in their very dissimilarity the members of the church are dependent on each other.

In the epistles to the Ephesians and to the Colossians, the image of the church as the body of Christ clearly has cosmic, universal components. Christ is the head of the church, which is his body, but he is also the sovereign head over all the universe's superhuman powers and principalities.[13] In Christ, God has bridged the gulf which separated Jews from Gentiles; the church by her very existence testifies to God's intention to reconcile what has been at odds. The church is the initial realization of God's plan to restore and unify the universe.

Paul has no interest, scientific or theosophic, in the structure of the universe or in the celestial hierarchy of powers and angelic beings, even though he takes their existence for granted. Paul stood at the boundary of a religious revolution which transformed fascination with the universe's divine order, and with the regular movement of the sun, the moon, the planets and the stars, into cosmic anxiety. The individual strove to win release from inexorable fate, from the power of the stars and from imprisonment in the material world by undergoing initiations into secret cults, by participating in religious rites, and by seeking to learn the knowledge which gave the knower the ability to escape (*gnōsis*). Astrology and other forms of mythological pseudo-science erased the boundaries between matter and energy and personal beings. In Paul we read both of powers and principalities and of the elements of the world (*RSV* - "the elemental spirits of the universe," Gal. 4:3). This second expression does not designate the four material elements of early natural philosophy (earth, water, air and fire), but rather the fundamental forces which govern existence, especially, perhaps, the power of the stars. Behind such conceptions lies the human

---

[13]The epistles to the Ephesians and Colossians represent a Pauline school of thought even if they were not written by Paul himself or at this request. My own position on the authorship of these letters has shifted somewhat over the years. Today I am most inclined to think that they were written after the death of the Apostle. See my article "Ephesians," in *IDBSup*, 268-269.

experience that man is not master of his own fate, but subject
to powers beyond his control, the hidden forces that govern
nature, society and even the life of the individual.

Against this background, the Christian confession that
Jesus is Lord includes the proclamation that all powers and
principalities are subject to him. Those who believe are
free from the cosmic powers, whatever they are. Christians
have no need of rites and ceremonies which honor these beings
in order to attain salvation, nor do they need to engage in
ascetic practices in order to escape their realm of influence.
Christians are free to use everything which God has created,
giving thanks.[14] They have no reason to fear the cosmic powers:
"For I am sure that neither death nor life, nor angels, nor
principalities, nor things present, nor things to come, nor
powers, nor height, nor depth, nor anything else in all creation
will be able to separate us from the love of God in Christ Jesus,
our Lord" (Rom. 8:38-39). Christian faith means freedom from
the world and its powers as well as freedom from the Mosaic Law
and its commandments.

On occasion, Paul speaks about freedom from the world
using ordinary language rather than cosmic terms. The Christian
cannot commit himself completely to earthly cares, to human ties,
sorrows and joys: "(Let) those who deal with the world (live)
as though they had no dealings with it" (1 Cor. 7:31). In
antiquity, liberty implied the contrast to slavery, or to bondage,
far more than it does today. But the liberty of which Paul
speaks even the slave who is in Christ can share. Christian
liberty does not confer moral license: the man who commits sin
soon becomes the slave of Sin.

The concept of liberty is part of Western culture's Greek
heritage. Paul too owes some debt to Greek philosophical ideas
about the liberty of the wise man who knows that some things lie
beyond his power. But Paul goes further; the freedom of which he
speaks is not stoic apathy, the undisturbed peace of mind of a
man who maintains an inner distance from worldly affairs. Paul
integrates freedom with an engaged concern: that man is free
who is Christ's slave, and who, moved by love, becomes the slave
of other men. The free member of a Christian community respects

---

[14]See Rom. 14:6, 14; 1 Cor. 10:23-30. Cf. also Col. 1 - 2
and the comments upon Colossians in F. O. Francis and W. A. Meeks,
Conflict at Colossae, SBLSBS 4 (Missoula: Scholars Press, 1973),
esp. 197-200.

the freedom of his brothers. Paul exhorts the Corinthians
not to become the slaves of men, while at the same time reminding
them: "For though I am free from all men, I have made myself
a slave to all, that I might win the more" (1 Cor. 7:23; 9:19).

Impact on Western Thought

Paul's formulation of the relationship between faith in
Christ and the Law of Moses, his central theological concern,
had a decisive impact on the church in its formative years.
Paul was neither the first nor the only early Christian to carry
the Christian message beyond the borders of Judaism. But without Paul, Christianity might very easily have split into two
camps, one a sect within Judaism, and the other, entirely
separate from Judaism, a mystery cult association which would
soon have lost its identity in the welter of contemporary
syncretism. Our knowledge of primitive Christianity before and
contemporary with Paul is too limited for us to assess the
probability of this danger with any accuracy. There is no doubt,
however, that Paul made an important contribution which helped
enable the church to retain the Old Testament while refusing to
adopt specifically Jewish traditions. Only by combining both
these elements could the church have developed as it did, into
a universal institution, accessible to all, with a historic
consciousness of its vocation as the People of God. Paul's
penetrating theological analysis of these problems had a decisive
impact on the whole subsequent history of the church, and thereby
on subsequent world history.

Paradoxically, we can continue by saying that the Pauline
problematic of the relation of the church to the Law and to
Israel soon became irrelevant. The fall of Jerusalem to the
Romans in 70 marked the end of the powerful influence of the
Jerusalem church. Few Christians any longer perceived that the
unity of Jews and Gentiles in the church was a problem. In a
dramatic reversal of the situation which Paul had confronted, Jews
who wished to become Christians had to abandon Judaism. The
church retained the Old Testament, but read it as a Christian
book; the use of the anachronism "Old Testament" itself helps
convey the early Christian outlook.

As time went on, the hope faded that Christ would soon
vindicate Christian faith by his coming again; Christians no
longer felt in their own lives, as Paul and his contemporaries

had, that a new Creation had dawned with Christ and with his
resurrection. First generation problems gave way to those of
the second and third. For those who had always been Christians,
the Pauline contrast between "once" and "now," so vivid for
mission congregations, lost its force. Christians continued to
honor Paul, they collected his letters and read them, but more
because they valued their general religious content than because
they understood and approved Paul's solutions to his specific
problems.

Paul's attempt to express his basically non-Greek thought
structure using Greek language and concepts colored by Greek
philosophy, made it easier for later Christian generations to
combine Greek philosophy with Christian faith. In the second
century, Gnostics and other heretics displayed an interest in
Paul which the orthodox did not share, at least not to the same
degree. The most important of these second century heretics,
Marcion, even prepared his own critical edition of the Pauline
letters, a process which may have prompted the church to fix
more firmly the apostle's place in the canon. At the end of
the second century, Irenaeus and other church fathers wrested
Paul away from the Gnostics and used his writings to confute
them. From that time on, Pauline elements have been an integral
part of Christian theology.

Through the centuries Paul has exerted influence not as
an original thinker but as the author of inspired writings. But
a thread of Paul's thought runs through the whole fabric of
Western intellectual history, in philosophical speculation
about man and history, liberty and unity, as well as in theology.
We cannot, however, distinguish the specifically Pauline from
other Christian elements, from the impact made by the Gospels and
other books of the New Testament, by the Old Testament, by church
tradition and by theological interpretation.

At two points in the history of the West specifically
Pauline ideas emerged with striking impact: at the time of
Augustine and at the time of the Reformation. In these periods
the Pauline doctrines of salvation by grace and justification by
faith, without works, gained such weight that subsequent Western
Christianity has continued to read Paul through the eyes of
Augustine, and for Protestants, of Luther. In the Eastern church,
the problem of the relation of faith to works has never had such
a central position. In the East, Christians regard Paul as a
saint, a mystic and a martyr. As to his theology, his image of
the church as the body of Christ was more important than his
doctrine of justification.

Augustine found Paul useful when, in his struggle against Pelagius, he emphasized the necessity of grace. Paul's belief that throughout history God chooses some and rejects others became the foundation for a doctrine of each individual's predestination to salvation or to condemnation. Luther found in Paul the solution to his personal problems of conscience, and took up Paul's insistence on Christian freedom in his struggle against monastic piety, ceremonial ritual and the church's hierarchical organization. Augustine and the reformers did recognize fundamental elements of Paul's thought, but they placed these elements in a non-Pauline context, a context shaped by the history of the church, by its practices of penance, and by a consciousness of sin far more introspective than that of Paul and of his congregations. Modern biblical study has attempted to take Paul's own situation seriously, to understand him as a man of his own time, to view his special contribution against the background of what his contemporaries and predecessors thought and said. The picture of Paul which has gradually emerged contains much that appears strange to us, but it has also shown that Paul was a thinker of wider scope and greater penetration than we would have guessed from the traditional stereotype.

CHAPTER II

PAUL AND POSSESSIONS

No reader of the New Testament can avoid confronting the sayings of Jesus about money: "Do not lay up for yourselves treasures on earth," "No man can serve two masters, ... You cannot serve God and mammon," "Go, sell what you have, and give to the poor," "Woe to you that are rich." Nor need one read too far in the prophets or in James to find harsh pronouncements about wealth and its dangers. We find no such judgments in Paul's letters. At a first reading, Paul does not appear to have much to say about the problems of wealth. This apparent silence is very striking. Paul, who traveled through large cities in the Roman Empire making his living as a tentmaker, must have had far more experience dealing with money than Jesus, who was a carpenter in a rural town, Nazareth, before beginning his public ministry.

Of course Paul does know something about the dangers of wealth; the word he most commonly uses to describe them is *pleonexia*. *Pleonexia* means the desire to have more. English translations use words like "covetousness," "ruthless greed," "rapacity," and "avarice." "Greed" occurs frequently in lists of pagan vices. Greed is idolatry. Just as adulterers, thieves and robbers cannot inherit the kingdom of God, neither can the greedy. Christians should not even mention greed; their lives should provide no opportunity to speak of its existence.[1] Here Paul speaks plainly.

_____

[1]Rom. 1:29; 1 Cor. 5:10f.; 6:10; Col. 3:5; Eph. 4:19; 5: 3,5. Ephesians and Colossians represent Pauline catechetical traditions even if not written by Paul. So do the Pastoral Epistles.

22

But it is difficult to avoid the impression that such warnings
are reminiscences of elementary Christian instruction, almost
truisms.   Paul is much more zealous and eloquent when he discusses
sins against moral purity and love.   Only 1 Timothy speaks about
greed as the root of all evil.[2]

Paul does not simply warn against economic abuses; he
advocates a positive economic ideal for the individual to work
quietly and eat one's own bread: "If anyone will not work, let
him not eat."   Everyone must manage his own affairs and work with
his own hands.   Nobody should have an opportunity to criticize
the way Christians live.   Christians must meet their economic
obligations, including the payment of taxes to the Roman authorities.[3]
To use a word current in Paul's time which in ours describes a
certain socio-economic ideal, Paul advocates autarchy.[4]   In Paul's
letters, this word means that the individual must be content
with what he has.   But there is more to the word than that; in
order to maintain his economic independence, the individual must
at least have enough to get by, and he must avoid the entrapment
of wealth.

The man who manages his own affairs prudently will also
be able to provide for those in need.   The Christian worker should
strive to earn more than is necessary to provide for his own
needs, in order to be able to relieve the suffering of those who
cannot provide for themselves.   The exhortation to do good, to
provide for those who have nothing, is a constantly recurring
element in Paul's moral teaching.[5]   For Paul, next to the sacrifice
of life itself, giving away all one's possessions is the greatest
act of love.   But he does not urge the members of his congregations
to such extremes of charity; he writes: "But have (I) not love,
I gain nothing" (1 Cor. 13:3).

There is no doubt that Paul advocates a high moral standard
concerning the use of money.   However, his exhortations are down-
to-earth, little more than commonplaces.   Paul neither condemns
wealth nor glorifies its renunciation.   He does not urge the
Christian to leave everything and to imitate Jesus' life of poverty.

---

[2] 1 Tim. 6:10; cf. 6:6-9, 17-19.
[3] See 2 Thess. 3:10-12; 1 Thess. 4:11f.; Eph. 4:28; and
Rom. 13:1-7.
[4] *autarkeia:*   2 Cor. 9:8 ("have enough"); 1 Tim. 6:6
("contentment"); *autarkēs:*   Phil. 4:11 ("content").   The idea
can also be present where the word is not used, e.g. 1 Thess.
4:12 :   "So that you may ... be dependent on nobody," or: be in
need of nothing.
[5] See Rom. 12:13; 2 Cor. 9:8; Gal. 6:6-10; Eph. 4:28; 2
Thess. 3:13.

What Paul demands of the Christian is honesty, industriousness, contentment and generosity. We get the impression that he demands solid middle-class respectability. It is obvious that Paul has appropriated the best of the ethical traditions of Judaism about possessions, traditions which largely coincided with the views of the Greek moralists. There is less of anything specifically Christian.

However, we have not yet presented the whole picture. There are elements which Paul adds to his treatment of money which make it unique. First, it is strange that Paul never speaks about money directly even though he writes several times about financial matters. This may reflect his environment, in which he had little reason to distinguish between money and other forms of property and income. He only uses the term "possessions" (or "property") once, in passing.[6] In every other case, he paraphrases. It appears that, consciously or unconsciously, he is striving to avoid using the appropriate nouns. His circumlocutions would not seem natural if they were not expressions of a unified outlook. Paul never looks at an individual's relationship to money in isolation.

References to money are always part of a total context, which includes the attitude to its use. Three factors in particular are decisive for Paul's attitude toward money: eschatology, the church, and his own situation as an apostle.

Second, Paul was aware that he was living in the last days. He expected to see Jesus' return and the end of the world. He knew that the Messiah had already come and that the process which would bring the world to an end had already started. The events which guaranteed the world's end, Jesus' death and resurrection, had already occurred. Christians, who were baptized into Christ Jesus, were already delivered from "this present evil age," they had already received the Holy Spirit as a first fruit and as a guarantee of their redemption.[7] In this situation property and money had little significance; they belonged to the age which was perishing. Paul uses phrases like "material benefits"

---

[6]1 Cor. 13:3: *panta ta hyparchonta mou* ("all I have"). Cf. e.g. Matt. 24:47 ("all his possessions"); Luke 11:21 ("his goods"), 12:33 ("your possessions").

[7]See e.g. 1 Cor. 10:11; 2 Cor. 1:21f.; 5:5,17; Gal. 1:4; 4:4-6; 6:15; Rom. 6:1ff.; 8:9ff.; 13:11-13. On the social and economic conditions of the members of the Pauline congregations, see Malherbe, 29-31, 71-87; M. Hengel, *Property and Riches in the Early Church: Aspects of a Social History of Early Christianity* (London: SCM, 1974) esp. 35-41. Cf. also E. A. Judge, "St. Paul and Classical Society," JAC 15 (1972) 19ff.

("carnal things": *KJV*) and "matters pertaining to this life."[8]
The contrast is to the spiritual good, i.e., to matters that
relate to God and to his kingdom. Economic affairs are trivial.[9]
For those who already have a share in the new age, money can no
longer have any real importance. Paul is far from "dropping out"
of society, however. He sharply rebukes those members of the
Thessalonian congregation who had stopped working because they
believed that the Day of the Lord was at hand.[10] Paul demands
that those living in the last days manage their economic affairs
with an inner integrity: "The appointed time has grown very
short; from now on, let those who have wives live as though they
had none, and those who mourn as though they were not mourning,
and those who rejoice as though they were not rejoicing, and
those who buy as though they had no goods and those who deal
with the world as though they had no dealing with it for the
form of this world is passing away."[11] A Christian shall obviously
continue to work and earn money, but he shall at the same time
maintain his independence.

This view echoes the teachings of the Cynic and Stoic
philosophers contemporary to Paul; they too spoke about autarchy
and about the wise man's independence of the external conditions
of his life.[12] But although the exhortations are similar, Paul's
advice had very different roots. Paul is not concerned with the
self-sufficiency and personal integrity of the wise man, with
his inner freedom and his mastery of the external conditions of
his existence. Paul states the consequences of the objective
situation in which Christians live at the end of the ages. What
matters is their relation to their Lord in heaven. The Christians
must not attach themselves to money or to other earthly concerns,
attachments which would weaken their commitment to the Lord. They

---

[8]*ta sarkika*, Rom. 15:27 ("material blessings"); 1 Cor.
9:11, ("material benefits"); *ta biōtika*, 1 Cor. 6:3 ("matters
pertaining to this life").

[9]*ta elachista*, i.e. the smallest things, 1 Cor. 6:2
("trivial cases").

[10]Thus 2 Thess. 3:6ff., cf. 2:1ff. The exhortation to
work in 1 Thess. 4:11-12 is part of traditional paraenesis, see
R. F. Hock, *The Working Apostle: An Examination of Paul's Means
of Livelihood* (Diss., Yale, 1974) 96-108. Nevertheless,
eschatological expectations and the presence of "idlers" (*ataktoi*)
seem to enhance its relevance for the Thessalonians, see 1 Thess.
4:13ff.; 5:14.

[11]1 Cor. 7:29-31.

[12]The Diatribes of Epictetus provide the best known illu-
stration of this attitude. For the necessity to distinguish between
Stoics and Cynics and between differing trends within both schools,
see A. J. Malherbe, "Cynics" and "Epictetus," *IDBSup*, 201-203;
271.

ought not to be anxious about anything but to please him.

Paul did not insist that those whose livelihoods involved dealing with money change their occupation. On the contrary, Christians had an obligation to continue working in the profession they practiced before becoming Christians: "Only, let everyone lead the life which the Lord has assigned to him, and in which God has called him," "Every one should remain in the state in which he was called."[13] The end is near at hand, earthly affairs have lost their significance, and therefore Christians have no reason to alter their position in life. Paul applies this logic to the married and to the unmarried, to the circumcised and to the uncircumcised, to slaves and to the free.[14] There can be little doubt that his attitude toward the rich and the poor was much the same. The poor and the rich have the same Lord, who gives both groups a share in his bounty and who joins them in the same church: this is the strikingly new element in Paul's thought. The congregation becomes the decisive social reality for the Christian way of life, and communal life by necessity involves the use of possessions. Herein lies an important difference from the ideals of the Stoic sages and Cynic preachers. Here too we find part of the explanation for the difference between what Jesus and what Paul say about money.

The customary ethical rules have even greater weight within the community: the Christian should "do good to all men,

---

[13]1 Cor. 7:20. Here *RSV* translates: "Every one should remain in the state in which he was called." In the Greek text (*en tē klēsei hē eklēthē*) the word *klēsis* refers, in accordance with normal Pauline usage, to God's effective call through the gospel. Paul's idea is that a person should remain in this call as it first reached him (whether he was or was not circumcised, was slave or free, married or single). Cf. 1 Cor. 7:17ff., esp. 7:24, *en hō eklēthē* ("in whatever state each was called"). Paul fails to take into account that his rule could not possibly apply to children as they grew up and to adults who had to find work in order to support themselves. He assumes that only a short period of time remains but, after all, he had been a Christian for some twenty years when he wrote 1 Corinthians. He may, in fact, presuppose that children continued to live in the house and to practice the trade of their parents. If so, this would provide some information about social conditions in the Pauline congregations. At least since Luther, the word *klēsis* in 1 Cor. 7:20 was taken to refer to the civil state or occupation as being a religious vocation. As a consequence, Paul's eschatologically motivated theory of status quo was turned into a biblical rationale for social conservatism.

[14]The advice to slaves who have an opportunity to gain freedom (1 Cor. 7:21b) remains enigmatic. For information on an attempt to reach beyond the alternative renderings in the text and footnote in the *RSV*, see S. Scott Bartchy, *First Century Slavery and 1 Corinthians 7:21* (SBLDS 11, Missoula: Scholars Press, 1973).

and especially to those who are of the household of faith" (Gal.
6:10). Greed is especially shameful when it victimizes a
Christian brother. Paul harshly rebukes Christians at Corinth
who have filed lawsuits against one another as a result of their
commercial dealings.[15] Worst of all for Paul is that they appeal
to pagan courts to settle their financial differences. But the
congregation has already suffered a defeat when its members sue
one another: "Why not rather suffer wrong? Why not rather be
defrauded?" The issue of lawsuits gives Paul the opportunity to
stress the basic idea that Christians must be willing to suffer
injustice.[16] He views the whole problem in the light of the
position that Christians will occupy when they participate in
the judgment of the world, and in the light of the reality in
which they already participate as a result of their baptism.

We know little about the social composition of the
Pauline congregations. We can guess that the majority consisted
of craftsmen and shopkeepers. We know that there were some slaves.
As a whole, however, the congregation did not belong to the
proletariat narrowly construed, though it did not come from
the upper class: "For consider your call, brethren; not many
of you were wise according to worldly standards, not many were
powerful, not many were of noble birth."[17] Paul could no doubt
have added: "Not many were rich." But he did not. For Paul,
the gospel is more a judgment on those who think they are wise,
who think they are noble, than a judgment on the rich. It is
quite likely that the congregation at Corinth did have some rich
members, even if they did not belong to the intellectual or
social elites. In any case, the congregation includes not only
slaves but also slaveowners. Paul provides moral instruction
for both groups. When Paul speaks of a man and his household,
he includes not only his immediate family but his slaves as well.[18]

---

[15]1 Cor. 6:1–11. See E. Dinkler, "Zum Problem der Ethik
bei Paulus," *ZTK* 49(1952), now in *Signum Crucis* (Tübingen: Mohr,
1967) 204–240.

[16]Paul shares the idea with Greek moralists in the
Socratic tradition that it is better to suffer injustice. See
also Matt. 5:39f.; 1 Peter 2:20; 3:9, 13f.

[17]See 1 Cor. 1:26. In Rome and other cities in the Empire
freedman and other people outside the families could be rich
without being fully accepted in the higher circles. The Christian
church, like other cults and associations, is likely to have
found recruits among people who were moving upwards in society,
as Wayne Meeks has pointed out in an unpublished paper.

[18]1 Cor. 1:16; cf. Acts 16:15; 18:8.

We know little about the individuals whose names we find in
Paul's letters or in Acts; what we do know indicates that they
were financially independent. Perhaps some of them were very
wealthy. The poor have probably remained anonymous. By and
large, that too indicates that we cannot assume that most of
the congregation's members came from the proletariat.

What is the relationship of rich to poor in the Pauline
congregation? Again, the texts provide little information. Paul
never says: "There is neither rich nor poor." This is not a
pressing question for Paul. But the Corinthian correspondence
makes it clear that economic differences did create problems.
Even at the liturgical center of the congregation's life, in
the Lord's Supper, groups formed along social lines. Here Paul
clearly rebukes the well-to-do for their behavior. The rich
have gorged themselves on the food they brought with them with
the result that those who could only arrive later, slaves and
workingmen, do not have enough to eat. Those who act in this way
"despise the church of God and humiliate those who have nothing."
Paul condemns the indifference to the significance of the sacrament implicit in such behavior.[19]

This is not the only image of congregational life at
Corinth which Paul provides, however. He also mentions Christians
who provide hospitality for the congregation gathered in their
homes. When Paul writes from Corinth to the Christians in Rome,
he refers to Gaius as: "host to me and to the whole church"
(Rom. 16:23). It is probable that Gaius not only allowed the
congregation to gather in his home, but also entertained it.
This reference hints that the Pauline congregations soon begin
to take wealth into the service of the church. It is not that
the rich man sells all that he has and contributes to the poor
or to the congregation's common fund; rather, he opens his home
to the congregation and, perhaps, provides for it at his own
expense.[20]

Philemon used his wealth in this way.   The letter Paul
wrote him gives us an example of Paul's attitude toward an
individual's management of his personal financial affairs. The
escaped slave Onesimus was Philemon's property. Paul begins by
assuring Philemon that he thanks God for the love and faith which

---

[19]See 1 Cor. 11:17-24.
[20]See the references to the churches in the house of
Prisca and Aquila (Rom. 16:3-5; 1 Cor. 16:19), of Philemon,
Apphia and Archippus (Philem. 2), and of Nympha (Col. 4:15), and
also the recommendation of Phoebe as the helper (*prostatis*) of
many in Rom. 16:1-2.

Philemon has displayed "toward the Lord Jesus and all the saints."
He mentions the joy and comfort Philemon's love have afforded
him, "because the hearts of the saints have been refreshed through
you" (Philem. 4-7). Paul alludes to the generosity which Philemon's
wealth has enabled him to show his Christian brothers, hoping
that he will once more demonstrate this generosity. Paul does
not mention the financial aspect directly, which is typical.
What is important is that Philemon has manifested Christian love
and that he has given his Christian brothers an opportunity to
experience the reality of that love. Here the material does not
stand in opposition to the spiritual; rather, the material becomes
a carrier, a medium, of the spiritual.

Paul writes to Philemon in order to intercede for an
escaped slave, Onesimus, who had come to Paul and whom Paul had
converted. Onesimus' escape from Philemon appears to have been
compounded by some financial wrongdoing. Though Paul may not
know exactly what happened, he presupposes that Philemon has
a valid claim to make against Onesimus. He writes to Philemon
with great solemnity that Philemon should charge Onesimus' debt
to Paul's account: "I, Paul write this with my own hand, I will
repay it" (Philem. 19). Indeed, the tone is so solemn that we
detect an element of irony in it. The irony becomes more evident
when Paul adds that he could have said that Philemon owed Paul
his very self, because it was through Paul that he had become a
Christian. Despite the irony, Paul is making a serious point.
There ought to be proper order in financial affairs, even (and
especially) among Christians. Paul is actually suggesting that
Philemon renounce his claim against Onesimus, but he leaves it
to Philemon to make his own decision. There is another suggestion
which Paul makes only implicitly. There can be little doubt that
Paul hopes not only that Philemon will welcome back his runaway
slave, but also that he will then send Onesimus back to Paul to
continue to serve him while he is in prison.[21] Paul refuses to
ask this favor of Philemon directly; he simply suggests it (though
indeed he suggests it very strongly!). He leaves it to Philemon
to do more than what Paul has asked him to do, "in order that
your goodness might not be by compulsion but of your own free will
(Philem. 14). Paul expects much of his fellow Christians, even

---

[21]See John Knox, *Philemon among the Letters of Paul*, (2.
ed., Nashville: Abingdon, 1959), 24-32. The evidence does not
prove that the legal question of Onesimus' status as slave or
freedman was important to Paul.

in financial matters. But he expects them to act freely and
lovingly, not under compulsion.

We find no trace of a communistic ideal in Paul's letters,
not even of a voluntary consumers' communism as an expression
of love. He does however mention the ideal of economic equality;
he quotes from Scripture: "He who gathered much had nothing
left over, and he who gathered little had no lack."[22] It is
when speaking of the relationship between different Christian
congregations that Paul speaks of equality (*isotēs*), viewing
them as economic units. But certainly the ideal of mutual help
and of equalizing abundance and scarcity applies to individuals
as well. The method that Paul endorses is that those who have
more than they need share what they have with those in want, not
that everyone surrenders his possessions to a communal fund.

There may well have been a common congregational fund,
but we have no real picture how that fund was managed. Paul
lists acts of helping among spiritual gifts, he talks about
serving, and about him who contributes.[23] It remains uncertain
whether he refers to those whose resources enable them to help
others or to those who administer a common congregational fund.
In the earliest period perhaps both functions belonged to a
single group of individuals. It is obvious that in his letter
to the Philippians Paul presupposes a church office whose
responsibilities include financial administration. When he
mentions bishops and deacons, he does so because they are the
ones who manage the congregation's common fund.[24] At the same
time, these officials preside over the congregation's worship.
Responsibility for the management of the congregation's financial
affairs, for carrying on its charitable work and for presiding
over its liturgies was inseparably joined together in these early
congregations. The community's celebration of the Eucharist was
also a common meal, the time when the congregation offered its
gifts, gifts which were later distributed to the poor.[25]

---

[22]See 2 Cor. 8:8-15 where Paul quotes Exod. 16:18.
[23]*antilēmpseis* (1 Cor. 12:28) ("helpers"), *diakonia*, Rom.
12:7; *ho metadidous*, Rom. 12:8 ("he who contributes"; the
reference to economic contributions is not beyond dispute). In
Rom. 12:8 *ho proistamenos* is probably "a leader" (*NEB*, cf. 1 Thess.
5:12), not "he who gives aid"; *ho eleōn* ("he who does acts of
mercy") probably refers to visiting the sick and similar charitable
acts, rather than to almsgiving.
[24]Phil. 1:1; cf. 4:10ff. and see below, note 37.
[25]The picture drawn in the text depends more on inferences
from what we know about early Christian practice in general than
upon exact information provided by the letters of Paul. From 1
Cor. 16:2 we may possibly draw the inference that gifts for
immediate use within the congregation were collected on the first
day of the week, when Christians gathered for worship. See also
Acts 2:44-47; 6:1-6.

When Paul mentions these matters, he never stresses the purely financial aspect which can be measured in dollars and cents. Paul stresses instead the giver's attitude: "Each one must do as he has made up his mind, not reluctantly or under compulsion, for God loves a cheerful giver" (2 Cor. 9:7). Paul concentrates on the joy and love which the gifts express, on the relationship to one another and on the community in Christ which the distribution of material goods realizes. Money becomes more than just money within the Christian church; it attains an almost sacramental significance: "A visible sign of an invisible grace."

The collection on behalf of the Jerusalem church makes this point most clearly. This collection was extremely important to Paul.[26] It became one of the principal foci of the last years of his work in Asia Minor and Greece; it was a project which Paul worked hard and long to complete. The economic need of the Jerusalem church was a fundamental presupposition underlying the project. But this is not the element which weighed most heavily on Paul. More important for Paul was that the collection was an obligation which he had assumed. At the Apostolic Council, which acknowledged that Gentile Christians were free from the requirements of the Mosaic Law, Paul and Barnabas had promised to "remember the poor" (Gal. 2:10). The fulfillment of this promise symbolized for Paul a ratification of the unity between Jewish and Gentile Christians. Paul's way of speaking about this gift is very characteristic. He uses words like "service," "fellowship," "blessing," and "grace." He regards the money itself as the embodiment of everything which giving the gift symbolizes, and he expresses himself in a way which is impossible to translate.[27] For Paul, the gift proves the reality of the love which binds all Christians together. The congregation in Macedonia has manifested exactly the right spirit: "Their abundance of joy and their extreme poverty have overflowed in a wealth of liberality on their part. For they gave according to their means, as I can testify, and beyond their means--not as we expected, but first they gave themselves to the Lord and to us by the will of God" (2 Cor. 8:2,5). Indeed, Paul can appeal to Christ as a model:

---

[26]On the collection, see D. Georgi, *Die Geschichte der Kollekte des Paulus für Jerusalem* (Hamburg: H. Reich, 1965); K. F. Nickle, *The Collection* (SBT 48, London: SCM Press, 1966).
[27]On the terms and metonyms for the collection to Jerusalem, see Appendix I below.

"Our Lord Jesus Christ, that though he was rich, yet for your
sake he became poor" (2 Cor. 8:9).[28]

Paul wants the members of his congregations to give
freely, willingly. Yet he regards the gift as a duty, as a
repayment, because the Gentiles have come to share in the
spiritual blessings which originally belonged to the Jews. The
spirit with which the Jewish Christians receive the gift is as
important to Paul as the spirit with which the Gentile Christians
give it. By accepting the gift the mother congregation in
Jerusalem ratifies its fellowship with Gentile Christians and
confirms its recognition that Gentile Christians are brothers
in Christ. If the gift is given and received with joy, it
unites Jewish and Gentile Christians so that as a single community
they can give thanks to God. In this way, the gift of money
expresses what is for Paul most important: the unity of Jews
and Gentiles in the church of Christ.[29] This is the reason that
it was so important to Paul to deliver the gift in person, even
though he fully understood the risk of a journey to Jerusalem.

Paul knew that his zeal to complete the collection exposed
him to criticism; some have clearly impugned his motives. Paul
took care to shield himself from such criticism as much as possible
by conducting himself very scrupulously. The congregations themselves chose representatives who supervised the local collection
and who accompanied Paul when he delivered it: "We intend that
no one should blame us about this liberal gift which we are
administering, for we aim at what is honorable not only in the
Lord's sight, but also in the sight of men." (2 Cor. 8:20-21).[30]

Even apart from the collection, Paul's actions exposed
him to criticism. The modern saying, "The pastor's purse is
never full," reflects an attitude toward wandering preachers,
sophists or philosophers widespread in antiquity. In his first
letter to the Thessalonians, Paul tries to make it clear that he
is not a preacher of that type: "For we never used either words
or flattery, as you know, or a cloak for greed, as God is witness"
(1 Thess. 2:5). Paul reminds them: "We worked night and day,

---

[28]For the purposes of the present study, it does not
make much difference whether 2 Corinthians 8 and 9 are fragments
of two separate letters or originally belong in the present
context. See Appendix II below.
        [29]See Rom. 15:27-31; 2 Cor. 9:10-14. I have dealt with
this aspect of the collection in other studies, see pp. 77, 110
and 141.
        [30]2 Cor. 12:14-16 shows that Paul's handling of the
collection was criticized. 2 Cor. 8:16-23 lists his precautionary
methods.

that we might not burden any of you." Paul can recommend his own
conduct as an example for them to follow.[31]

Even while stressing that he has worked with his own
hands, that he has renounced their financial support, Paul
emphasizes that he is entitled to that support. He uses arguments to support his claim: the analogy to soldiers, the image
of gardeners who share in the harvest and shepherds who have a
right to part of the flock, the commandments of the Mosaic Law
and Jesus' own words.[32] The saying of Jesus that the laborer
deserves his food appears in Paul in the form: "Those who
proclaim the gospel should get their living by the gospel."
Paul adduces only this positive statement. He does not refer to
the prohibitions against carrying a money belt or traveling bags,
or against efforts to obtain more than simple hospitality. Paul's
selection and interpretation of Jesus' instructions illustrate
the difference between preaching the gospel in rural Galilee
and preaching the gospel in the principal cities of the Empire.[33]

Why does Paul stress so heavily a right to support which
he has renounced? It is extremely important to him that his
churches acknowledge this right because that acknowledgment means
they recognize his legitimacy as an apostle. For this reason,

---

[31]See 1 Thess. 1:6 and cf. 1 Cor. 9 and 11:1. On 1 Thess.
2:3-12 see A. J. Malherbe, "Gentle as a Nurse," *NovT* 12 (1970),
203-217. On Paul's work with his hands, see Hock (note 10).
Both Malherbe and Hock draw attention to the similarities between
Paul and the Cynics.

[32]See 1 Cor. 9:6-14. On Paul's use of sayings of Jesus,
see D. Dungan, *The Sayings of Jesus in the Churches of Paul*
(Philadelphia: Fortress), 3-80. Dungan's analysis of Matthew's
redaction is unsatisfactory, but that does not impair the value
of his study of Paul's handling of the saying in 1 Cor. 9:14
(Matt. 10:9, Luke 10:7).

[33]As reported in Mark 6:8-11 (Luke 9:3-5) and Matt. 10:
9-14/Luke 10:4-11, Jesus' instructions call the disciples to
devote all their energy to their preaching and healing mission.
The prohibition against carrying money presupposes that they should
not earn money either, but trust that God would provide. According
to Paul's interpretation, Jesus had stated the principle that the
preacher of the gospel had a right (*exousia*) to receive support
(1 Cor. 9:4,6, 18; cf. Gal. 6:6). Missionaries like Paul and
Barnabas, who founded new churches in Hellenistic cities, had
either to carry money or to work in order to support themselves
when they first came to a new place. Paul's practice was opposed
by the itinerant charismatics who visited Corinth, but these
"apostles" could rely on receiving their livelihood without work
or money only because they visited cities where there was already
a Christian community (cf. 2 Cor. 10:12-16; 11:12-15; 12:11-15).
That the ancient practice of itinerant apostles and prophets could
lead to abuse is also attested by Didache 11, cf. Hermas 43
(Mand. XI). G. Theissen has devoted several studies to the
radicalism of itinerant charismatics and the contrast between them
and Paul's church-founding missionary practice. See esp.
"Wanderradikalismus," *ZTK* 70 (1973), 245-271, and "Legitimation
und Lebensunterhalt," *NTS* 21 (1974/75), 192-221.

Paul's congregations must understand that his renunciation of
support represents a purely personal decision, a free will under-
taking which exceeds his obligations. The financial sacrifices
others make, Paul wants them to make voluntarily, with joy,
not because of compulsion. He makes it clear that the same
rule applies to him. He has earned the right to the congregation's
support, but he has renounced it of his own free will. Thus, his
renunciation is praiseworthy, something in which he can take
justifiable pride.[34] To preach the gospel was the charge he had
received from God, about which he had no choice; but to preach
without asking for his deserved compensation was in itself his
reward (1 Cor. 9:18). His sacrifice removed a possible stumbling
block from the path of prospective converts; they had no cause
to believe that he was motivated by greed.

Indeed, Paul was criticized because he refused to accept
payment. When Paul speaks about the injustice he had done the
church at Corinth by refusing compensation, about the lack of love
he displayed by his sacrifice, the irony is obvious: "For in
what were you less favored than the rest of the churches, except
that I myself did not burden you? Forgive me this wrong!" (2
Cor. 12:13).[35] Paul assures them that he will not in the future
ask for any help from the congregation at Corinth or from neighbor-
ing congregations. The reason for Paul's attitude may well be
the criticism he has received at Corinth for the way he dealt
with money. Paul did receive help from the congregations in
Macedonia, even when he was living in Corinth. Paul says that
he "robbed" other congregations in order to spare the Corinthians.[36]
Perhaps some at Corinth accuse him of robbery because of his
efforts to promote the collection for the Jerusalem church.

The congregation at Philippi in particular distinguished
itself by helping Paul financially. They sent a gift to Paul
when he was a prisoner in Ephesus (or Rome). The letter which
Paul wrote to express his thanks for their gift is perhaps our
best evidence for his attitude toward money.[37] One must be

_____

[34]See esp. 1 Cor. 9:15-18; 2 Cor. 11:10, and. cf. E. Käsemann,
"A Pauline Version of the 'Amor Fati'," in *New Testament Questions
of Today* (Philadelphia: Fortress, 1969), 217-235.
    [35]Cf. 1 Cor. 9:3ff.; 2 Cor. 11:7-12; 12:14-18.
    [36]2 Cor. 11:8. See also 2 Cor. 11:9; 12:13 and Phil. 4:10ff.
    [37]The opening of Philippians adumbrates the thanks for
the gift at the conclusion of the letter (4:10-20). The bishops
and deacons (1:1) are likely to have administered the gift. The
phrase *epi pasē tē mneia hymōn* (1:3) most likely refers to the
support with which the Philippians had several times "remembered"
Paul. See P. Schubert, *Form and Function of the Pauline Thanksgiving*, 61. Their "partnership (*koinōnia*) in the gospel" was

cautious about describing anything in world history as unique;
but there is no letter of acknowledgement and thanks which
compares to Philippians. I need not say too much about the letter;
let me simply note that Paul gives thanks explicitly for the
gift only at the end of the letter. What he mentions at greater
length is fellowship in working for the gospel, joy and community
in Christ. Paul, who was proud that he supported himself, that
he did not burden anyone, was filled with radiant Christian joy
because of the gift which he had received.

     Paul is not expressing thanks merely for a gift of money.
He gives thanks for the fellowship in Christ which the gift
expresses. Here again we see that a gift of money within the
Christian congregation can be an act of worship, nearly sacramental. Paul describes their gift as "a fragrant offering, a
sacrifice acceptable and pleasing to God" (Phil. 4:18). Paul
had not asked for the gift and he would have managed without it.
As he told the Philippians: "For I have learned, in whatever
state I am, to be content. I know how to be abased, and how
to abound; in any and all circumstances I have learned the secret
of facing plenty and hunger, abundance and want. I can do all
things in him who strengthens me " (Phil. 4:11-13).

     With this quotation we could have concluded. But we
inquisitive modern men and women want the answer to one more
question: what was Paul's own financial situation? His financial
condition during the time he spent as a missionary seems fairly
clear: working with his own hands enabled him to survive, with
a minimum of outside help. Probably, he knew want more often
than plenty. But what was the financial situation in the home
in which he grew up? There can be little doubt that Paul came
from a rather well-to-do family. Though he worked as a tentmaker,[38]
the self-conscious pride he takes in earning his living by working
with his own hands makes it unlikely that he came from a working-
class family. Paul had learned to make tents because every Jew
had to learn a trade, not because it was necessary in order for
him to support himself.[39]

---

manifested in financial support of Paul (Phil. 1:5; cf. 1:7). A
note of joy pervades the whole letter (Phil. 1:18, 25f.; 2:2,17f.;
3:1f.; 4:1,4). The gift from Philippi was, certainly, one factor
that made Paul rejoice. See also R. D. Webber, *The Concept of
Rejoicing in Paul* (Diss., Yale 1970). 164-167, 178-183, 216-217,
245-250, 268-276, 286-288, 315-319, 353ff.).

     [38]Only Acts 18:3 makes a reference to Paul's trade. The
meaning of *skēnopoios* ("tentmaker") is not quite certain.

     [39]In his dissertation (see note 10), Hock points out that
the evidence to which scholars usually refer is later than Paul.
Hock therfore prefers to think that Paul followed the practice of

What little information we have about Paul's family and
adolescence confirms the impression his letters create. The
rabbinic training Acts attributes to Paul, if true, would not
provide conclusive evidence about his economic status. Several
of the rabbis were rather poor. If Paul did study in Jerusalem,
however, that would suggest that he came from a family of independent means; not many working-class Diaspora Jews could have
afforded to send their sons to Jerusalem for an education. That
Paul's father was a Roman citizen also makes it more likely that
he was well-to-do.[40] Perhaps it is not too rash to suggest that
the close cooperation and friendship between Paul and Barnabas
had its roots in similar social backgrounds. We know from Acts
that Barnabas had a farm which he sold. He gave the money he
received to the congregation's common fund, which the apostles
in Jerusalem managed. He obviously belonged to the group which
contributed most.[41]

If what I have suggested is true, what happened to the
money which Paul inherited from his father? It is difficult to
imagine that he did not receive an inheritance, though he might
have been disinherited because of his conversion to Christianity.
More likely Paul, like Barnabas, gave his property to the congregation's common fund, or perhaps he used the money to support himself during his early years of service as a missionary for Christ.
We do not know, because the extant letters describe only his
later, more successful work. If my conjecture is correct, then
the silence of the sources is eloquent indeed. Paul's financial
sacrifice is likely to have been greater than we can determine
from his letters, but he chooses not to talk about it.

There is a pervading but quiet heroism which characterizes
Paul's attitude toward money; to use Paul's words: "The love
of Christ controls us." (2 Cor. 5:14).

---

some Cynics, e.g. Simon the Shoemaker. See pp. 6-21, etc., esp.
"Conclusions," 163-165.
        The Cynic analogies, however, in no way exclude the
possibility that Pharisees also combined study with the practice
of a craft. On Cynic influence on rabbinic Judaism, see H. Fischel,
Rabbinic Literature and Greco-Roman Philosophy (SPB 21, Leiden:
Brill, 1973).
        [40]See Acts 22:28 on Paul's Roman citizenship and 23:16-22
on the son of his sister.
        [41]See Acts 4:36-37. On the theme of possessions in Luke-
Acts, see L. Johnson, *The Literary Function of Possessions in Luke-
Acts*, (Diss., Yale, 1976, to be published in the SBL Dissertation
Series).

APPENDIX I

WORDS AND PHRASES REFERRING TO THE COLLECTION

The following list illustrates the variety of terms and circumlocutions which Paul uses to speak about the collection for Jerusalem. The translation of the *RSV* is given in quotation marks, with the addition of parentheses where I have first given elementary lexical information. The list begins with more or less technical terms and proceeds to metonyms, metaphors, and other words and phrases which refer only within a specific context to the collection.

logeia, collection, 1 Cor. 16:1,2 ("contribution").

koinōnia, partnership, sharing, etc., Rom. 15:26; 2 Cor. 9:13 ("contribution"); 2 Cor. 8:4 ("taking part").

diakonia, service, Rom. 15:31; 2 Cor. 8:4 ("relief"); 2 Cor. 9:12 ("offering"); 2 Cor. 9:13 and, possibly, 1 Cor. 16:15 ("service"). The verb *diakonein*, serve, refers to the collection in Rom. 15:25 and 2 Cor. 8:19,20.

leitourgia, voluntary public service, or (priestly) ministry, 2 Cor. 9:12 (*hē diakonia tes leitourgias tautēs*, "the rendering of this service"); *leitourgein*, "to be of service," Rom. 15:27.

charis, (gift of) grace, favor, 1 Cor. 16:3 ("gift"); 2 Cor. 8:6,7,19 ("gracious work"). Cf. 2 Cor. 8:1 ("grace," as in 2 Cor. 8:9; 9:14).

haplotēs, simplicity, sincerity (in giving), 2 Cor. 8:2 ("liberality"), 9:11,13 ("generosity").

eulogia, blessing, 2 Cor. 9:5 ("gift," "willing gift"). Cf. 9:6, *ep' eulogiais* ("bountifully").

hadrotēs, plenitude, 2 Cor. 8:20 ("liberal gift").

perisseuma, "abundance," 2 Cor. 8:14.

endeixis tēs agapēs hymōn, "proof of your love," 2 Cor. 8:24.

karpos, fruit, Rom. 15:28 ("have delivered to them what has been raised," with the footnote: "Greek *sealed to them this fruit*").

sporos, seed, sowing, 2 Cor. 9:10 ("resources"); cf. the quotation from Ps. 112:9 in 2 Cor. 9:9 and the allusion to Isa. 55:10 in 9:10. *ho speirōn*, "he who sows," 2 Cor. 9:6.

ta genēmata tēs dikaiosynēs hymōn, "the harvest of your righteousness," 2 Cor. 9:10, with allusion to Hosea 10:12.

meros, part, etc.; *en tō merei toutō,* "in this case," 2 Cor.
   9:3.

hypostasis, substance, reality, matter, etc., but hardly ever
      confidence; see Bauer-Arndt-Gingrich and H. Koester in *TDNT,*
      VIII, 572-589. *en tō hypostasei tautē,* 2 Cor. 9:4 ("for being
      so confident") probably means either "in this state of mind"
      (referring to Paul's boasting,. 2 Cor. 9:3, cf. 11:17) or
      simply "in this matter." Only on the last interpretation
      does the word belong to this list.
Translation becomes especially difficult where Paul combines
several of these words to speak about the collection; e.g.
2 Cor. 8:4: *tēn charin kai tēn koinōnian tēs diakonias tēs*
      eis tous hagious, the grace of and the participation in the
      service for the saints ("the favor of taking part in the
      relief of the saints").
Some other words are associated with the collection without ever
denoting it: *prothymia,* "readiness" or "good will," 2 Cor.
8:11,12,19; 9:2; *spoudē,* "earnestness," 2 Cor. 8:7,8; cf. 8:16,
17; *agapē,* "love," 2 Cor. 8:7,8,24; *ergon agathon,* "good work,"
2 Cor. 9:8.

APPENDIX II

ON THE LITERARY INTEGRITY OF 2 CORINTHIANS 1-9

        According to fairly widespread opinion, 2 Corinthians 8
and 9 are two fragments of separate letters which a redactor
incorporated into the composite document which we know as 2
Corinthians. See e.g. D. Georgi, "Corinthians, Second Letter to
the," in *IDBSup* 183-186. For the purposes of my study, it
does not make much difference whether or not this is really so.
Nevertheless, I would like to set forth some counter-arguments
for which I am indebted to former and present students at Yale.

1. 2 Cor. 7:4 contains a thematic statement which is spelled
out in 7:15-16; the argument here prepares for, and is continued
in, chapter 8. See R. D. Webber, *The Concept of Rejoicing in*
Paul (Diss., Yale, 1970) 225-245.

2. Throughout 2 Cor. 1-7 Paul expresses his confidence in the
Corinthians and seeks to reestablish his own credibility. Only

when mutual confidence is restored can Paul hope that the Corinthians will heed his advice concerning the collection for Jerusalem. See S. N. Olson, *Confidence Expressions in Paul: Epistolary Conventions and the Purpose of 2 Corinthians* (Diss., Yale, 1976) 99-215.

3. In terminology, in the use of examples, and in other features, the argument in 2 Cor. 8 (and 9) conforms to the style of deliberative or symbouleutic rhetoric. The most obvious examples occur in 2 Cor. 8:10: *gnomēn...didōmi*, "I give my advice," and *touto...sympherei*, "it is best." In symbouleutic rhetoric, the credibility (or "ethos") was a matter of great importance, and so it is in 2 Corinthians. (S. Olson, D. Wilcox, D. Worley).

4. By handling the affair with the wrongdoer to Paul's full satisfaction, the Corinthian Christians had already passed a first test, see 2 Cor. 2:5-11; 7:7-13. The completion of the collection will be a second, decisive test of their faith, love, earnestness, and loyalty to Paul, see 2 Cor. 8:8,24, 9:4ff., 13. Cf. also 13:5-10. (J. Espy).

5. The formula *peri men gar*, "now...about," in 2 Cor. 9:1 could, but does not need to, introduce a new topic. It could mark the transition from the recommendation of Titus and two brothers in 2 Cor. 8:16-24 to the resumed treatment of the collection itself in chapter 9. Even in 2 Cor. 9:3-5 Paul refers to the anonymous brothers, who apparently were representatives of the churches and members of the delegation that was to bring the collection to Jerusalem.

It is possible and even likely that Paul in his letter referred to the two brothers by name. If so, their names would for some reason have been deleted at an early stage of the textual history. Thus, there is indeed a possibility that the document which we read as 2 Corinthians underwent some editorial redaction at an early stage. But even if the document were composite, the seams should be located between chapters 8 and 9 and/or between chapters 9 and 10 but not between chapters 7 and 8 or between 7:4 and 7:5. On the special problem of 2 Cor. 6:14 - 7:1, see Chapter IV below.

CHAPTER III

PAUL AND THE CHURCH AT CORINTH
ACCORDING TO 1 CORINTHIANS 1:10-4:21

When Ferdinand Christian Baur in 1831 published his famous article on "The Christ-party in the Corinthian Church,"[1] he was not raising a new question but making a fresh contribution to a discussion which had already begun. Yet his article is generally considered to have inaugurated a new epoch in the history of New Testament scholarship. Dealing with one specific question, Baur in his article gave a first sketch of his understanding of the historical dialectic in primitive Christianity. The main ideas were later developed in voluminous works by Baur and his pupils in the "Tübingen School," and have exerted a considerable influence upon students of the New Testament up to the present day.

In his essay Baur argued that in spite of the four slogans reported in 1 Cor. 1:12 there were, in fact, only two parties involved in the strife at Corinth: over against the adherents of Paul and Apollos stood those of Cephas, who claimed to be those who belonged to Christ. As the weaknesses of this theory have often been pointed out, there may be some reason for calling attention to its strengths. Baur observed that in 1 Cor. 1-4 Paul does not deal with a variety of parties, but in "this

---

[1]"Die Christuspartei in der korinthischen Gemeinde, der Gegensatz des paulinischen und petrinischen Christentums in der ältesten Kirche, der Apostel Petrus in Rom," *Tübinger Zeitschrift für Theologie* (1831), Heft 4, pp. 61-206. Cf. Baur, *Paulus* (Stuttgart, 1945), 259-332.

first apologetic section" gives a justification for his apostolic
authority and ministry. Further, he was able to trace a
continuity between 1 Cor. 1-4 and the later controversy of which
2 Corinthians, especially chapters 10-13, is evidence. Baur
could also relate the enigmatic slogan "I belong to Christ" to
Paul's remark in 2 Cor. 10:7: "If any one is confident that he
is Christ's, let him remind himself that as he is Christ's, so
are we." Finally, Baur was able to integrate the Corinthian
controversy into a comprehensive view of the earliest history
of Christianity which he found to be determined by the tension
between Paulinists and Petrine Judaizers. Yet, the arbitrary
reduction of the four slogans to two parties caused numerous
modifications of Baur's theory even within his own school.

More than one hundred years of research since Baur's
essay has made it clear that there is no real trace of Judaizers
at Corinth, at least not at the time of 1 Corinthians. According
to Wilhelm Lütgert, Paul's chief opponents at Corinth, identified
with the Christ party, were spiritualistic enthusiasts, an early
type of libertinistic Gnostics.[2] This theory has been very
influential in Germany. Adolf Schlatter modified it by tracing
a Palestinian background for the "Corinthian theology."[3] The
philologist Richard Reitzenstein explained both Paul's terminology
and the Corinthian piety on the background of contemporary
Hellenistic religiosity, mystery religions and syncretistic
Gnosis.[4] More recently W. Schmithals[5] and, in a different way,
U. Wilckens[6] have tried to reconstruct the doctrines of the
Gnostics in Corinth.

Outside Germany scholars have been more reluctant to
assume that Paul's polemic had to be directed either against
Judaizers or against Gnostics. Johannes Munck published an essay
on 1 Cor. 1-4, later incorporated in his book *Paul and the
Salvation of Mankind*, with the provocative title "The Church

---

[2]*Freiheitspredigt und Schwarmgeister in Korinth* (BFCT 12,
3, Gütersloh, 1908).
[3]*Die korinthische Theologie* (*Ibid.* 18, 2, Gütersloh, 1914).
Cf. also Schlatter's commentary, *Paulus, der Bote Jesu* (Stuttgart:
Calwer, 1934).
[4]*Die hellenistischen Mysterienreligionen* (3rd ed., 1910;
Leipzig: Teubner, 1927), esp. 333-393, "Paulus als Pneumatiker."
[5]*Gnosticism in Corinth* (1st ed., 1956; ET; Nashville:
Abingdon, 1971).
[6]*Weisheit und Torheit* (BHT 26; Tübingen: Mohr, 1959).
See the critical review by H. Koester in *Gnomon*, 33 (1961),
593ff.

without Factions."[7] He held that there were neither parties nor
Judaizers, and, we may add, no Gnostics at Corinth. What caused
the trouble was that the Corinthians, owing to their Greek back-
gound, misunderstood Christianity as wisdom: they took the
Christian leaders to be teachers of wisdom, like rhetors and
sophists who took themselves to be wise and made all this a
cause for boasting. More recently, John C. Hurd, Jr., has
written a very stimulating book on *The Origin of 1 Corinthians*.[8]
Following solid traditions of American scholarship, he avoids
the generalizations of theology and comparative religion and
tries to reconstruct the stages of the relations between Paul
and the church at Corinth prior to 1 Corinthians. The result
is that the controversies behind 1 Corinthians were not due to
any extraneous influence upon the congregation, but to Paul's
own change of mind in the time between Paul's Corinthian ministry
and the previous letter referred to in 1 Cor. 5:9-11. This change
is explained as due to the apostolic decree to which Paul in
his previous letter felt obliged to be loyal; in accordance with
John Knox and others, Hurd argues that the Corinthian ministry
preceded the Apostolic Council, according to a chronology based
on Paul's letters and not on the secondary evidence of Acts.[9]

This brief and eclectic, but fairly representative
summary shows that while there is a wide negative agreement that
in 1 Corinthians Paul is not opposing Judaizers, there is no
consensus with regard to the background and nature of the controversies. As to the questions of exegesis, it is quite generally
agreed that in 1 Cor. 1-4 Paul is addressing the church at Corinth
as a whole, and that it is not possible to take any one section
to refer to any one of the parties, if there were such parties.
Likewise, while 1 Cor. 5-16 may attest the presence of various
trends within the congregation, it has not proved possible with
any degree of certainty to relate these trends to the slogans
reported at the beginning (1:12). But this exegetical consensus
is only a negative one.

No clear interpretation has been given to the slogans
of 1:12. If there were no factions, but merely quarrelling,
jealousy and strife, the difficulties are increased. Why, then,
does Paul give the slogans such a prominent place? The major

---

[7]"Menigheden uden Partier," *DTT* 15 (1952), 251-253. Incorporated as chapter 5 of *Paul and the Salvation of Mankind.*
[8]*The Origin of 1 Corinthians* (New York: Seabury, 1965).
[9]Cf. John Knox, *Chapters in a Life of Paul* (New York:
Abingdon, 1950), 13-88 (in *Apex Books* edition).

difficulty lies in the words "I belong to Christ" which quite a
few scholars regard as a gloss.[10] The combination with 2 Cor.
10:7 favored by Baur and, on different presuppositions, by Lütgert.
and Schmithals, seems to provide the relatively best possibilities
of interpretation, but the theories of these scholars are open
to other objections.

No clarity has been reached with regard to the relation
between chapters 1-4 and the rest of the epistle. An increasing
number of scholars doubt the integrity of 1 Corinthians; the
present epistle is assumed to be a composition of fragments
from two or more letters.[11] Hurd offers a valuable survey and
critique of these theories, but fails to provide a reasonable
explanation of the function of the first major section (1:10-
4:21) within the letter as a whole. On the fairly dubious
principle that "clearly the greater objectivity attaches to the
written portion of the information,"[12] he bases his understanding
of the background of 1 Corinthians entirely upon the hypothetical
reconstruction of the letter from the Corinthians to Paul and
Paul's previous letter. This may represent a sound reaction
against other scholars who have based their theories mainly
upon 1 Cor. 1-4. Munck deals only with these chapters, and
Wilckens concentrates on 1 Cor. 1-2 alone! But personally I
cannot share the optimism with regard to the objectivity of
written documents such as statements issued by ecclesiastical
bodies, and often find oral information more revealing with
regard to what has been going on. In fact, Hurd is hardly able
to make anything out of 1 Cor. 1-4, and the "tentative suggestion"
which he finally makes is a bad relapse into a method which he
has in principle overcome.[13]

Finally, no clarity has been reached with regard to
the relation between the situations reflected in 1 Corinthians
and in 2 Corinthians. Is Paul in 2 Corinthians, or in the
fragments of which the epistle is often assumed to be composed,
dealing with later developments of the same controversy as in

---

[10]J. Weiss and others, including Wilckens. For references
cf. Hurd, 96-107, and (Feine-Behm) W. G. Kümmel, *Introduction
to the New Testament* (Rev. ed.; Nashville: Abingdon, 1975), 273.

[11]Cf. Hurd, 43-47, 69-71, 86-89, 131-142. Kümmel,
Introduction, 202-205.

[12]Hurd, 62. But cf. also p. 113: "Paul knew from his
oral information that the Corinthians had not been altogether
candid with him in the letter they addressed to him."

[13]*Ibid.*, 269-270. Cf. the summary on p. 295: "I Cor.
1-4 and II Cor. 11:17-33 concern the 'parties' which we suggested
were the result of disagreement over the effect of the Previous
Letter on the table fellowship between Jewish and Gentile Christians."

1 Cor. 1-4, or is he facing entirely new problems? Both views are held, and there are arguments which seem to favor both of them.[14] In the following pages it will be argued that while Baur was wrong in taking Paul's opponents in 1 Cor. 1-4 to be Judaizers, he was fully right in speaking of these chapters as an "apologetic section" in which Paul justifies his apostolic ministry. It is a main failure of theories like those of Munck and Hurd that they do not really take this into account.[15]

An attempt to reach beyond the present impasse in the interpretation of 1 Cor. 1-4 must be performed according to a strict method if the result is not going to add to a chaos which is already bad enough. I would suggest the following principles:

(1) The controversy must be studied as such. Due account must be taken of the perspective under which Paul envisages the situation at Corinth. But as far as possible, we must also try to understand the Corinthian reaction to Paul.

(2) While 1 Cor. 1-4 must be understood against the historical background, any reconstruction of that background must mainly be based on information contained within the section itself. Relatively clear and objective statements concerning the situation at Corinth must serve as a basis. Evaluations, polemical and ironic allusions, warnings and exhortations may next be used to fill out the picture. Only when these possibilities have been exhausted, and with great caution, should Paul's own teaching be used as a source of information concerning views held by the Corinthians; Paul may have adapted his language to theirs, but this assumption remains highly conjectural.

(3) The integrity of 1 Corinthians may be assumed as a working hypothesis which is confirmed if it proves possible to understand 1 Cor. 1:10-4:21 as an introductory section with a definite purpose within the letter as a whole. Materials from 1 Cor. 5-16 should therefore be used for the sake of comparison. Special attention should be paid to chapters 5 and 6 which in the present context stand at the transition from 1-4 to those

---

[14]Examples are given by Kümmel, *Introduction*, 284-286.
[15]Without making any impression upon Munck, I tried to draw attention to the apologetic aspect in an article, "Paulus apostel og menigheten i Korinth (I. Kor. 1-4)," *NorTT* 54 (1953), 1-23. The present essay is an attempt to restate and elaborate my case, with less attention paid to exegetical details, and with the addition of some new, more conjectural hypotheses. My interest in the topic has been renewed by the work of Hurd, but it is not a main purpose to discuss his theories.

sections of the epistle in which Paul handles questions raised
by the letter from Corinth.

(4) In so far as they do not directly serve the purpose
of philological exegesis, but provide materials for a more
general historical and theological understanding, information
from other Pauline epistles, Acts, and other early Christian,
Jewish, Greek, or Gnostic documents should not be brought in
until the epistolary situation has been clarified as far as
possible on the basis of internal evidence. Points of similarity,
especially with 2 Corinthians, should be noted, but not used in
such a way that the results of contextual exegesis are pre-judged.

(5) Any reconstruction of the historical background
will at best be a reasonable hypothesis. A hypothesis will
recommend itself to the degree to which it is able to account
for the total argument and all details within 1 Cor. 1-4 with
a minimal dependence upon hypothetical inferences derived from
extraneous sources. The results achieved will gain in probability
if they can without difficulty be integrated into a comprehensive
picture of the history of primitive Christianity in its contemporary setting.[16]

The basic information contained in 1 Cor. 1:10-4:21 is
what was reported by Chloe's people: there was quarrelling
(*erides*) among the Christians at Corinth, each one of them saying,
"I belong to Paul," or "I to Apollos," or "I to Christ." In
3:3-4, where only the names of Paul and Apollos are mentioned,
Paul speaks about "jealousy and strife" (*zēlos kai eris*). As
the implication of the slogans is controversial, only the fact
of the quarrels is unambiguous. Another piece of evidence is,
however, added at the end of the section: "Some are arrogant
(*ephysiōthēsan*, lit. have been puffed up) as though I were not
coming to you" (4:18). That the persons in question were
"arrogant" (*RSV*), or "filled with self-importance" (*NEB*), is
Paul's evaluation. But we do get the information that some
assumed that Paul would not come back to Corinth. It seems likely
that they expressed their view openly.[17] In view of this statement, the idea that Paul always deals with the congregation as
a whole needs some modification; there are certain persons whom

---

[16]The statement of methodological principles will make it
clear why I discuss the theories of Munck and Hurd rather than
those of Schmithals and Wilckens. This does not reduce the value
of the immense amount of material gathered, especially by Wilckens.

[17]This is made fairly clear by the emphatic *eleusomai de*
at the beginning of verse 19, cf. verse 21 and 16:5-7.

he regards as "arrogant." As often, he uses the indefinite
pronoun *tines* to refer to definite persons whose names he does
not want to mention.[18] This indicates that Paul is aware of
the existence of some center of opposition to him within the
church at Corinth.

The results of this search for objective information may
seem to be very meager. But if combined the pieces of information
disclose that the quarrels and the slogans at Corinth were
related to the assumption that the apostle would not return. The
general context supports this combination.

The whole section begins with Paul's appeal to his
brethren in Corinth that they should agree and avoid divisions
(1:10). It ends with an equally urgent appeal that they should
be imitators of Paul: to that purpose he sends Timothy who
will remind them of his instructions (4:16-17). Both in 1:10
and 4:16 we find periods headed by the verb *parakalō* ("I appeal,"
"beseech," or "urge"), a formal pattern which Paul uses when
he sets forth what is a main purpose of his letters, expressing
what he wants the addressees to do.[19] The *parakalō*-periods are
distinguished from strict imperatives in that they call for a
voluntary response. But Paul makes it quite clear that as the
Corinthians' only father in Christ he does have authority to
command, even if he does not do so, He hopes that he will not
have to use his rod when he comes to Corinth which he plans to
do if that is the will of the Lord (4:14-15, 19-21). At the
beginning Paul asks for the mutual concord of the brethren; at
the end of the section if not before, the reader understands
that Paul at the same time asks his children to concur in harmony
with their father in Christ. This is well brought out by John
Knox, who has written, with reference to 1 Cor. 1-4: "He wants
his converts to stand firm, not only in the Lord, but also in
their loyalty to him."[20]

The general content of the section adds further confirmation to this. It deals with four main themes:

(1) Unity in Christ and the quarrels at Corinth, 1:10-13.
This initial theme is taken up again in 3:3-4 and 21-23.

---

[18]Cf. Rom. 3:8; 1 Cor. 15:12, 34; 2 Cor. 3:1; 10:2, 12;
Gal. 1:7; Phil. 1:15; 2 Thess. 3:11 (1 Tim. 1:6, 19; 4:1; 6:10,
21). Sometimes even *tis* or *ei tis* is used in a similar way.
[19]The clearest example of this epistolary use of *parakalō*
is found in Philem. 8ff. Cf. John Knox, *Philemon among the
Letters of Paul* (1935; 2nd ed.; New York: Abingdon, 1959), 22f.;
Bjerkelund, 118ff., 162ff.
[20]*Chapters in a Life of Paul*, 95.

(2) Wisdom and foolishness, the power and wisdom of God over against the wisdom of men. Various aspects of this main theme are handled in 1:17-3:2, and taken up again in 3:18-21 and 4:7-10.

(3) The function of the apostles and Christian leaders, and the esteem in which they should be held, 3:5-4:6, cf. 4:9-13.

(4) Paul's relations to the church at Corinth. This theme is implicit throughout the whole section from 1:13 onwards and comes into the foreground at the end, 4:14-21.

It is clear how the first and the third theme are related to one another. The Corinthians are quarrelling because they "boast of men," i.e. of one of the teachers, and are "puffed up in favor of one (of them) against the other" (3:21; 4:6). It is somewhat less evident why the wisdom theme is given such a prominent place. However, Paul takes the Corinthians' boasting of the teachers to imply boasting of their own wisdom (cf. 3:18-21; 4:7-10). At the same time, he sees the quarrelling as clear evidence that the Corinthians are not as wise and spiritual as they imagine themselves to be (3:3-4). But in order to understand the structure of the total argument we have to realize that the fourth theme, the apostle and his relations to the church at Corinth, comes in at all important points of transition.

The initial appeal for unity immediately leads to Paul's activity at Corinth and to his commission as a messenger of the gospel (1:13-17). In 2:1-5 and 3:1-2 Paul returns to his own first preaching at Corinth, so that this provides the framework within which he deals with the word of the cross and with the way in which the Corinthian brethren were called (1:18-25, 26-31), as well as with the wisdom which is reserved for the mature (2:6-16).

From his first preaching at Corinth Paul returns to the present situation (3:2c-4; cf. 1:11-12). Even when he deals with the questions, "What then is Apollos? What is Paul?" he not only makes statements of principle, but points to the special ministry assigned to him (3:10-11), and asserts that no human court, but only the Lord, is to pass judgment upon him (4:3-4). Even when he contrasts the predicaments of the apostles with the riches of the wise Corinthians, Paul has first of all his own ministry and sufferings in mind (4:8-13). Thus the whole argument quite naturally leads to the conclusion, "For though you have countless guides in Christ, you do not have many fathers. For I became your father (*hymas egennēsa*) in Christ Jesus through

the Gospel." It would be unfair to say that preparation for this
statement is the main function of everything that has been said;
yet, one aim of what Paul has to say about the strife at Corinth
about wisdom and foolishness, and about the function of Christian
leaders, is to re-establish his authority as apostle and spiritual
father of the church at Corinth.[21]

From the statement, "With me it is a very small thing
that I should be judged by you or by any human court" (4:3), we
may safely infer that some kind of criticism of Paul has been
voiced at Corinth. And it is not difficult to find out what
the main content of this criticism must have been. That becomes
evident in phrases like, "Not with eloquent wisdom" (*ouk en
sophia logou*, 1:17), "Not in lofty words of wisdom" (*ou kath'
hyperochēn logou ē sophias*, 2:1), "Not in persuasiveness of
wisdom" (*ouk en peithoi sophias*, 2:4),[22] "Milk, not solid food"
(*gala . . . ou brōma*, 3:2). To what extent the phrases, and
not merely their content, allude to what was reported to have
been said, is immaterial. Since the Corinthians evidently
understood themselves as wise because they thought themselves
inspired, pneumatic persons (cf. 3:1), we must conclude that Paul
was not merely held to lack the oratorical ability of a Greek
rhetor, but also the gift of pneumatic wisdom. In 4:8 the
apostles are not only said to be "fools for Christ's sake," but
also "weak," and "in disrepute."[23]

In addition to Paul's alleged lack of wisdom, Paul's
critics may have mentioned other failings. He had not baptized
many (cf. 1:14). The catalog of sufferings in 4:11-13 deserves
close attention. Hunger, thirst, and nakedness are common

---

[21]On several occasions the point that is most directly
relevant to the actual situation comes towards the end of a section
or an epistle, cf. 1 Cor. 10:23-11:1; 11:33-34; Rom. 15:30-33;
Gal. 6:11-17; Phil. 4:10-18; 2 Thess. 3:6-15. Thus there are
good analogies for the assumption that the issue involved in
1 Cor. 1-4 is most clearly to be seen in 4:14-21.

[22]I am inclined to take this as the original text which
by an early error was misspelled as *ouk en peithois sophias*.
The other variant readings can all be understood as attempts to
improve this. The problem has no material importance.

[23]Adducing very interesting evidence, Munck demonstrates
that Greek rhetors and sophists could be regarded as wise, powerful,
and honored: *Paul and the Salvation of Mankind*, 158f. and 162f.,
with notes. But he does himself see that the Corinthians thought
of their power as participation in the kingdom of God (p. 165).
The Greek analogies therefore do not suffice. At this date there
were hardly any sharp distinctions between philosophers, sophists,
rhetors, hierophants and mystagogues. For Jewish analogies cf.
D. Georgi, *Die Gegner des Paulus im 2. Korintherbrief* (WMANT 11;
Neukirchen: Neukirchener Verlag, 1964).

features in descriptions of persons in need (cf. e.g. Matt.
25:35-36). That he is "roughly handled" (*NEB, kolaphizometha*)
refers in a more specific way to afflictions suffered during
the apostolic ministry (cf. 2 Cor. 11:23-25). The lack of
stability (*astatoumen*) is characteristic of the apostle who is
"homeless"(*RSV*) and has to "wander from place to place" (*NEB*);
but the choice of the term may very well allude to what was
said at Corinth about the unstable apostle who was not likely
ever to come back (4:18; cf. 2 Cor. 1:15ff.). An unambiguous
reference to a practice of Paul which is known to have caused
objections at Corinth is contained in the clause "We labor,
working with our own hands" (cf. 1 Cor. 9:3-18; 2 Cor. 11:7-11;
12:13). Paul goes on: "When reviled, we bless; when persecuted,
we endure." This is what a follower of Christ should do (cf.
Luke 6:27-9; Rom 12:14). But adding, "When slandered, we make
our appeal" (*parakaloumen*, in *RSV*: "we try to conciliate"),
he once more alludes to the actual situation; at Corinth he is
slandered and responds, not with harsh words, but by making his
friendly--though not exactly "humble"(*NEB*)--appeal.

Since the entire section contains an apology for Paul,
and since the strife at Corinth was linked up with opposition
against him, it becomes possible to interpret the slogans reported
in 1:12. Those who said "I belong to Paul" were proud of him
and held that his excellence surpassed that of Apollos or Cephas.
The other slogans are all to be understood as declarations of
independence from Paul. Apollos is mentioned as the most
outstanding Christian teacher who had visited Corinth after Paul.
Cephas is the famous pillar, the first witness to the resurrection,
an apostle before Paul. The slogan "I belong to Christ" is not
the motto of a specific Christ-party but simply means "I myself
belong to Christ--and am independent of Paul." Understood in
this way, all the slogans have a clear meaning in the context
and in the situation. Paul had no reason to deal in detail with
the various groups, and it becomes quite natural that he should
concentrate his presentation on the relationship between himself
and Apollos.

It may be added that on the interpretation proposed, the
analogy between 1 Cor. 1:12f. and 2 Cor. 10:7 becomes clear. In
2 Cor. 10:7 there is no trace of a specific Christ-party: the
wandering apostles simply attacked Paul and claimed to belong to
Christ as his servants (cf. 11:23). Paul's answer is that he too
belongs to Christ, and, more than they, he is distinguished as
a servant of Christ by his sufferings. Here and there Paul finds

it an anomaly that someone at the same time can claim to belong
to Christ and yet oppose his apostle and faithful servant.

There is no reason to think that either Apollos or Cephas
was in any way responsible for the use that was made of his name
by people at Corinth who claimed to be independent of Paul.[24]
Paul himself stresses their solidarity and dependence upon God's
work (3:5-9, 22; 4:6; 15:11; 16:12). But what then was the
occasion for the strife and the opposition to Paul? One fact,
especially, needs explanation. The church at Corinth had sent
Stephanas, Fortunatus and Achaicus as a kind of official delegation
to Paul. In all probability, the Corinthians had commissioned
these delegates to bring a letter from the congregation to Paul,
asking for his opinion on a number of questions. In this letter
it was stated that the Corinthians remembered Paul in everything
and maintained the traditions he had delivered to them.[25] Thus,
the official attitude of the congregation seems to have been
one of loyalty to the apostle. Yet, Chloe's people could orally
report that there was strife in Corinth and that there was some
opposition to Paul. This tension between the written document
and the oral report requires some explanation.

We do not know anything either about Chloe or about her
people. From what Paul writes we do, however, learn one thing,
namely that it was not Stephanas and the other members of the
delegation who reported the quarrels at Corinth. It may mean
that the quarrels had started after the departure of the delegation,
or it may mean that the delegates had not gossiped. In any
case, Paul had his information about the quarrels and the opposition from some other source, and this may have been important
both to him and to the recipients of his letter. The name of
Stephanas is mentioned at the beginning of our section, in a very
curious fashion. Paul first states that he baptized none of the
Corinthians except Crispus and Gaius. But he has to correct
himself and add that he also baptized the household of Stephanas.
This lapse of memory may simply reflect that at the moment
Stephanas was with Paul and not at Corinth. But even without
much depth psychology one might suspect that Paul first forgot

---

[24]The Corinthians may well have derived their knowledge
of Cephas from what Paul had told them; at least Peter may have
been a great authority far away, in spite of the renewal by
C. K. Barrett of the theory that he had visited Corinth, "Cephas
and Corinth," *Abraham unser Vater: Festschrift O. Michel (Arbeiten
zur Geschichte des Spätjudentums und des Urchristentums*, 5;
Leiden: Brill, 1963), 1-12.

[25]1 Cor. 11:2. It is fairly generally agreed that Paul
here alludes to what was said in the letter from Corinth. Cf.
Hurd, 52 and 90f.

to mention the household of Stephanas because he did not wish
to involve Stephanas in his discussion of the divisions at
Corinth.

Much more important is the way Paul mentions Stephanas at
the end of the letter. First Paul recommends Stephanas and his
household; they were the first-fruits, i.e. the first converts
of Achaia, and have devoted themselves to the service of the
saints, which may mean that they have taken an active part in
the collection for Jerusalem.[26] With remarkable emphasis Paul
urges the congregation to be subject to such men and to every
fellow worker (16:15-16). After 1:10 and 4:16 this is the third
parakalō-period of the letter! Next Paul speaks about his joy
at the presence of the delegation, adding a new injunction:
"Give your recognition to such men" (16:17-18). It is risky
to draw conclusions from such injunctions as to the state of
affairs which they presuppose. But the double emphasis gives
some reason to suspect that not everybody in Corinth was inclined
to give due recognition to Stephanas, his household, and his
fellow delegates. The evidence is so far inconclusive, but a
hypothesis may be ventured: the quarrelling Corinthians were
opposing Stephanas as much as they were opposing Paul. As
Stephanas was the head of the delegation, he was quite likely
also its initiator, and a chief advocate of writing a letter to
Paul to ask for his opinion on controversial questions.[27]

The advantage of my conjecture is that it makes it
possible to explain in a simple, perhaps somewhat trivial way,
the data contained in 1 Cor. 1:10-4:21. The delegation and
the letter it carried were themselves the cause of the quarrels.
I can imagine myself hearing the objections, and I put them in
my own language:

> Why write to Paul? He has left us and is not likely
> to come back. He lacks eloquence and wisdom. He
> supported himself by his own work; either he does
> not have the full rights of an apostle, or he did not
> esteem us to be worthy of supporting him. Why not
> rather write to Apollos, who is a wise teacher? I
> am his man! Or, if we do turn to anybody, why not
> write to Cephas, who is the foremost of the twelve.

---

[26]R. Asting mentions this possibility, but is more inclined
to think that Paul refers to service rendered to Christian
preachers, including himself. *Die Heiligkeit im Urchristentum*
(FRLANT 46, nF 29; Göttingen: Vandenhoeck & Ruprecht, 1930), 151
and 182-183.

[27]Hurd argues that the Corinthians' questions were veiled
objections (113 and chapter 5, 114-209). In that case, the role
of Stephanas may have been that of a mediator who succeeded in
persuading the brethren that the objections should be presented
to Paul in the form of a polite letter. But cf. notes 39 and
40 below.

> I am for Cephas! But, why ask anyone for counsel?
> Should we not rather say: I myself belong to
> Christ? As spiritual men we ought to be wise
> enough to decide for oursleves.

The details of this picture are of course pure imagination.
But they may help us visualize the delicate situation Paul was
facing when he set out to write his answer to the Corinthians.
He had to answer a polite, official letter that asked for his
advice. But he had also received an oral report stating that
some brethren at Corinth had objected to the idea of asking
Paul for instructions. Quite likely, latent objections had
become more open and had caused a good deal of quarrelling after
the departure of the delegation. As a consequence, Paul had
to envisage the possibility that his letter containing his reply
might easily make a bad situation worse. Quarrel and strife
might develop into real divisions of the church, if his recommendations were enthusiastically received by one group and rejected
by others.[28]

If the situation was anything like what I imagine, Paul
could not possibly go right ahead and answer the questions raised
in the letter from the Corinthians. He had first of all to make
it clear that he did not speak as the champion of one group but
as the apostle of Christ, as the founder and spiritual father of
the whole congregation. The first section, chapters 1-4, is
therefore a necessary part of the total structure of the letter
and has a preparatory function. This also explains the somewhat
unusual pattern that a short thanksgiving (1:4ff.) is immediately
followed by the first *parakalō*-period.[29] Paul had first of all
to urge the Corinthians to agree, to be of one mind. Only on
the presupposition that they did so, and that no divisions arose,
would whatever else the apostle had to write be of any help.

Answering his critics, Paul is very careful to avoid
giving the impression that he favors any one group in Corinth.
There is no competition between himself and Apollos or Cephas,

---

[28]While Munck rightly argues that the term *schismata* used
in 1 Cor. 1:10 (cf. 11:18 and 12:25) does not prove that there
were "parties" or "factions," he has a tendency to play down the
serious danger of divisions within the church, *Paul and the
Salvation of Mankind*, 136-139. I am still inclined to think that
schismata corresponds to the term *maḥalākōt* used in rabbinic
literature. Jonathan ben Uzziel, for instance, is said to have
translated the prophets "in order that divisions should not
multiply in Israel," b.Megilla *3a*. Cf. my book, *Das Volk Gottes*
(1941, repr.; Darmstadt: Wisenschaftliche Buchgesellschaft,
1963) 224.

[29]The closest analogy is the period introduced by the
equivalent *erōtōmen* in 2 Thess. 2:1. See Bjerkelund, esp. 189ff.

and still less between Christ and himself. Therefore even the
slogan "I belong to Christ" is fittingly countered by the questions,
"Is Christ divided? Was Paul crucified for you? Or were you
baptized in the name of Paul?" There is only one Christ, and
therefore no distinction between the Christ to whom the Corinthians
belong and the Christ preached by Paul. Paul is Christ's delegate
and in no sense his rival. At Corinth he laid the foundation,
and it is impossible to belong to Christ without building upon
this foundation, which is Jesus Christ himself (cf. 3:10-11,
21-23).[30]

That Paul did not baptize many is for him a reason for
thanksgiving. There is no risk that anyone will say that he was
baptized in Paul's name and has been made his man. The task of
the apostle was not to baptize but to proclaim the gospel (1:14-17).
That he did not preach with eloquent wisdom was to the benefit of
the Corinthians, and in accordance both with his own commission
and with the nature of the gospel, which is the word of the cross.
What may appear as sheer folly is God's saving power and wisdom
(1:18-25). The Corinthians ought to know this from their own
experience (1:26-31). When Paul in Corinth concentrated on
preaching Jesus Christ as the crucified one, this was due to a
conscious decision. He renounced all the effects of rhetoric
and human wisdom, in order that the faith of the converts might
rest in the power of God alone (2:1-5). But when he did not
in Corinth elaborate the secret wisdom of God's way of acting,
it was not because Paul lacked the pneumatic gift of wise speech,
but because the Corinthians were immature (2:6-3:2).

My one-sided and incomplete summary of 1:14-3:2 may be
sufficient for the purpose to show that everything Paul here
says was relevant to the situation he faced. From 3:3 onwards he

[30]Even in 2 Cor. 11:4 the point is the identity of Jesus
and not a variety of Christologies. Paul preached the true Jesus
and made him the foundation of the church at Corinth. A Jesus who
does not fit this teaching must be a false Jesus. The same holds
true for a Spirit and a gospel which is received as if Paul had
not already preached the gospel and as if those who then believed
had not already received the Holy Spirit. Hurd (104-105) has
well summarized the arguments against the existence of a separate
Christ party. Paul's replies would "simply further the claims"
of the party. But Hurd has failed to take into account the
possibility that "I belong to Christ" could be an anti-Pauline
slogan even if it is not the device of a special party. On that
presupposition the replies become highly relevant just because
"It is axiomatic that Christ is a unity," as Hurd says himself;
Paul is not a rival, but the apostle, servant, and steward of
Christ. The argument in 1 Cor. 1:13-15 is analogous with 3:5-11
and 3:21-23; 2 Cor. 10:7; 11:1-4, and 11:23.

turns more directly to the present state of affairs. Using himself and Apollos as examples, he stresses their solidarity as
servants and fellow workers for God. Those who make comparisons
and are proud of the excellencies of their favorite fail to
realize their own dignity as God's field, building, and temple
(3:5-17). All things, including Paul, Apollos, and Cephas,
belong to those who themselves belong to Christ (3:21-23). Yet
it is also stressed that Paul had a special task of his own. He
was the one who planted and laid the foundation, and this he did
as a skilled master builder (*hōs sophos architektōn*). Certainly
he did not lack wisdom (3:6, 10). While Paul has no authority
of his own, all others have to build on the foundation laid by
him. They have to take care, lest they build with materials that
will perish, or even destroy the temple of God (3:10-17). The
context suggests that those who vaunt their wisdom might easily be
guilty of these offences.[31] When speaking about faithfulness
as the one duty required of stewards, Paul once more immediately
turns to the relations between the Corinthians and himself (4:2-5).

Even the riddle of the enigmatic statement in 1 Cor. 4:6
may possibly find a solution. The phrase *mē hyper ha gegraptai*
("not beyond what is written") is widely assumed to be the quotation
of a slogan used in Corinth.[32] I would suggest that even this
slogan was part of the discussions and quarrels connected with
the delegation and the letter to Paul. The point would then
be: "We need no instructions beyond what is written. As spiritual
men we can interpret the Scriptures for ourselves. Why ask Paul?"
Paul picks the slogan up and returns it. There is no contrast
between the apostle and "What is written," but there might be one
between the scriptures, Paul and Apollos on the one side and the
assertive and quarrelling Corinthians on the other. By the example
of Paul and Apollos they should learn not to go beyond what is

---

[31] I see no reason for making 3:18 the beginning of a new
section.

[32] In addition to the commentaries, cf. O. Linton,"'Nicht
über das hinaus was geschrieben steht' (1 Kor. 4. 6)," *TSK* 102
(1930), 425-437; L. Brun, "Noch einmal die Schriftnorm 1. Kor. 4,
6," *ibid.* 103 (1931), 453-456; M. D. Hooker, "'Beyond the things
which are written'," *NTS* 10 (1964), 127-132. Miss Hooker deals
very well with the terminology and context, but I have not been
convinced by her renewal of Lütgert's and Schlatter's suggestion
that the Corinthians ventured to go beyond what was written. It
seems much more likely to me that they exercised their wisdom as
interpreters of scripture as suggested by the terms *sophos*, *grammateus*,
and *suzētētēs* in 1 Cor. 1:20. Only in 1 Corinthians does Paul use
quotation formulas like, "It is written in the law," and "The law
says" (9:8, 9; 14:21, 34); the reason might be that he agrees to
play the game according to the rules set by the Corinthians themselves.

written, viz., not to be puffed up, but faithfully to perform
the appointed service, knowing that everything is a gift of God.
In the context the slogan gets its content from the preceding
citations from and allusions to what is written concerning the
wisdom of God in contrast to the wisdom of men (cf. 1:19f.;
1:31; 2:9; 3:19f.).

Paul does not, as his adherents are likely to have done,
deny the facts which his opponents alleged against him. But
what they meant as objections Paul interprets as indications of
the faithfulness with which he has carried out his commission.
Lack of wisdom, power, and honor is part of the lot that God
has assigned to the suffering apostles of the crucified Christ
(4:9-13). In order to forestall the possibility that quarrels
could lead to divisions, Paul the whole time deals with the
church at Corinth as a unity. Only at the end does he single
out some persons and flatly deny what they have asserted (4:18f.),
that he will not return to Corinth, and, therefore, that he no
longer cares for the brethren there; it is simply not true.
They are his dear children, and certainly he will come very
soon, if the Lord wills. This assertion is repeated at the end
of the epistle (16:5-7, cf. also 16:24).

We can now draw some conclusions:

(1) The section 1 Cor. 1:10-4:21 is correctly, even if not
exhaustively, to be characterized as an apology for Paul's
apostolic ministry.

(2) The quarrels at Corinth were mainly due to the
opposition against Paul.

(3) Probably, the quarrels were occasioned or at least
brought into the open by the letter and the delegation which
were sent to Paul.

(4) The section has a clear and important function within
the total structure of 1 Corinthians; before Paul could answer
the questions raised, he had to overcome both false appraisals
and false objections, and to re-establish his apostolic authority
as the founder and spiritual father of the whole church at Corinth.[33]

A number of problems remain. I have to deal briefly with
some of them. The first is the function of 1 Cor. 5-6. Why doesn't
Paul after the introductory section immediately proceed to give

---

[33]As to Paul's authority, cf. 1 Cor. 5:3-4; 7:40b; 9;
11:16, 34b; 14:37-38; 15:1-2, 10, and 2 Corinthians, *passim*.

his answer to the questions raised by the Corinthians? It is hardly more than a partial answer that in chapters 5-6, and in 1-4, he deals with matters about which he has only oral information.[34] In spite of theories that fragments from several letters are combined, chapters 5-6 seem to be closely related to their context. There are several points of contact between the preceding section and the beginning of chapter 5.[35] 6:12-20 anticipates several items in the latter part of the epistle.[36] 6:1-11 is related to chapter 5 by the idea of judgment, by the question of the relations to those outside the church, and especially by the catalogs of sinners in 5:10 and 11 and 6:9-10. Finally, 6:9-11 serves not only as a conclusion to 6:1-8 but also as an introduction to 6:12-20. There is no reason to doubt the literary integrity. The problem is that of the epistolary function of these short sections.

The most important point in this connection may be the allusion to the previous letter, 5:9-11. I have elsewhere argued that the content of what Paul wrote may best be reconstructed by a combination of 5:9-10 with 6:9-10.[37] He must have written something like: "Neither immoral men, nor the greedy, nor robbers, nor idolaters, etc., will inherit the kingdom of God. Do not associate with them, nor even eat with them." If this reconstruction is approximately correct, the fragment 2 Cor. 6:14-7:1 is hardly likely to have been part of the previous letter.[38] Closer parallels are found in the catechetical instructions in Eph. 5:3-7 and Gal. 5:19-21, cf. also Col. 3:5-6; 1 Thess. 4:3-6, and the free, epistolary variation in Rom. 1:18-2:11. Thus, the previous letter is likely to have contained a restatement of Paul's oral instructions, just like 1 Thess. 4:2ff.[39]

---

[34]The section 11:17-34 is an example of material based on oral information and dealt with at a later place in the letter. Cf. Hurd, 79-82.

[35]*pephysiōmenoi*, 5:1; cf. 4:19. Paul's absence and presence, 5:3; cf. 4:19f.; *kauchēma*, 4:6; cf. 3:21; 4:7. Cf. Hurd, 89, n. 1.

[36]Cf. Hurd, 87-9.

[37]See my article, "Der Epheserbrief und der verlorene, erste Brief des Paulus an die Korinther," *Festschrift O. Michel* (see note 24), 65-77.

[38]See Chapter IV below.

[39]Hurd has seen that there are some signs of similarities between 1 Thessalonians and the previous letter. (231-233). In addition to the analogies between 1 Thess. 4:2-6 and 1 Cor. 5-6, statements like 4:4-5, 4:13-18, and 4:19-20 might in fact have occasioned questions like those which are treated in 1 Cor. 7, 12-14, and 15. But, instead of following this track, Hurd has elaborated the much less attractive hypothesis that the previous letter was occasioned by the Apostolic Decree.

It is fairly generally assumed that in Corinth what Paul
had written was taken to imply that all social relations with
unbelievers had to be broken off, and that, in 1 Cor. 5:9-13,
Paul is correcting this idea, whether (as is sometimes assumed)
it was his own original intention, which he subsequently altered,
or whether it was the Corinthians' misunderstanding of what he
wrote. Certainly the scope of his instruction may have been
open to several interpretations, as can be seen by the analogous
passage in Eph. 5:3ff. But neither theory--self-correction or
misunderstanding--is necessary.[40] The point in 1 Cor. 5:9ff.
may simply be a matter of clarification, with the purpose of
stressing that what Paul wrote was highly relevant to the church
at Corinth. I am therefore inclined to think that chapters 5-6
are still closely related to the controversies which the first
main section of the epistle sought to clear up.

At Corinth someone may have felt that even in his previous
letter Paul had only given them milk and not solid food; why
ask for a new letter from him? Dealing with two concrete cases,
and adding some general warnings against sexual license, Paul
is able to illustrate his point, viz., that the brethren at
Corinth are still badly in need of the milk of elementary instruction concerning a Christian way of life. Understood in this
fashion, chapters 5 and 6 can be seen to have an important
function as the transition from the introductory section to the
answers given to the questions raised by the letter from Corinth.
To put it more bluntly: Paul did not want to shame his children
at Corinth by what he wrote concerning their quarrels and the
opposition to him (4:14), but before he proceeded to answer their
questions he did point out that there were cases of which they
ought to feel ashamed (5:1-6; 6:5). If the incestuous man is to
be identified as one of those who were puffed up, assuming that
Paul would not return (4:18), the reasons for this would be quite
obvious; but I see no possibility for deciding whether he was
or not.[41]

---

[40]I owe this observation to C. Douglas Gunn. To state
"that we have in 1 Cor. 5:9-11 Paul's own word for the fact that
his earlier statement on the subject had been misunderstood by
the Corinthians," as Hurd does on p. 215, is not correct. But
even if one accepts the probability of the inference, as I have earlier
done myself, there is not sufficient evidence to justify the shift
from Hurd's first conclusion that it is not possible to know whether
or not the section 5:9-13a was occasioned by the Corinthians'
letter, to his later assumption that this was indeed the case
(Hurd, 83, 149-154, 215, 219f.).
[41]In case he was, the further identification with Paul's
opponent in 2 Cor. 2:5ff. and 7:12 would not be as improbable
as most contemporary commentators think.

In my essay I have explained the controversies reflected
in 1 Cor. 1-4 in terms of the church policy and personal matters
involved. This does not mean that I think the theological aspects
of minor importance. But in practice theological debates usually
involve questions of church policy and personal relations. I
see no reason to assume that this was different at the time of
Paul. Though we regard theology, church policy, and personal
relations as separate and yet allow them, illegitimately, to
influence one another, Paul makes no such distinctions. He does
not distinguish person and office, but identifies himself and
wants to be identified by his apostolic ministry.[42] Even his
theology and his policy cannot be kept separate from one another.
His theology is flexible, responsive to different situations.
Yet it has a firm core. In shorthand fashion it may be called
a theology of the cross, a term that is especially appropriate
with regard to 1 Cor. 1-4. From this basis, he evaluates the
trends within the church at Corinth. He finds that the Corinthians
do not recognize the wisdom of God, manifested in the cross of
Christ. Claiming to have a wisdom of their own, they fail to
appreciate that wisdom which, to paraphrase a Lutheran term, is
an alien wisdom, *sapientia aliena*. They think that they already
possess the coming power and glory, not realizing that in this
world the glory of the church and its leaders is, like the glory
of Christ himself, veiled under weakness and sufferings (cf.
4:8ff.). Likewise, by passing judgments themselves, they fail
to take account of the judgment that is to come, which both the
apostle and his critics have to face (3:11-15; 4:5). Boasting
that they are pneumatic, they prove by their behavior that they
are psychic, sarkic, that they are just ordinary men (2:14-3:4).
Still using the language of Lutheran theology, we may say that in
the eyes of Paul the Corinthians uphold a false theology of glory.

To an adherent of *theologia crucis* any doctrine which
he dislikes may appear to be *theologia gloriae*. The term is not
very useful for characterizing any specific type of theology. We
have to raise the question whether or not this does in an analogous
way hold true to Paul's picture of the Corinthian theology. And
certainly, Christians at Corinth may have quarrelled and passed
critical judgments, both against Paul and against one another,
they may have appreciated wisdom and rhetoric, and they may have
been proud and even arrogant, without having any profound

---

[42]On Paul as an "eschatological person" cf. Fridrichsen,
p. 3 and *passim*.

theological reasons for all this. Much of what Paul writes does
not give us any information whatsoever about what was involved
in the theological aspects of the controversies. And yet, there
are some clear indications that Paul really did hit the nail on
the head when he found that the main tendency in Corinth was to
anticipate the eschatological glory to such a high degree that
almost nothing was left for the future. To use modern slogans:
the Corinthians upheld an "over-realized eschatology", over-
stressing the "already" and neglecting the "not yet".

The clearest evidence is to be found in 1 Cor. 15. Whatever may have been the exact views of those who said, "There is
no resurrection of the dead," they evidently saw no reason for
a future resurrection, since those who were baptized already
participate in heavenly glory.[43] That this was their attitude
both the sacramentalism and the pneumatic enthusiasm at Corinth
confirm (1 Cor. 10:1-13; 12-14).[44] The encratitic tendencies
with regard to marriage and sexual intercourse, as well as the
custom of allowing women to prophesy and speak in the assembled
congregation, without restrictions, are likely to reflect the
idea that there was no longer a distinction of male and female,
since those who belonged to the new mankind were like the angels
(1 Cor. 7; 11:2-15; 14:34-35). Even the knowledge and liberty
claimed in relation to meat sacrificed to idols point in the
direction of eschatological enthusiasm (chapters 12-14).

To Paul this type of enthusiasm is a perversion of the
message he had preached at Corinth. Yet it is conceivable that
it may have emerged spontaneously as a result of Paul's own
activity.[45] To some degree the tendencies may also have been
stimulated by the preaching of Apollos. I see no necessity for

---

[43]Cf., long ago, Schlatter, *Die Korinthische Theologie*
(see note 3), 28, 62-66, etc. Many details are still under
discussion, as, for instance, how far 2 Tim. 2:18 is an adequate
summary of the Corinthians' position; but a fairly wide consensus
seems to be emerging, cf. Hurd, 195-200 with references, and
further Munck, *Paul and the Salvation of Mankind*, 165-167, and
E. Käsemann, "On the Subject of Primitive Christian Apocalyptic,"
in *New Testament Questions of Today*, 131-137.

[44]In their letter the Corinthians must have written about
their zeal for spiritual gifts, 1 Cor. 14:12 and 39. This explains
the somewhat forced transitions in 12:31 and 14:1. This allusion
is more obvious than others which have been widely recognized,
but is not taken account of in the literature surveyed by Hurd,
67-68.

[45]Hurd's reconstruction of Paul's first preaching in
Corinth is reasonably independent of the dubious theory concerning
the impact made upon the previous letter by the Apostolic Decree.
Several points deserve serious attention. Cf. 273-288.

assuming any other extraneous influence at work. If the term
"Gnosis" is to be applied, one would probably have to assume
that in the spiritual climate of those days various types of
Gnosis could emerge, mutually independent of one another.[46]
But these are complicated questions. This short survey of
theological trends at Corinth has only one purpose in this
context: to show that the section 1 Cor. 1:10-4:21 not only
has the function of re-establishing the authority of Paul as the
founder and father of the entire church at Corinth, but also
prepares for the content of the answers given to the questions
raised and indicates the theological basis on which these answers
are given.

The way in which Paul identifies his cause and his person,
his policy and his theology, may be astonishing and strange to
us. We know that even at Corinth the reactions were mixed. The
letter apparently made its impact. In 2 Corinthians we hear no
more about the concrete questions discussed in 1 Corinthians;
probably Paul's instructions were accepted. The proposals to
appeal rather to Apollos or to Cephas may not have been very
serious, and proved to be failures. What did not come to an
end was the criticism directed toward the apostle. Many of the
objections which Paul countered in 1 Cor. 1-4 were voiced again,
partly in modified, partly in sharpened forms.[47] The relations
between the apostle and the church at Corinth in the time
between 1 and 2 Corinthians were both complex and troublesome.
It is easy to understand that many were quite willing to listen
when some new, wandering apostles arrived. And thus, the apostle
had once more to write an apology for his apostolic ministry, this
time in a sharper and more direct form (2 Corinthians, especially
chapters 10-13). The picture here drawn of the situation in
Corinth at the time of 1 Corinthians does therefore harmonize
very well with our general knowledge of the Corinthian church
and of primitive Christianity as a whole.

In later days, and even in scholarly literature, the
Corinthians' mixed feelings with regard to Paul have found many

---

[46]If Wilckens is right that there was a fully developed
Gnostic Christology at Corinth, the balance of probability would
weigh in the other direction. The data discussed in my paper is
not favorable to this hypothesis, but it is not excluded by my
own reconstruction.
[47]When Paul is said constantly to recommend and defend
himself, this might well be a direct reaction to 1 Corinthians.
Cf. 2 Cor. 3:1; 5:12; 12:19. It was admitted, however, that
"His letters are weighty and strong," 10:10.

echoes. Paul has been hated and loved more than most persons of
the past. The book on Paul by Vilhelm Grønbech, the Danish
historian of religion, might be mentioned as a highly sophisticated
version of such reactions with many features in common with the
Corinthians' portrait of Paul.[48] John Knox is one of the few who
have tried to do justice both to the opponents and to the admirers
of the apostle past and present.[49] While the debate will go on,
we should not forget that Paul did not care about judgments passed
by the Corinthians or by any human court. He would hardly have
cared more about the tribunal of history if he had been familiar
with that concept. His only ambition and passion was to be found
a faithful servant in the judgment of his Lord. For the historian,
the chief task must be not to express sympathy or antipathy or to
evaluate virtues and shortcomings, but to try to understand Paul
as he wanted to be understood, as an apostle of Jesus Christ.
He is an amazing person. In 1 Cor. 1-4 he proves able to handle
delicate matters of church policy or trivial matters of church
politics in such a way that his words are still worth reading.
He has something to say which is potentially most important, and
which remains reasonably clear in spite of the hypothetical nature
of our historical reconstructions.[50]

---

[48]V. Grønbech, *Paulus. Jesu Kristi Apostel* (Copenhagen,
1940). Cf. E. Hirsch, *ZNW* 40 (1941), 229-236.

[49]"The Man and His Work," *Chapters in a Life of Paul*,
89-107.

[50]Conversations with colleagues and students have convinced
me that the characterization of 1 Cor. 1:10-4:21 as an apologetic
section is one-sided and may be misleading, for two reasons:

A. In contrast to parts of Galatians (esp. chapters 1-2) and
    2 Corinthians (esp. chapters 10-13), 1 Corinthians 1-4 is
    not written in the style of an apologetic letter.

B. To call the section "apologetic" is to downplay the degree to
    which Paul is critical of his own adherents as well as of
    his opponents.

Nevertheless, the section lays a foundation for the subsequent
parts of the letter, it serves to reestablish Paul's true authority,
and it does contain apologetic elements, see esp. 1 Cor. 4:2-5
and 18-21. I have therefore decided not to rewrite this study
but to let it remain fresh, one-sided, and at some points conjectural.
For other approaches to 1 Cor. 1-4, see e.g. R. W. Funk, "Word and
Word in I Corinthians 2:6-16," in *Language, Hermeneutic, and the
Word of God* (New York: Harper & Row, 1966) 275-305; W. Wuellner,
"Haggadic Homily Genre in I Corinthians 1-3," *JBL* 89 (1970) 199-204;
J. H. Schütz, *Paul and the Anatomy of Apostolic Authority* (Cambridge
University Press, 1975) 187-213.

CHAPTER IV

A FRAGMENT AND ITS CONTEXT:
2 CORINTHIANS 6:14-7:1*

It is generally recognized that the section 2 Cor. 6:14-7:1 is a self-contained unit, beginning with the exhortation, "Do not be mismated with unbelievers," and concluding with the injunction "Since we have these promises, let us cleanse ourselves from every defilement of body and spirit, and make holiness perfect in the fear of God." The injunctions are motivated by a series of rhetorical questions, "For what partnership have righteousness and iniquity? etc. The central affirmation, "We are the temple of the living God," is supported by a chain of scriptural quotations freely adapted. Read in isolation from its context, the section makes perfectly good sense, whether one reads it as addressed to some particular issue, such as mixed marriages or participation in pagan religious ceremonies, or as a general warning against association with outsiders.

Taken at face value, the section is not related to its context. If it is left out, there is a smooth transition from 6:11-13 to 7:2. I quote the key sentences: "Our mouth is open to you Corinthians; our heart is wide ... In return, widen your hearts also. Make room for us..." As a consequence of such observations a number of scholars have drawn the conclusion that 2 Cor. 6:14-7:1 is an interpolation.[1] There has been a good deal

---

*A paper read at the Annual Meeting of the Society of Biblical Literature in Toronto, 1969, unaltered but with footnotes added.

[1]See e.g. D. Georgi, *IDBSup* 183f.; Kümmel, 287ff.

of discussion as to whether the fragment was taken from some
other letter of Paul, presumably the lost "previous letter" to
the Corinthians, mentioned in 1 Cor. 5:9-11, or whether it was
derived from a non-Pauline source.[2] The vocabulary and phraseology are not typically Pauline. If the fragment had recently
been discovered on a sheet of papyrus, the idea of Pauline
authorship would hardly have occurred to anybody. Yet, Paul's
style and language are so flexible that it is difficult to say
with certainty that Paul could not possibly have written the
text.[3] I would think that this problem has been solved by the
discovery of the Qumran documents. Even persons like myself who
are reluctant to assume much direct influence of the Qumran
sectarians upon the New Testament will have to admit that 2
Cor. 6:14-7:1 is a slightly Christianized piece of Qumran
theology. Christ has been substituted either for God or for the
Prince of Light (resp. Michael) as the opponent of Belial (Beliar);
the designation of the members of the holy community as *pistoi*
(believers) and of the outsiders as *apistoi* (unbelievers) seems
to be Christian. But most of the other terms and ideas, the
dualism between light and darkness, the term Belial, the notion
of the community as the temple of God, the chain of quotations,
the call for separation and for purification, are all typical
for the Qumran documents. This has been demonstrated conclusively
by Joseph Fitzmyer and others, whose arguments need not be repeated.[4]

---

[2]Theories about the composite nature of the Pauline
Epistles started with the conjectures that 2 Cor. 6:14-7:1 was a
fragment of Paul's lost "previous letter" to the Corinthians
mentioned in 1 Cor. 5:9-11; that 2 Cor. 10-13 belonged to the
letter which Paul wrote "with many tears" (2 Cor. 2:4), and that
Romans 16 was (part of) a letter to Ephesus. In the course
of time hypotheses have multiplied and become increasingly
complicated--and less credible. See Harry Gamble, "The Redaction
of the Pauline Letters and the Formation of the Pauline Corpus
of Letters," *JBL* 94 (1975) 403-418.

[3]Several words and phrases used in 2 Cor. 6:14-7:1 do
not occur elsewhere in the Pauline Epistles, as pointed out in
commentaries and special studies. Yet, other words and phrases
indicate that the fragment has been reworked in a Pauline style,
see note 13 below.

[4]See esp. J. Gnilka, "2 Cor. 6:14-7:1 In The Light of
The Qumran Texts and The Testaments of the Twelve Patriarchs
(1963) E. T. in J. Murphy O'Connor, ed., *Paul and Qumran* (Chicago,
Priory Press, 1968) 46-68; J. A. Fitzmyer, "Qumran and the
Interpolated Paragraph in 2 Cor. 6:14-7:1," *CBQ* 23 (1961) 271-
280, repr. in *Essays on the Semitic Background of the New Testament*
(SBLSBS 5, Missoula: Scholars' Press, 1974) 205-217. In some
respects, the Book of Jubilees contains even closer parallels to
2 Cor. 6:14ff. than any of the clearly sectarian writings, cf.
Jubil. 1:15-26, 2:19-22, 22:14-24, (30:11, 33:11-20).

Assuming that the fragment is of non-Pauline origin, I
see no reason to think that it was originally part of Paul's lost
letter and only later incorporated into our 2 Corinthians. There
is no exact agreement, but only a vague similarity, between the
fragment and what must have stood in the previous letter. It
is unnecessarily complicated to conjecture that a non-Pauline
text was first quoted by Paul in one letter and later on interpolated into another. I therefore assume that 2 Cor. 6:14-7:1
is a fragment of non-Pauline origin, now to be read as part of
our 2 Corinthians. The fragment may be either pre-Pauline or
post-Pauline. Neither of these possibilities can be excluded
a priori. On the one hand, David Flusser has shown that the
most striking New Testament parallels to Qumran texts belong to
the layer of tradition common to Paul, John, 1 Peter, Hebrews,
etc., presented by Bultmann under the heading "The Kerygma of
the Hellenistic Community."[5] On the other, a writing as late
as the Shephard of Hermas contains parallels to Qumran as close
as those of any New Testament document. Thus neither the content
nor the affinities help us to decide whether the fragment was
quoted by Paul or interpolated by a later redactor. Whoever
incorporated the fragment can, possibly, also have altered its
wording.

Scholars who have upheld the integrity of 2 Corinthians
have tried to show that a warning against intermingling with
the Gentiles fits the context. Most of these explanations have
been somewhat strained and far-fetched.[6] Many of those who
assume a secondary interpolation argue that our 2 Corinthians
as a whole was contrived by a redactor who combined fragments
from a number of Pauline letters into a new composition.[7] Some
of them, especially Günther Bornkamm, have been able to trace
some pattern for the redactional arrangement. But none of them

---

[5]See D. Flusser, "The Dead Sea Sect and Pre-Pauline
Christianity," *Scripta Hierosolymitana*, 4 (1958), 215-266.
On the general problem of Qumran and the New Testament, see
the cautious comments of P. Benoit in *NTS* 7 (1960/61), esp.
288-295, the comprehensive study of H. Braun, *Qumran und das
Neue Testament*, I-II (Tübingen: Mohr [Siebeck], 1966) esp. II,
165-180; on our passage, see I, 201-203, and the summary of
J. A. Fitzmyer in *IDBSup* 216-219.

[6]One example may suffice: In his supplement to Lietzmann's
commentary (*HNT* 9, 4 ed. 1949), Kümmel considered 2 Cor. 6:3-10
as an excursus on the apostolic ministry, whereas Paul in 6:14ff.
continues the ethical paraenesis he had begun in 6:1-2.

[7]See e.g. Georgi, *IDBSup* 183ff., who thinks that 2
Corinthians is a composition of five different letters (accepting
6:14-7:1 as non-Pauline).

seems to have offered a rational explanation for the interpolation
of our fragment between 6:13 and 7:2. A cautious scholar like
Kümmel takes this to be a major weakness of the whole interpolation theory.[8] Thus, the apparent lack of meaningful
connection between the fragment and its context can be used as
an argument in both directions.

Under these circumstances I propose that we temporarily
bracket the whole question of the integrity or composite nature
of 2 Corinthians and simply try to read the text as it stands.
We should not only ask for the original meaning of the fragment
but try to understand its function in the present context. Once
the question is put this way, the answer follows. The transition
from Paul's interrelations with the Corinthians to the contrast
between light and darkness is created by two injunctions: "Widen
your hearts also," and "Do not be mismated with unbelievers!"
If the exhortation and the warning are read in conjunction, the
meaning is clear: "Widen your hearts for us (i.e., Paul), and
do not be mismated with unbelievers who refuse to do so." The
rest of the fragment serves to support this exhortation and this
warning. As there is no accord between light and darkness,
and between Christ and Belial, the Corinthians should not make
common cause with the unbelievers, who reject the apostle. They
ought to welcome him; that is the only behavior appropriate for
those who are the people of God. Obviously the fragment was
not originally written to serve this function, but it is equally
obvious that read this way it makes good sense in the context.

The possibility of this simple solution has not even
occurred to the majority of commentators.[9] Yet if the total
context of 2 Corinthians is taken into account, the section 6:11-
7:4 can hardly be read in any other way. The term *apistoi* occurs
only once in 2 Corinthians outside our fragment, in 4:3-4: "And

---

[8] See Kümmel, 288.

[9] Ph. Bachmann (in *Kommentar zum N.T.*, ed. Zahn [Leipzig:
A. Deichert, 1909] 294), considered the possibility that Paul
suggested that the Corinthians would join forces with the unbelievers by locking the door to Paul, but rejected it in favor of
the theory of a misplaced fragment from the "previous letter."
In *A Commentary on the Second Epistle to the Corinthians* (New
York: Harper & Row, 1973), C. K. Barrett finds the transition
from 6:13 to 14 abrupt but by no means impossible. He paraphrases
(on p. 194): "If you turn to God and to me as his messenger,
it means a break with the world." This makes sense, but in the
context it makes better sense to turn the logic of the argument
around: "If you really break with the world, it means acceptance
of God and of me as his messenger."

even if our Gospel is veiled, it is veiled only to those who are
perishing. In their case the God of this world has blinded the
minds of the unbelievers, to keep them from seeing the light
of the glory of Christ, who is the likeness (*eikōn*, image) of
God." Within its context this passage contains an indirect
warning to the Corinthians; they should take care not to side
with the unbelievers to whom Paul's gospel is veiled. A similar
idea is suggested by the passage in 2:15-16: "We are the aroma
of Christ to God among those who are being saved and among those
who are perishing, to the latter a fragrance of death to death,
to the former a fragrance of life to life." The contrast between
life and death in this passage is as sharp as the contrast
between righteousness and iniquity, light and darkness, in 6:14ff.
Two groups of men, those who are saved and those who perish, are
separated by their opposite reactions to the gospel and to the
apostle. In chapter 3 the apostle is further identified as the
minister of the new covenant, a covenant with glory and righteousness.

The fragment in 6:14ff. has to be read against this
background. The apostle of Christ is the representative of
righteousness and light. A refusal to welcome him would mean
that the Corinthians sided with unbelievers, with iniquity,
darkness, and Belial against righteousness, light, and Christ.
We may paraphrase the injunctions in 6:13-14 by supplementing
them from what has been said earlier: "Widen your hearts to me,
and do not be mismated with the unbelievers whose minds the god
of this world has blinded."

The immediately preceding section, from 5:11 onwards,
reinforces this way of reading our fragment and its context. Here
the nature of Paul's ministry, including his dealing with the
Corinthians, is defined by means of references to the love of
Christ and to the action of God, who in Christ reconciled the
world to himself and entrusted Paul with the ministry of reconciliation. As an ambassador for Christ, through whom God makes
his appeal, Paul makes a petition (*deometha*): "Be reconciled to
God" (5:14-20).[10] Applied to the Corinthians, this appeal takes
a special form, "We entreat you not to accept the grace of God
in vain" (6:1). After a parenthetical citation of Isa. 49:9
with the comment "Behold now is the day of salvation" etc., Paul

---

[10]Paul has begun to exhort the Corinthians in 2 Cor.
5:20: "We beseech" (*deometha*). 5:21 is a delayed conclusion to
5:17-19; cf. Rom. 3:22b-23; 7:25b; 10:17, and see "The Missionary
Theology in the Letter to the Romans," Chapter V, 77, 85 n. 22.

continues by stressing that he in no way poses any obstacle but in all his sufferings and doings commends himself as God's servant (6:3-10). The reason for this self-recommendation is, no doubt, the presence at Corinth of people who are said to pride themselves on external matters and to be in need of letters of recommendation (5:12; 3:1), letters which probably, as argued by Dieter Georgi, contained enumerations of their charismatic performances, their *res gestae*.[11] Paul engages in an emulation (a *emulatio, sygkrisis*) of them, but not without a sense of irony in stressing the paradox of strength in weakness. Thus he gives the Corinthians cause to take pride in him, in the hope that, knowing him, they may be able to answer his critics (5:11-12).

After inserting this self-recommendation, Paul formulates his appeal more specifically. The exhortations to be reconciled to God (5:20) and not to receive the grace of God in vain (6:1) are narrowed down to the request that the Corinthians should be open to Paul as his heart is open to them. The three appeals are not identical in content, yet the sequence suggests that it would be difficult to conform to the former injunctions without also accepting the last one. Thus the insertion of the fragment in 6:14-7:1 only reinforces the note of urgency which is already present in the context. For the Corinthians, to refuse to welcome Paul might mean to receive the grace of God in vain or, in other words, to be mismated with unbelievers.

Within the context, the final exhortation in the fragment, like the first one, takes on a very specific meaning. The first seven chapters of 2 Corinthians, from 1:12 onward, stress the integrity and purity of Paul's conduct towards the Corinthians (cf. 1:17; 1:23; 2:4,17; 4:1-2). Listing his afflictions in 6:3-10 (a "peristasis catalog"), Paul again asserts his integrity and reliability (vv. 6-8). Immediately after the inserted fragment he writes: "Open your hearts to us; we have wronged no one, we have corrupted no one, we have taken advantage of no one" (7:2). In this context the injunction, "Let us cleanse ourselves from every defilement of body and spirit, and make holiness perfect in the fear of God," must be read as a call for reciprocity. The Corinthians' attitude toward Paul ought to be marked by the integrity and sincerity which characterized his conduct towards them.

---

[11] See D. Georgi, *Die Gegner des Paulus im 2. Korintherbrief,* (WMANT, 11, Neukirchen, Neukirchener Verlag, 1964) 241-246; A. Fridrichsen, "Peristasen-katalog und Res Gestae," *SO* 8 (1928) 78-82.

The interpretation might be further elaborated. What I
have said should be sufficient to prove that the fragment makes
good sense within its present context. The contextual sense is
different from the original meaning, but just as a more or less
verbatim quotation, the fragment has a clearly definable
function where we now read it. Its present location cannot be
due to an accident; whoever inserted the fragment must have
known what he was doing. Whether this person was Paul himself
or a later redactor remains an open question, dependent upon the
literary analysis of 2 Corinthians as a whole.[12] The text of the
letter seems to have been altered before it came into the Pauline
collection of epistles. Personally, I find the deletion of the
names of the brethren who accompanied Titus to be most unambiguous
evidence for this (cf. 8:18, 22, 23; 12:18). Other problems
are well known. I would, therefore, consider it unfair to assign
the whole burden of proof to those who deny the integrity of our
2 Corinthians.[13] Although I am presently unwilling to commit
myself to any definite solution of these complex issues, I am
fairly convinced about one thing, namely, that the person who
inserted the fragment in 6:14-7:1 is the same one who added
chapters 10-13 at the end of the letter.

The quotation of the fragment serves as a serious warning
to the Corinthians and makes the situation envisaged in chapters
1 through 7 resemble the difficult situation envisaged in
chapters 10-13 much more than the text of 1-7 would do without

---

[12]While I remain convinced that 2 Cor. 6:14-7:1 is based
on a fragment with remarkable similarities to the Dead Sea Scrolls
and the Book of Jubilees, I am also convinced that the fragment
has been reworked and adapted to its present context: The phrase
echontes oun...(since we have ...) in 2 Cor. 7:1 has analogies
in 3:12 and 4:1, cf. 3:4; 4:7; 5:1. The clause, "For we are
the temple of the living God," (6:16), has a closer analogy in
1 Cor. 3:16 than in any of the Dead Sea Scrolls. The address
agapētoi (beloved) in 7:1 occurs also in 2 Cor. 12:19, and the
verb *epitelein* (7:1) occurs also in 2 Cor. 8:6,11. Concepts
like "righteousness," "light," or "unbelievers" are even elsewhere in 2 Cor. used in a dualistic context, see e.g. 3:9ff.;
4:3-6; cf. 2:15-16.

[13]In his article, "2 Cor. 6:14-7:1: An Anti-Pauline
Fragment?", *JBL* 92 (1973), 88-108, H. D. Betz has suggested
that the fragment originated among the opponents Paul combats
in his letter to the Galatians or in a similar group. It is
not impossible that both Paul's opponents and Paul himself, or
a later disciple of Paul's, made use of the same traditions and
scriptural passages, reworking them in opposite ways and using
them in different contexts. I refrain here from a fuller
discussion of Betz's conjecture, and of other problems. In a
seminar paper in the fall of 1976, David Rensberger presented a
more comprehensive study of 2 Cor. 6:14-7:1. Hoping that it
will some day be published, I have not here incorporated his
observations.

the fragment. Moreover, the admonition to cleanse away every
defilement in 7:1 is paralleled by the harsh statement about
those "who have not repented of the impurity, immorality and
licenciousness which they have done," in 12:21. The false
apostles are branded as servants of Satan (11:14). Most important, what is implicit in 6:11-7:4 is made explicit in a
slightly different form in 11:2-4:   "I am afraid that as the
serpent deceived Eve by his cunning, your thoughts will be
led astray from a sincere and pure devotion to Christ." The
reference here is to the false apostles who preach Christ as
if he had not already been preached by Paul and who make the
Corinthians receive the Spirit as if they had not already
received it when they accepted the gospel preached by Paul.
Disloyalty to the apostle is equated with infidelity to Christ
who sent him, to the Spirit originally received, and to the
gospel proclaimed by Paul. The willingness of the Corinthians
to welcome the "superlative apostles" to the neglect of their
own apostle makes Paul fear that Satan will seduce them. What
is merely suggested by the insertion of the fragment (in 6:14-
7:1) is here stated in plain words: to join the false apostles
in their opposition to Paul would mean to side with Satan/Belial
in his opposition to Christ.

     Read in isolation, the fragment 2 Cor. 6:14-7:1 is a
very important piece of evidence for some kind of connection
between the Qumran community and the early church. Read within
the context of 2 Corinthians, the same fragment attests an
understanding of Paul which tends to identify rejection of the
apostle with rejection of Christ and siding with the devil. If
the fragment is a secondary interpolation, its insertion would
be a most interesting example of early "Paulinism", to be
considered along with the deutero-Pauline epistles. The lack
of links with the context and the absence of any full analogy
to a quotation of this type and extent may still favor the theory
of interpolation. But I have to confess that I find it somewhat
difficult to imagine a later redactor who was capable of expressing
his understanding of Paul's unique apostolic ministry in such an
indirect and subtle way, leaving it to the readers to understand
the function of the fragment within its context. The possibility
that the apostle himself incorporated the fragment may after all
have to be reconsidered.

CHAPTER V

THE MISSIONARY THEOLOGY
IN THE EPISTLE TO THE ROMANS

Paul has been acclaimed as the first Christian theologian and as the greatest Christian missionary of all time. Scholars have, however, often failed to realize how closely these two aspects are interrelated. In modern times there has often been a separation between theology and mission.[1] Foreign missions have frequently been conducted with more enthusiasm than theological reflection, and the study of Christian mission has only slowly obtained its proper place in the theological curriculum. This modern separation between theology and mission has had a great impact on the image of Paul. Many scholars have described his theology as a dogmatic system without much inner relationship to his missionary work. Other scholars have gone to the opposite extreme and argued that Paul's genius was that of a great missionary and religious personality. Only recently have an increasing number of scholars begun to recognize that there is something wrong in the very distinction between Paul's mission and his theology. His theology and his missionary activity were inseparable from one another.[2]

Paul's theology was no academic dogmatics thought out at the desk and presented in the classroom. A systematic outline of

---

[1]The classical example of this reaction is A. Deissmann, *Paul* (1911, 2.ed. 1925; ET, London: Hodder & Stoughton, 1911, tr. W. E. Wilson). See also G. Warneck, *Paulus im Lichte der heutigen Heidenmission* (Berlin: M. Warneck, 1914).

[2]In contrast to the works of Bultmann and Ridderbos, those of J. Munck and K. Stendahl are characteristic, in some respects extreme, examples of the more recent trend, as is also, in another manner, the booklet of C. J. Roetzel. For references, see the general bibliography.

his theological doctrines becomes at best an accurate and useful map, a two dimensional projection without depth or movement. Paul does not develop a system like the scholastic philosophers, orthodox Protestants, or German idealists. This, however, does not mean that Paul's theology has no inner unity. The word "system" applies to structures as diverse as the array of the planets around the sun and as a language where an infinite number of statements, which may even contradict one another, are possible. This flexibilty enables us to call Paul's theology a "system" which has one center of gravity, Jesus Christ, and in which variegated statements are interrelated with one another as parts of an encompassing totality. The perimeter is conditioned by the sacred Scriptures and traditions of Israel, including faith in God, biblical history, and eschatology, as well as by the social world and the changing circumstances that Paul had to face.

Paul does not stand outside the history of salvation and reflect on it. He is much more actively involved and has a special role to play in the period between the death and resurrection of Christ and his coming in glory. Thus he is not developing a Christian philosophy of history, even though portrayals of his theology from a "history of salvation" perspective run the risk of giving that impression.[3] He argues theologically in order to make the missionary congregations understand their own place within the divine economy, what God has granted and promised to them and therefore also what he can expect of them. To put it very briefly, we may characterize Paul's theology as a christocentric theology of mission with biblical history and eschatology as its framework.

Paul understands himself as an apostle of Jesus Christ, commissioned to preach the gospel to Gentiles who had not previously heard it. In Pauline usage, the words "gospel" and "apostle" are correlates,[4] and both are missionary terms. But Paul's concept of an apostle implies much more than our word missionary. The apostle has his commission from the risen Christ himself with authority to be his ambassador and representative, as long as he

---

[3]See Bultmann's critical review of O. Cullmann, *Christ and Time* in *TLZ* 73 (1948) 659-66 (= *Exegetica*, Tübingen: Mohr, 1967, 356-366).

[4]Already in his early article, "TO EUAGGELION hos Paulus," *NorTT* 13 (1912), 153-170, 209-256, A. Fridrichsen stated that gospel and apostle are correlated concepts (p. 250). See also his later study, *The Apostle and His Message*, 8ff., and my critical review in *Nuntius Sodalicii Neotestamentici Upsaliensis*, 2 (1949) 11-14.

does not disregard his commission but remains faithful to the
gospel. Paul maintains that he preached the same gospel as
Peter and the others who were apostles before him (e.g. 1 Cor.
15:11). What made Paul's "gospel to the uncircumcised" different
from Peter's "gospel to the circumcised" was Paul's special
commission: to preach the good news about Christ to the non-Jews.
That meant that the time had already arrived when salvation was
to be offered to the nations.

When Paul summarizes the content of the gospel, he often
adds something about his own call and work.[5] Quite likely, he
referred to his own conversion and commission even in his missionary
preaching. That would explain that he could be accused of
proclaiming himself (see 2 Cor. 4:5). In his letters, he not
only calls the congregations to imitate his conduct, he also
presents himself as an example of God's grace, which makes all
Jewish privileges and zeal for the Law irrelevant (see Phil 3:
4-11; Gal. 1:11-16; 2:19-20). At least in retrospect, Paul claims
that he received the call to preach among the Gentiles when the
risen Christ appeared to him. But his experience was at the same
time a conversion which changed the direction of his life and
turned his convictions upside down.[6] Thus, an inner unity of
mission and theology can be traced back to the beginnings of Paul's
life as a Christian, even if the theology which we know from the
letters was articulated under the impact of Paul's later missionary
experience.

Paul's apostolic ministry was not limited to missionary

---

[5]See Rom. 1:1-6; 1 Cor. 15:3-11; 2 Cor. 4:4-6; 5:17-21;
Gal. 1:6ff.; 2:7-9. Cf. also Phil. 2:5-3:17 and 1 Thess. 1:3-
2:11. In Ephesians, Colossians, and the Pastoral Epistles the
correlation between the gospel and the apostle is expressed in
more stereotyped phraseology, see Eph. 3:1-12; 6:19f.; Col. 1:23-
29; 1 Tim. 1:11ff.; 2:5-7; 2 Tim. 1:8-12; Titus 1:1-3. There is
a more distant analogy to this correlation in the kerygmatic
speeches in Acts, which not only summarize the story of Jesus,
relating it to Old Testament testimonies, but also refer to those
who are witnesses to this story, Acts 2:32; 3:15; 5:32; 10:39,41;
13:31; cf. Luke 24:48. For the author of Acts, Paul does not
belong to the primary witnesses, but his calling is reported
three times, in Acts 9, 22 and 26. From Gal. 1:23-24 we learn
that the story of Paul's conversion circulated at a very early
date. See my article, "Evangelium og Apostel," *NorTT* 44 (1943),
193-217. Cf. also J. H. Schütz, *Paul and the Anatomy of Apostolic
Authority* (SNTSMS 26, Cambridge Univeristy Press, 1975) esp.
35-158.

[6]Stendahl, 7-23 ("Call rather than Conversion"), objects
to the phrase "Paul's conversion" -- for good reasons if the
term "conversion" carries connotations of a change of religion.
But certainly, the call of Paul resulted in a radical change of
direction.

proclamation of the gospel. He aimed further than that. In
Rom. 15:16 he refers to his ministry as priestly service whose
goal is "that the offering of the Gentiles may be acceptable,
sanctified by the Holy Spirit." In 2 Cor. 11:2 he uses nuptial
imagery: "I betrothed you to Christ to present you as a pure
bride to her one husband." In several letters Paul states the
goal of his intercession and whole endeavor in terms like these:
"so that you...may be pure and blameless for the day of Christ,"
or "guiltless in the day of our Lord Jesus Christ."[7] Paul was
not just a herald who hurried to proclaim the gospel to all
nations. His ministry also had a more pastoral aspect. He is
the intercessor on behalf of his congregations who pleads their
cause before God and he is the advisor who counsels them, in order
to be able to present them to Christ at his coming, which Paul
expected in the near future.

It is only when we are aware of the various aspects of
Paul's ministry that we can fully understand how intimately his
theology is bound up with his missionary activity. He is the
herald of the gospel, Christ's ambassador to the Gentiles, an
example for his churches and their intercessor and counselor,
and all of this is part of his eschatological mission. It is
therefore one-sided to see Paul's theology as an existential
interpretation of the kerygma which he proclaimed as a missionary.[8]

---

[7]See Phil. 1:10-11; 1 Cor. 1:8, and cf. 1 Thess. 3:13;
5:23; Phil. 1:6 (Col. 1:22f., 28). On Paul as an intercessor
(or paraclete), see my article "Paulus som förespråkare," *STK*
18 (1942), 173-182 (a reaction to N. Johansson, *Parakletoi,*
Lund: Gleerup, 1940). Cf. also the recent study of G. P. Wiles,
Paul's Intercessory Prayers (SNTSMS 24, Cambridge University
Press, 1974).

Since L. Bieler, *Theios Anēr* (Vienna: O. Höfels, 1935)
it has become customary to use the term "divine man" (*theios anēr*)
in a wide sense and to apply it to Paul's opponents (esp. in
2 Cor.). But in this wide sense, one would have to consider Paul
himself as a divine man, albeit as a very peculiar representative
of the category--as H. Windisch did in his book *Paulus und Christus*
(Leipzig: Hinrichs, 1934). Paul was a divine messenger, a
missionary, preacher and teacher, tested in the agony of suffering,
a charismatic person and miracle worker, and he was a paraclete,
the intercessor of the Gentile churches and of his own people.
One ought, however, to use the term in a more restricted sense,
as the ancient sources do. See Carl Holladay, *Theios Anēr in
Hellenistic Judaism: A Critique of the Use of the Term in Christology*
(Diss., Cambridge, 1974, to be published in the SBLDS).

[8]Bultmann tends, in his *Theology of the New Testament,* to
substitute an existentialist systematization of Paul for the
traditional dogmatic interpretation. See my review article in
The Crucified Messiah, 90-128.

It would also be one-sided to see Paul's theology mainly as a
rationale for his Gentile mission and as a defense of its results.[9]
Paul develops his theology in ongoing dialog, reminding, warning,
exhorting and counseling his churches, polemicizing against
misunderstandings of the gospel and against anything that might
distort the integrity of the communities which he hopes to present
to Christ. For this reason each of his letters has its own
distinctive features, depending on the audience and the circumstances to which Paul speaks. Writing letters and "doing theology"
was part of his mission.

In most of his letters Paul deals with practical issues
in young churches or, as in 2 Corinthians, with the relationship
between them and himself. The letters move back and forth from
specific problems to matters of principle which provide guidelines
for their solution. Only the Letter to the Romans stands apart.
Here the epistolary introduction and conclusion serve as a framework for discussion of theological themes that apparently have
little or no close relationship to the immediate concerns of
the recipients. For this reason, the Letter to the Romans has
been the starting point for presenting a systematic outline of
"Pauline Theology," or what German scholars in the 19th century
called "Paulinism." The interpretation of Romans is therefore
decisive for testing the interrelation of Paul's theology and
his missionary work to see whether or not it is really as close
as I have maintained. The following comments are intended to
show that it is.

The prescript of Romans (1:1-7) is as unique in the
history of epistolography as is the letter itself. Its pattern
follows the Pauline variant of epistolary convention and includes
three elements: 1. The name of the sender. 2. The recipients.
3. A greeting formula.[10] The first of these three parts, however,
has been expanded in a very unusual way. Paul introduces himself as "a slave of Christ Jesus, called to be an apostle,"
adding that he has been set apart for the gospel of God. Then
he inserts a reference to God's promise in the Old Testament and
a summary of the gospel and concludes by returning to his own
commission. It is from the promised Son of God, Jesus Christ our

---

[9]Stendahl, e.g. 27, 80f., 130f., views Paul's teaching
about justification under this perspective. To me that seems to
be a one-sided approach, even if a necessary corrective. See
Chapter VI.

[10]See e.g. W. G. Doty, *Letters in Primitive Christianity*
(Philadelphia: Fortress, 1973) 29-31; Roetzel, 29-30. Cf. also
J. A. Fitzmyer, "Some Notes on Aramaic Epistolography," *JBL* 93
(1974) 201-225: F. X. J. Exler, *The Form of the Ancient Greek Letter*

Lord, that Paul has received grace to be an apostle and to bring
about obedience of faith among all the Gentile nations. Due to
these expansions, the opening identification of the sender has
almost become an exordium, a prologue to the whole letter. A
closer analysis would show that the prescript of Romans anticipates
a number of themes that are elaborated in the body of the letter.
The primary function of the opening paragraph is to set forth
Paul's full credentials for addressing the Christians in Rome
with an apostolic and didactic letter.

In a Greek letter prescript, the second part is the
identification of the addressees. The normal form is a dative in
the third person, as in Rom. 1:7a: "To all God's beloved in Rome,
who are called to be saints." It is one of the peculiar stylistic
features of the prescript to Romans that before he has formally
identified the addressees, Paul has already turned directly to
them, addressing them, using a second person plural pronoun to
state that they too are included among the nations to whom the
Lord has sent Paul, giving him grace to carry out his apostolic
task. This irregularity is an example of the freedom with which
Paul varies epistolary conventions, combining formality with
intimacy.

Paul had made it a rule that he would not build on an
"alien foundation," by preaching the gospel where others had
preached the gospel before him and had already laid the foundation
of a Christian community (see Rom. 15:20-21; 2 Cor. 10:13-16).
In the case of Rome, however, he intended to make an exception,
hoping to reap some harvest in the world capital by his missionary
work as he had among the rest of the Gentiles (Rom. 1:13-14). In
Greço-Roman antiquity, a written message was regarded as a substitute for personal presence and oral communication.[11] Thus, that
Paul addressed an apostolic letter to the Christians in Rome,
preaching the gospel in writing, was a departure from his rule,
not to intrude upon churches which he had not founded himself.
Using the prescript to give his full credentials, Paul makes it
clear that his apostolic commission to preach the gospel and
bring about obedience of faith extends to all nations, including
Rome. At the same time, he also makes it clear that he respects
the independence of the Christians in Rome: they are already
"God's beloved, called to be saints," and "called to belong to
Jesus Christ," just as Paul is himself "called to be an apostle."

---

[11]On the practice and theory of ancient letter writing,
see my article, "Letter," in *IDBSup* 538-540, with bibliography.

As usual the prescript is followed by some opening
sentences that express the sender's attitude toward the addressees
of the letter.[12] Paul usually assures his audience of his thanksgiving and intercession. That is an expression of appreciation,
appropriate for the apostle, as the spiritual father and counselor
of a congregation. Writing to the Christians in Rome, Paul is
not in this position. The reason for his thanksgiving is that
their faith is reported far and wide, i.e., it has become generally
known that Christianity has spread to Rome. Giving a very polite
twist to a conventional epistolary phrase, Paul does not write
that he prays for the well-being of the addressees but that he
prays for his own well-being, that he may at last succeed, by the
will of God, in coming to visit the Christians in Rome.[13] Having
written that he hopes to strengthen them with some spiritual gift
he corrects himself. What he has in mind is mutual encouragement
(Rom. 1:12). Paul is very careful to make it clear that he does
not want to intrude upon the Roman Christians, but at the same
time he excuses himself for his failure to come earlier (Rom. 1:13).

The epistolary conclusion confirms that the writing of the
letter to the Romans was a delicate task that called for diplomatic
tact and politeness. Paul assures the addressees that he is
confident of their ability to take care of themselves and to
instruct one another (Rom. 15:14). He considers his own letter
a reminder; he concedes that he has written somewhat boldly, and
he goes on to give a further explanation of his apostolic mission
and his future plans (Rom. 15:15-33). Here we learn that the letter
was written towards the end of Paul's missionary activity in the
Eastern provinces, probably during his last visit to Corinth. At
this moment Paul can write: "I no longer have any room for work
in these regions" (Rom. 15:23). I take the meaning of this
astounding statement to be that representative churches had finally
been so well established that they would, with the help of God, be
able to prepare themselves for the day of the Lord, without the
supervision of the apostle. What had hindered Paul from going
to Rome earlier was, obviously, trouble in some of the congregations
and the delayed conclusion of the collection for "the saints" in
Jerusalem.

Paul wrote his letter to the Romans at a turning point in

---

[12]Schubert (See General Bibliography).
[13]Cf. Rom. 1:10, *ei pōs ēdē pote euodōthēsomai* ("that I
may now at last succeed") with 3 John 2, *euchomai se euodousthai*
("I pray that all may go well with you," followed by: "I know
that all is well with your soul"). A similar use of *euodousthai*
is fairly common in papyrus letters.

his career, shortly before he left on his last journey to Jerusalem.
Various circumstances at the time of writing are reflected in the
letter. It is easy to find reminiscences of the conflicts in
which he had recently been involved and of which we have evidence
in his letters to the Corinthian and Galatian Christians. It is
also possible to read the letter as a draft of the "collection
speech" which Paul intended to deliver in Jerusalem. One obvious
purpose of the letter was to prepare for Paul's arrival at Rome.
One does not have to read much between the lines to see that Paul
also wanted to refute objections to, and forestall possible
misunderstandings of, his teachings and whole attitude. But we
should not belittle the stated purpose of the letter either; Paul
wrote to the Christians in Rome in order to exhort and strengthen
them without intruding upon them and without doubting the genuineness
of their Christian faith. What Paul does in his letter is what he
had for a long time hoped to do in person: he preached the gospel
to those in Rome (see 1:15). He had all the more reason to do so
in writing as troubles in Jerusalem might possibly hinder him from
ever coming to Rome (see 15:31f.). To some extent, the letter
anticipates the mutual encouragement that Paul hopes to enjoy in
Rome (1:12). He not only suggests that the Christians in Rome
will support his mission to Spain, but he also explicitly asks
for their intercession for his journey to Jerusalem (see 15:24,
30-32). The appeal for intercession may, indeed, be a main
reason why Paul wrote *this* letter to the Romans. The Christians
in Rome needed to know what Paul taught and how he understood
his own mission if they were going to ally themselves with other
Pauline churches and intercede for a favorable reception of the
collection.[14]

Like Paul's other letters, Romans has the characteristics
of a genuine letter. It is a written communication between two
parties who are spatially separated and is a substitute for
personal presence. The letter form serves to provide information
and to make requests, and also to promote friendly relations
between sender and addressees. Even the didactic nature of the
main body of the letter is conditioned by the specific epistolary
situation. The relationship between theology and missionary

---

[14]On recent studies on the composition and purpose of
Romans, see G. Klein, "Romans, Letter to the," *IDBSup* 752-754,
who concludes by stating an emergent consensus: "In any case,
recent debate shows that Romans can be adequately interpreted only
by seriously viewing it as an occasional letter in the form of an
essay that goes beyond the occasion." Cf. also Käsemann's commentary
on Rom. 15:29 (see General Bibliography).

activity is as intimate in Romans as in any of Paul's letters,
but the perspective is different. The letter contains little,
if anything, that gives us specific information about the origin
and organization of Roman Christianity. Paul may himself have
been fairly well informed.[15] But if he was, it is all the more
remarkable that he does not address more directly any internal
problems. He was not the spiritual father of the Roman Christians,
and he leaves it to them to make specific applications of his
teaching. It would almost seem as if he was more in need of
their understanding, intercession and loyal support than they
were in need of his advice. It is not the problems of a local
church but the universal gospel and Paul's own mission which in
this letter provide the point of departure for theological
discussion. This is made very clear by the way in which Paul
introduces the theme of the letter.

Writing about his travel plans, Paul states: "I am
indebted to Greeks and to barbarians, both to the wise and to
the simple" (Rom. 1:14). What Paul owes to mankind is nothing
but the gospel of Christ.[16] The thematic statement about the
gospel as God's power of salvation is introduced as a motivation
for Paul's disposition not to be ashamed of the gospel but to
confess it boldly to all people everywhere, even in Rome. We
should also observe the back reference to the letter opening:
the gospel in which the righteousness of God is revealed is
identical with the missionary kerygma that Paul summarized in
Rom. 1:2-6.

In Rom. 1:16-18 Paul sets forth three thematic statements:
1. The gospel is God's power for salvation, for Greeks as well as
for Jews. 2. In the gospel the righteousness of God is revealed,
"from faith to faith." 3. The wrath of God is revealed from
heaven against all ungodliness and wickedness of men. Editors
and commentators usually make the third thesis, Rom. 1:18, begin
a new paragraph and a new section of the letter. They are uncertain
whether the thesis in 1:16-17 should be considered part of the

---

[15]This would certainly be the case if the list of greetings
in Romans 16 is an original part of the letter to Rome, as I think
it is. A strong case for the integrity of the letter has been
made by Harry Gamble, Jr., *The Textual History of the Letter to
the Romans* (SD 42, Grand Rapids: Eerdmans, 1977). On p. 91ff.,
Gamble rightly stresses the commendatory character of the greetings.
Cf. also W. Wuellner, "Paul's Rhetoric of Argumentation in Romans,"
CBQ 38 (1976) 330-351.
    [16]Cf. my article, "Evangelium og plikt" (Gospel and Duty), in
Festskrift til Regin Prenter (Copenhagen: Gyldendal, 1967) 142-154.

letter opening (1:8-17) or a short thematic paragraph by itself.
But in the Greek text, the four sentences in Rom. 1:15-18 are
all logically connected with one another by means of a *gar* ("for").
The thematic statements all serve as a warrant for the preceding
one. The question of whether a sentence belongs to the preceding
or to the following paragraph is anachronistic since the text
was to be read aloud and the original handwriting did not set the
paragraphs off from one another. In many manuscripts not even the
words are separated from one another. As the text was to be
heard, rather than seen, the transition from one unit of thought
to another had to be indicated by other means than by typographical
or scribal arrangement. In Romans, as elsewhere, the conclusion
of one section frequently introduces the theme of the following
section. Greek prose style was in general closer to oral speech
than are modern literary products.[17] In order to follow the flow
of thought in the Pauline letters, one should pay more attention
to thematic statements, gradual transitions, and "ring composition"
than to the division into chapter and verse or to headings and
systematized outlines supplied by modern translations and
commentaries.

The last two of the three thematic statements in Rom.
1:16-18 are formulated in antithetical parallelism and spelled
out in reverse order. Paul first deals with the revelation of
the wrath of God (Rom. 1:18-3:20) and only after that with the
revelation of his righteousness (3:21ff.). At the point of
transition, Paul links the two units of thought. In 3:21 Paul
has turned to the theme of God's saving righteousness, but in
3:22b-23 he inserts a delayed conclusion to the preceding section:
"There is no distinction, for all have sinned and fall short of
the glory of God." The opening statement in 1:17 had already
referred to "all ungodliness and wickedness of men." In 1:19-32
Paul spells this out with respect to Gentiles, who are without
excuse for their idolatry and punished by their vices. But then
Paul gives his accusation an unexpected twist, indicting any
person, even the Jew, who condemns Gentile vices but does similar
things (2:1-5). The chapter division between 1:32 and 2:1 is
misleading because it obliterates the central position of the
description of God's impartial judgment in 2:6-11 which repeats
the phrase "the Jew first and also the Greek" from 1:16, concludes
the treatment of the revelation of God's wrath and introduces the
theme of divine impartiality.

---

[17]At this point I owe important insights to A. Wifstrand,
"Grekisk och modern prosastil" (Greek and Modern Prose Style), in
Tider och Stilar (Lund: Gleerup, 1944) 5-38.

Theologians and exegetes have long struggled with the
problem that Paul teaches justification by faith, without works
of the Law, but at the same time asserts, without any qualification,
that the outcome of the last judgment will depend upon what a person
has done.   There is indeed a problem here, but apparently Paul
himself did not pay much attention to it.   The most obvious reason
for this is that Paul stressed the same point in both cases.
There is no distinction between Jew and Greek, because God shows
no partiality, neither when he justifies the ungodly nor when he
renders to every man according to his works.

In Rom. 2:12-29 Paul applies the dogmatic axiom of God's
impartiality to the Gentiles who have sinned "without the law"
and to the Jews who sinned "under the law."[18]   The Gentiles can
get a fair trial because they know what the Law requires (2:14-16).
The Jew will have no advantage in possessing the Law if he has
broken it (2:17-24).   It is not the external circumcision of the
body but only the inner circumcision of the heart that counts
before God (2:25-29, cf. 2:13).   Having reached this point, Paul
raises the question: "Then what advantage has the Jew?" (Rom.
3:1).   The condensed series of questions and answers in 3:1-8
shows how important it was to Paul to refute false consequences
drawn from his teaching and objections raised against it.   He
will return to a fuller refutation later in his letter (see esp.
chapts. 6-7 and 9-11).

Undergirding his accusation against Jews and Greeks with
a catena of scriptural quotations, Paul draws the conclusion that
no human being will be justified by works of the Law (3:9-20).
Against this negative background he turns to its positive counter-
part, the theme that was first stated in Rom. 1:17, the revelation
of the righteousness of God.   The basic exposition of the theme
in 3:21-26 deals with "the redemption in Christ Jesus," in whom
God has set things right.   The consequences are drawn in a new
series of questions and answers (3:27-31) and supported by an
interpretation of Abraham's faith in God attested in Gen. 15:6

---

[18]I have found the most convincing analysis of the argument in Romans 1-2 to be that of M. Pohlenz, "Paulus und die Stoa,"
ZNW 42 (1949) 69-104   (repr. 1964).   As I suggested in *STK* 18
(1942, see note 7), Paul's argument would gain in force if it
presupposes the idea that the Torah and/or the *mitzvoth* (commandments observed) will act as advocates for the Israelites in the
judgment of God.   Cf. Aboth 4:13 and other passages collected by
N. Johansson, *Parakletoi*, 174-178.   Paul's idea would then be that
the Gentiles have similar defenders (or accusers).   Jouette Bassler
is preparing a dissertation on the idea of God's impartiality,
esp. in Rom. 2:11 and context.

(Rom. 4). Paul insists that there is no distinction, that God is
the God of Gentile nations as well as of Jews, and that Abraham
is the father of all believers, whether they are circumcized or
not (3:21, 29f.; 4:11f.). To Paul, the existence of uncircumcized
Gentile believers is fully legitimate because it is based on
faith in the God in whom Abraham believed (see Rom 4:5, 17, 24f.).[19]

Through the end of chapter 4 the composition of Romans is
fairly clear in so far as Paul has first treated the theme of
God's wrath and righteous judgment (1:18-2:11 + 2:12-29 and 3:
1-8 and 9-20) and after that has taken up the theme of God's
righteousness (1:17; 3:21-26 + 3:27-31 and 4). The analysis of
chapters 5-8 has created more difficulties. Older Protestants
tended to think that Paul first dealt with justification (1:16-
5:21) and then with sanctification (6-8). In the 19th century
it became more common, especially in Germany, to distinguish
between two lines of thought in Paul: Rom. 6-8 contained a
"mystical-ethical doctrine of salvation" to be distinguished from
the "forensic" doctrine in the earlier chapters.[20] In either case,
the exegetes failed to pay sufficient attention to the formal
composition of Romans and to the eschatological and missionary
dimensions of Paul's theology. A number of more recent scholars,
however, have preferred to connect Rom. 5 with 6-8 rather than
with 1-4, since already in Rom. 5:1-11 Paul proceeds from justification to the final salvation and the life of those who are
justified by faith.[21]

---

[19]See Käsemann's commentary, with bibliography. H. Moxnes,
Oslo, is working on a fresh investigation of Abraham's faith in
God, centering on Rom. 4:17ff.

[20]The distinction between two separate lines of thought in
Paul goes back to H. Lüdemann, *Die Anthropologie des Apostels
Paulus* (Kiel: Universitätsbuchhandlung, 1872); cf. A. Schweitzer,
Paul and His Interpreters, 28ff. Schweitzer's own eschatological
approach contributed much, although largely in an indirect way, to
the overcoming of the duality. In recent decades, the problem has
receded into the background; cf. e.g. H. D. Wendland, *Die Mitte
der paulinischen Botschaft* (Göttingen: Vandenhoeck & Ruprecht,
1935); P. Schubert, "Paul and the New Testament Ethic in the Thought
of John Knox," in W. Farmer, ed., *Christian History and Interpretation,* 363-388. Most recently, the problem has been restated by
E. P. Sanders, esp. 474-511. This important book appeared so late
that a discussion is impossible. Sanders distinguishes between
"juristic" and "participatory" (rather than "ethical" or "mystical")
categories, and thinks that "the main theme of Paul's theology is
found in his participationist language rather than in the theme of
righteousness by faith" (p. 552). One question would be if Paul's
theology is not, in its very center, more polemical than Sanders
will allow for.

[21]See e.g. the commentaries on Romans by Dodd, Nygren,
Barrett, and Käsemann.

There is no doubt that Rom. 5:1-11, like 3:21-26, has a
fundamental importance within the total composition and serves as
a basis for subsequent comments and elaboration. The analogy
between Adam and Christ in 5:12-19 illuminates and supports the
main thesis in 5:1-11, that justification is a sure ground for
the hope of final salvation and life. Moreover, Romans 8 restates
more fully several ideas that are already present in 5:1-11: the
sufferings that believers experience are not contrary to their
standing in grace; the Holy Spirit, which they have received, and
the love of God, evidenced by Christ's vicarious death, assure
them that their hope is not in vain.[22]

Yet, Rom. 5:1-11 can also be seen as a (preliminary)
conclusion to the preceding argument. The transition from an
argument in the third person to the use of an inclusive "we"
begins already in 4:24-25 and continues through 5:1-11. It is
clear that Rom. 5 is part of the exposition of the first theme
introduced in Rom. 1:16ff.: "The gospel is a power of God for
salvation," etc. But the exposition of that theme continues
through Rom. 9-11 ("Jew first and Greek") and right up to the
conclusion of the paranaesis in 15:7-13. We should therefore not
take Rom. 1:16 as a specific theme for the section Rom. 5-8. It
is, rather, the encompassing theme for the whole main body of the
letter (1:16-15:13). The theses about the revelation of God's
righteousness and of his wrath (1:17-18) are subthemes, and are
treated in a reverse order. Whether the main line of division
should be drawn before or after chapter 5 is a minor problem. More
important, analysis of the composition confirms that the over-
arching theological theme of Romans coincides with the motivation
for Paul's missionary zeal. "Justification by faith" is not in
itself the theme of the letter but part of, and a criterion for,
Paul's missionary theology.

Even within Romans 5-8 the chapter divisions and inserted
headlines tend to obscure the flexible, yet orderly progression
of Paul's argument. Here, too, discrete units of thought conclude
with theses that are then elaborated or that give rise to questions.
The main examples are: 5:9-11 + 5:12ff.; 5:20-21 + 6:1ff.; 6:14 +
6:15ff.; 7:5-6 + 7:7ff.; 7:12 + 7:13ff. (7:25a + 8:1ff; see below);

---

[22]See my synopsis of Rom. 5:1-11 and 8:1-39 in my article
"Two Notes on Romans 5," *ST* 5(1951) 37-48. A revised version of
the synopsis is included as Appendix I to this article. For a
more detailed argument, see P. van der Osten-Sacken, *Römer 8 als
Beispiel paulinischer Soteriologie* (FRLANT 112, Göttingen: Vandenhoeck
& Ruprecht, 1975) esp. 57-60.

8:17b + 8:18ff. The problems raised and discussed in chapters
6 and 7 cause some difficulties for analysis since they are not
directly related to the main positive argument set forth in
chapters 5 and 8. One might consider the discussions of problems
related to sin and the Law as digressions,[23] but would then have
to add that they feed into the main argument and enrich it, as
can easily be seen by a comparison between Rom. 5 and Rom. 8.
It would be more appropriate, however, to consider the units
introduced by the questions in 6:1, 6:15, 7:7 and 7:13 as
refutations of objections against Paul's doctrine and thus as
integral parts of his argumentation.[24] Earlier in the letter Paul
has already envisaged the objection that his doctrine gave free
rein to sin and abrogated the Law (see 3:4-8 and 31). It is
obvious that this objection or false consequence posed a real
threat to Paul's missionary work. If left unrefuted, it would be
fatal to Paul's credibility in Rome.

But why, then, does Paul in Rom. 6 drop the terminology of
faith and justification and shift to a baptismal imagery of death,
burial and resurrection with Christ and later to an argument from
moral philosophy (6:15ff.) and to a somewhat strained comparison
with marriage law (7:1-4)? It is not satisfactory to answer that
Paul shifts to another, more "Hellenistic" and mystical line of
thought. Outside the Letter to the Romans, the attempt to distinguish between "forensic" and "mystical-ethical" terminology becomes
artificial.[25] Even in Romans, Paul ascribes a "forensic" importance
to the sacramental death with Christ (see Rom. 6:7 and 7:1-4).
It would seem to have been entirely possible for Paul to move
directly from the reign of grace through righteousness (Rom. 5:21)
to the moral consequences of being under grace (6:15ff.). The

---

[23]In *ST* 5, 41 (see note 22), I spoke about Rom. 6:1-7:6
and 7:7-25 as "two digressions." Cf. also J. Jeremias, "Zur
Gedankenführung in den paulinischen Briefen," in *Studia Paulina in
honorem J. de Zwaan* (ed. van Unnik, Haarlem: Bohn, 1953) 146-154;
J. Dupont, "Le problème de la structure littéraire de l'Epître
aux Romains," *RB* 62 (1955) 365-397; B. Noack, "Current and Back-
water in the Epistle to the Romans," *ST* 19 (1965) 155-166. On
the function of Romans 5:12-21 within this context, see Appendix
II to this chapter.

[24]A digression may, of course, carry as much weight as the
main argument but, in ancient rhetoric, refutation of real or
possible counterarguments is an integral part of the art of persuasion. For this insight I am indebted to Stan Stowers, who is
preparing a study of "Paul and the Diatribe," centering upon the
dialogical elements in the style of Romans.

[25]Cf. e.g. 2 Cor. 5:14-21; Gal. 2:16-21; 3:23-4:6; Phil.
3:8-11 (Eph. 2:1-10; Col. 2:9-15). See, e.g., R. C. Tannehill,
Dying and Rising with Christ (Berlin: Töpelmann, 1963).

main reason for the introduction of a new set of terms and images
in Rom. 6:1ff. may be very simple. Paul wanted to persuade his
Roman audience. The juridical terminology of righteousness and
judgment, transgression and pardon was most appropriate for the
argument that, ultimately, it made no difference whether or not
a person knew the revealed Law, since God is the impartial judge
and had set things right by letting his Son die for all, without
any distinction. Having argued that the Law was only an interim
order that came in to make the crime greater, he is faced with a
different task. Refuting the alleged consequence, that his
doctrine favored sinning, he turns the point around and exhorts
his readers that they should put themselves and their capacities
for action at the disposition of God, in the service of righteousness. To further this purpose he appeals to their own experience:
they have been baptised into the death of Christ, they have become
obedient to the "standard of teaching" to which they have been
handed over as to a master, and they have received the Spirit of
Christ (see Rom. 6:3ff., 17ff. and 7:5-6 + 8:2-17).

     Having refuted the notion that his teaching favored
sinning, Paul has to face other objections that he equated the Law
with sin and made the Law responsible for the death of the sinner
(Rom. 7:7, 13). In the answers to these objections the wider,
missionary perspective seems to drop out of sight. Paul speaks
in the first person singular, and even if the "I" is rhetorical,
used to express a typical experience, the distance from the
description of social vices in Rom. 1:24ff. and 2:17ff. is
obvious. Parts of Rom. 7:14-25 read like a confession of sin with
inserted comments.[26] The point of these comments, and already
of 7:7-12, however, is the exculpation of the Law. The blame is
to be put on sin, the power that reigns over mankind since Adam.
Just because it is holy and righteous and good, the Law made an
end to the state of moral indifference and caused evil desire
(7:7-12). Recognizing that the results of his actions do not
correspond to his good intentions, the sinner bears testimony to
the goodness of the Law - and to his own slavery under sin.

     The confession in Rom. 7:14-15, 18-19, 22-23 concludes
with a cry for deliverance and a thanksgiving (vv. 24-25a). As
the thanksgiving marks the transition to the assertions of liberation
and new life in Romans 8, many commentators have assumed that the

---

[26]See Appendix III to this chapter. Stendahl, 83, has
rightly stressed that Rom. 7:7-25 is part of an argument about the
Law but overreacted in considering the "supporting argument"
simply "a common sense observation."

final comment in v. 25b has been misplaced, or that it is a
secondary gloss. I prefer to see it as a "delayed conclusion"
that refers back to the statements in 7:5-6 and clarifies them.[27]
There Paul spoke about "sinful passions, aroused by the law" and
about slavery "under the old written code" (lit. "under the oldness
of the letter" *palaiotēti grammatos*) which he contrasted with
enslavement in the new order of the Spirit (*en kainotēti pneumatos*).
In the conclusion Paul makes it clear that he does not blame the
Law but sin for the enslavement and death of the carnal man, who
lives in the flesh without the lifegiving power of God. His mind
may be subservient to the Law of God and recognize it to be good,
but with his flesh (and that means in practice) he is a slave
to the law of sin. For Paul, the Law requires deeds and not good
intentions. Just by bringing about evil in spite of his own good
intentions, man proves that he is enslaved, incapable of liberating
himself.

The treatment of Law and sin (Rom. 7:7-25) has a double
function in the context, to refute objections and exculpate the
Law, and to provide the dark background for the liberation in
Christ and the new life in the Spirit. Under both aspects, the
section gives a fuller elaboration of ideas that Paul had earlier
stated in a condensed form (see Rom. 3:7-8, 19-20; 5:20-21, and
also 3:31). In Rom. 1:18-3:20 Paul accused Gentiles and Jews
because of the vices that were current among them. In Rom. 7:7-25
he analyzes more deeply the general human predicament in this
world, which since the fall of Adam has been under the sway of
sin. In Romans 8 Paul elaborates what was already said in 5:1-11
about the reasons for confident hope in the midst of sufferings,
but he does so against the background of man's slavery under sin,
as described in 7:7-25. The Holy Spirit, given to those who
believe in Christ, is the lifegiving and guiding power which makes
it possible to fulfill the just requirement of the Law, as well as
the surety of future life and glory. In order to refute objections
and to encourage and admonish the Christians in Rome, Paul has
added depth to his missionary theology.

In Rom. 9-11 Paul returns to the role of Jews and Gentiles,
resuming the question about the faithfulness of God to his people
(see 3:1-4). We find similar compositional devices as in the
rest of the letter. A brief introduction is followed by a thematic

---

[27]For other examples of delayed conclusions, see Rom. 3:
22b-23; 10:17; 2 Cor. 5:21. The correspondence between Rom. 7:6b
and 7:25b is an example of rhetorical inclusion.

statement which covers the following discussion: "It is not as
though the word of God failed" (9:6a). Two subthemes (9:6b and
7) are treated in a reversed order. Paul proves from Scripture
that "not all are children of Abraham because they are his
descendants" (9:7-13). Later on, he develops the other theme
that was introduced first: "Not all who are descended from Israel
belong to Israel" (9:6b, cf. 9:22-29, 30-33; 10:16-21; 11:1-10).
At this point, the argument becomes somewhat complicated because
Paul also refutes objections (9:14ff. and 19ff.), supports his
argument with scriptural quotations and, at a remarkably late
point, states the reason why he had to deal with the question
of whether or not the word of God to Israel had failed (cf. 10:
1-17).[28] There is no need to go into detail here. The inner
unity of Paul's mission and theology is nowhere more obvious than
in Rom. 9-11. Within the doctrinal body of the letter, it is
only here that Paul explicitly refers to his own ministry as
apostle to the Gentiles - and as intercessor for Israel.[29] Moreover, Paul's vision of future salvation for all Israel provides
the right perspective for the collection with which Paul is, at
the moment of writing, ready to go to Jerusalem, pleading that
the Christians in Rome should intercede with their prayers that
it might be well received.

There is no need to discuss the exhortations in Rom. 12:
1-15:13 in any detail either. By and large they represent the
same type of paraenesis that we find in 1 Thess. 4-5 and in other
letters as well. Various subsections are introduced by thematic
appeals. Most of the exhortations pertain either to the mutual
relations between Christians or to their relations to those outside, including the governing authorities. Especially the discussion
of the strong and the weak in Rom. 14:1-15:6 seems to presuppose
that Paul had some knowledge of internal problems in Rome, but
even here he deals with typical rather than with specific cases,
thus avoiding intruding on a church that he had not himself founded.
We can further note that the warning against haughty thoughts in
Rom. 12:3 and 16 picks up a theme from the more specific warning
that Paul addressed to the Gentiles in 11:20.

---

[28]Rom. 10:4 is another example of a conclusion that introduces the theme of the following section. Rom. 10:17 is the
conclusion to 10:4ff., but already in 10:16 Paul has introduced
his next theme, the disobedience of (part of) Israel. Rather,
he returns to this theme, cf. 9:30-33; 10:1-3.

[29]For a fuller treatment of Rom. 9-11, see Chapter IX.
On Paul as intercessor for Israel, see Wiles, *Paul's Intercessory
Prayers*, 253-258.

Not only in 11:18ff. but already in 6:11-13 Paul had
shifted to a hortatory mood. This is one indication among others
that the paraenesis is organically related to the theological
argument in Romans. The initial, and thematic, request in Rom.
12:1: "to present (*parastēsai*) your bodies as a living sacrifice,
holy and acceptable to God," especially, recalls 6:13: "yield
(*paristanete*, present) yourself to God." The difference is that
in 6:13 Paul used military rather than sacrificial metaphors.
The sacrificial imagery reappears in Rom. 15:16, where Paul
speaks of the goal of his own ministry: "that the offering
(*thysia*, sacrifice) of the Gentiles may be acceptable, sanctified
by the Holy Spirit." Here the Gentiles are seen as the sacrifice
to be presented by Paul, whereas Paul in Rom. 12:1 calls his
readers to sacrifice themselves. Neither the similarity nor the
difference between the formulations in 12:1 and 15:16 can be
accidental. As a minister of Christ Jesus to the Gentiles, Paul
is to present them as a sacrifice to God. But he can only achieve
this goal if his constituency responds with a voluntary obedience
and learns to discern what is the will of God for themselves (see
Rom. 12:2 and cf. Phil. 1:9-11 and Rom. 15:14). Both the opening
sentences in 12:1-2 and the whole paraenetic section in Romans
confirm that Paul considers the Christians in Rome to be part of
his constituency and yet he is careful to respect their independence.

Concluding his exhortations, Paul writes: "Welcome one
another, therefore, as Christ has welcomed you." The formulation
is a generalized resumption of 14:1: "As for the man who is weak
in faith, welcome him." We are hardly to identify the weak and
the strong in Rom. 14:1-15:6 with Christian Jews and Gentiles.
Christ's ministry to the circumcised, that confirmed the promises
to the patriarchs and made the Gentiles praise God for his mercy,
is rather to be seen as a paradigm for Christian conduct in general
(Rom. 15:7-13). The conclusion to the paraenesis and to the main
body of the letter refers back to the thematic statement in Rom.
1:16: "a power for salvation...to the Jew first and also to the
Greek," and even to the opening summary of the gospel which God
had promised beforehand (1:2-6). The conclusion reaches beyond
the opening, however, in making the praise of God's faithfulness
to his people and his mercy toward the Gentiles the ultimate goal
(see the Psalm quotations in Rom. 15:9-12).

The analysis of the composition of Romans could easily
have been carried on at greater length and in more depth. I hope
that my somewhat scattered remarks have been sufficient to

illuminate the inner correspondance between the form, the content,
and the setting of the letter. Paul's letter to the Romans
gives us the most comprehensive representation of Paul's theology
because it was written for a very particular purpose. The theology
of Romans is closely tied to the Pauline mission with its historical
and eschatological perspectives. If we are to take the letter
seriously as a canonical, normative writing, it will neither
suffice to use it to nurture personal piety nor to integrate Paul's
teachings into a systematic theology. The task is rather to
regain the unity of theology and evangelism, and of justification
by faith and world mission.

APPENDIX I

A Synopsis of Romans 5:1-11 and 8:1-39

The parallelism between the two segments of the letter
pertains to themes and argumentation rather than to vocabulary,
phraseology, or order. I have therefore not written out the text
of Rom. 8, assuming that the reader will have a Bible at hand.
In order to draw attention to verbal similarities, I have inserted
some transliterations of the Greek text. The equivalent English
words and phrases can easily be identified in a translation.

Romans 5:1-11	Romans 8
1. Therefore, since we are justified (*dikaiōthentes*) by faith,	1-2 30 (*edikaiōsen*) 33 (*ho dikaiōn*)
we have peace with God through our Lord Jesus Christ.	
2. Through him we have obtained access to this grace in which we stand, and we rejoice in our hope (*ep' elpidi*)	20 (*eph'* (h)*elpidi*) 24-25 (*te...elpidi... elpis ...*)
of sharing the glory of God (*tēs doxēs tou theou*).	17b (*hina kai syndoxathōmen*) 18 (*tēn mellousan doxan...*) 21 (*eis tēn eleutherian tēs doxēs tōn huiōn tou theou*) 29-30 (*toutous kai edoxasen*)
3. More than that, we rejoice	17b (*eiper sympaschomen ...*), 18
in our sufferings (*en tais thlipsesin*)	35-37 (*thlipsis ē stenochoria*)
knowing that suffering produces endurance (*hypomonē*)	25 (*di' hypomonēs...*)

Romans 5:1-11	Romans 8

4. but endurance
    produces a tested mind
    and a tested mind
        produces hope (*elpis*),
	24-25

5. and hope does not disappoint us,
        because God's love (*hē agapē tou theou*)
        has been poured into our hearts
        (*en tais kardiais hēmōn*)
 	
        through the Holy Spirit
        which has been given to us.
	17, 28-30, 35-39
	31-32
	
	26-27 (*ho de ereunōn*
	          tas kardias)
	2, 4, 9-11, 13-17a, 26-27
	23 (*...pneuma theou oikei*
	          en hymin)

6. While we were yet helpless,
        at the right time Christ died
        (*apethanen*) for the ungodly.
	34 (*X. I. ho apothanōn*)

7. - - -	

8. But God shows his love for us
        in that while we were yet sinners
 	
        Christ died for us.
	35, 39 (*apo tēs agapēs*
	              tou theou tēs
	              en Christō Iēsou)
	34 (*X. I. ho apothanōn*)

9. Since, therefore we are now justified
        by his blood,
    much more shall we be saved by him
        from the wrath of God.
	30, 33
	34
	31-34

10. For if (*ei gar*) while we were enemies
        we were reconciled to God
        by the death of his Son (*...huiou...*),
    much more (*pollō mallon*),
        now that we are reconciled,
        shall we be saved
        by his life (*en tē zoē autou*)
	10, 11, 13b, 17a (*ei de...*)
	31-32 (*ei ho theos...*
	              tou idiou huiou...
	              pōs ouchi kai...)
	
	33-34
	34 (*mallon de egertheis...*)

11. Not only so,
        but we also rejoice in God
        through our Lord Jesus Christ,
    through whom we have now received
    our reconciliation.
	31-39, *passim.*

Comments: Apart from the climactic chain in Rom. 5:3-4 and the aside in Rom. 5:7, all major themes in Rom. 5:1-11 reappear in Romans 8: Justification and a restored relationship to God as the basis for the hope of future salvation and glory, in spite of present sufferings; the gift of the Holy Spirit, the death of Christ, and the love of God as warrants for this hope; a note of exultation. Yet, the difference between the two segments of the letter is not simply one of order, style, and phraseology. As the terminology shows, 5:1-11 is still closely linked to chapters 1-4 and brings

the argument there to a preliminary conclusion: "By faith" and
"grace" in 5:1-2; Christ's death for the ungodly, while we were
still "helpless," "sinners," "enemies" in 5:6-10; "by his blood"
and salvation "from the wrath" in 5:9. By contrast, the restatement
of the argument in chapter 8 is set forth against the background
of 5:12-7:25: Liberation from the sway of sin and death; the
contrasts between the flesh and the Spirit, i.e. between our mortal
bodies and the Spirit of God, and between slavery and freedom;
participation and conformity with Christ; the Holy Spirit as guide
and power for moral life and as helper and intercessor in weakness
and sufferings, not only as a warrant of salvation.

APPENDIX II

The Argument in Romans 5:12-21

Since the main text did not deal with the Adam - Christ
analogy in Rom. 5:12-21, I may add some comments here.[30] The
main function of this segment of the letter is to support the
argument in 5:1-11, in much the same way as the interpretation of
the story of Abraham in chapter 4 supports the main thesis in 3:
21-26. Paul argues that Christ's "act of righteousness" (*dikaiōma*),
i.e. his obedience unto death, will bring life as well as justification to all who receive God's grace through him. The fall of
Adam, which made sin come into the world and which became the
cause of death for all mankind, provides an analogy and a warrant
for this conclusion. In this respect, Rom. 5:12ff. restates the
argument in 5:1-11, using the analogy between Christ and Adam to
add a universal perspective. But in the course of his argumentation,
Paul changes direction, going from an argument from analogy to an
argument from a minor to a major cause (*a minori ad maius*, see
esp. Rom. 5:15,17). One reason for this is a conviction which Paul
shared with the rabbis: the mercy (or grace) of God is greater,
and will have more far-reaching effects, than the judgment with
which he reacts to sin (cf. Exod. 20:5-6 and 34:6-7). But this is
hardly the whole explanation.

---

[30]This is a summary and restatement of the second of my "Two
Notes on Romans 5," *ST* 5 (1951) 37-48.

The breakdown of the sentence structure in Rom. 5:12ff.
indicates that there is a specific factor which makes the analogy
between Christ and Adam less than complete. It was only in the
period before Moses that everybody died as a consequence of Adam's
fall which had brought sin and death into the world (cf. Rom.
5:13-14). Later on, sinners were also accountable for their own
transgressions of the Law (cf. *ek pollōn paraptōmatōn* ("following
many trespasses"), Rom. 5:16). By contrast, Christ's act resulted
in a righteousness that remains a free, undeserved gift, a grace
that outweighs the many transgressions of the Law as well as the
sin of Adam. Thus, it was only in the time between Adam and Moses
that the relation between the one and the many was the same in the
order of sin and death as in the order of righteousness and life.
Paul can draw the conclusion that it is all the more certain that
all who have received justification through Christ will also obtain
life through him.

Thus, the Law is the factor which disturbs the analogy
in contrast between Adam and Christ. That this is indeed so is
confirmed by the conclusion of the chapter, Rom. 5:20-21. Here
Paul raises the question of the function of the Law and of its
relation to sin, a question that had remained unanswered, or had
only received partial answers, in the preceding parts of the letter
(see Rom. 3:20, 31; 4:13-15). The answer given in Rom. 5:20-21
introduces the theme of the argumentation that follows in Rom.
6-8. All of this means that Rom. 5:12-21 supports and extends
the argument in 5:1-11, but at the same time serves as a transition
to the renewed treatment of sin and the Law in chapters 6-7, which
in turn provides the background for the restatement of themes
from 5:1-11 in chapter 8. The whole of Romans 5 is connected with
both the preceding and with the following sections of the letter,
5:1-2 serving as a transition from the exposition in 3:21-4:25,
and 5:20-21 serving as a transition to the questions raised in
6:1ff. The problem of whether a main line of division should be
drawn between chapters 4 and 5 or between 5 and 6 or, possibly,
between 5:11 and 5:12 becomes acute only if we ask for some
systematic outline and fail to follow Paul's vivid argumentation.

APPENDIX III

Confession and Comments in Rom. 7:14-25

Confessional Statements	Comments
14. We know that the Law is spiritual, but I am carnal, sold under sin.	
15.	I do not understand my own actions.
For I do not what I want, but I do the very thing I hate.	
16.	Now, if I do what I do not
17.	want, I agree that the Law is good. So then it is no longer I that do it, but sin
18.	which dwells within me. For I know that
nothing good dwells within me, I can will what is right, but I cannot do it.	that is, in my flesh.
19. For I do not do the good that I want, but the evil I do not want is what I do.	
20.	Now if I do what I do not want, it is no longer I that do it,
21.	but sin which dwells within me. So I find it to be a law that when I want to do right, evil lies close at hand.
22. For I delight in the Law of God, in my inmost self,	
23. but I see in my members another law, at war with the law of my mind and making me captive to the law of sin which dwells in my members.	
24. Wretched man that I am! Who will deliver me from this body of death?	
25. Thanks be to God through Jesus Christ our Lord!	
	So then, I of myself serve the Law of God with my mind, but with my flesh I serve the law of sin.

The text might have been arranged in other ways, but the distinction between confessional statements and comments is fairly clear. The comments in the right column undergird Paul's rejection of the idea that the Law is responsible for the death of the sinner. Sin is to be blamed. The left column, by contrast, reads like a confession of sin, a lamentation over slavery under the power of Sin, introduced by the phrase "but I ..." which is used in a similar

way in some of the Psalms and in Qumran hymns.[31] The concluding
cry for deliverance and the thanksgiving in 7:24-25a are also in
harmony with the confessional style.[32]

The comments are obviously made in retrospect, from Paul's
Christian point of view. The confession of sinfulness contrasts
sharply with Paul's self-evaluation as a Pharisee: "As to righteousness under the law blameless" (Phil. 3:8). It contrasts equally
with his evaluation of himself as a Christian: "I am not aware of
anything against myself" (1 Cor. 4:4). But the common opinion
that Rom. 7:7-25 gives Paul's Christian evaluation of existence
under the Law[33] is not quite satisfactory either, as it fails to
give a satisfactory explanation for the confessional style.
Especially the cry for deliverance at the end would seem artificial
if the intention was simply to give a Christian interpretation of
pre-Christian existence.

In spite of all that has been written about Romans 7, there
is still room for a careful, comparative investigation of the
style. Here I shall only make some common sense remarks:

1. The "I" form is no doubt used as a rhetorical device, but the
   use of this form would hardly be meaningful unless both the
   speaker and his audience can in some way identify with the
   experience of the typical "I".

2. If genuine, a confession of sin is a very personal matter.
   Yet, the confession may be best expressed in stereotyped
   language, perhaps in the form of a ritual prayer.

3. When we confess our sins before God, our self-evaluation is
   very different from what it normally is when we communicate
   with other people. The Dead Sea Scrolls contain very clear
   examples of this, but I would think that the observation also
   holds true for Pharisees, for saints, and for ordinary people.

---

[31]See Psalms 22:7; 69:29(30); 73:2; 1 QS 11:9; 1 QM 1:21;
3:23f.; 4:33,35; 11:19; 12:24; 18:25,31 and fragm. 1:4; 3:11; 52:3.
For the sequence in Rom. 7:14, "We know ... but I am ...," see
1 QH 1:21: "These things I have known..., yet I am but a creature
of clay and a thing kneaded with water," etc., and 3:20-24: "And
I knew there was hope ... But I, a creature of clay, what am I?"
For similarities and differences between Rom. 7 and analogous
passages in the Dead Sea Scrolls, see esp. H. Braun, "Römer 7,7-25
und das Selbstverständnis der Qumran-Fromme," in *Gesammelte Studien
zum Neuen Testament und seiner Umwelt* (Tübingen: Mohr, 1962), 100-
119 (repr. from *ZTK* 56, 1959).
[32]Cf. E. W. Smith, "The Form and Religious Background of
Romans 7:24-25a," *NovT* 13 (1971) 127-135.
[33]See esp. the very influential study of W. G Kümmel, *Römer
7 und die Bekehrung des Paulus* (Leipzig: Hinrichs, 1929). In spite
of many variations, Kümmel's main thesis has been accepted by a
great number of scholars.

The confessional statements are so general that everybody
can make them their own. They are not autobiographical in any
narrow sense, but they do express Paul's personal experience. His
intention was good, as he was motivated by zeal for the Law. Yet,
the result of his action was evil: he persecuted the church of
God. The "I" who makes the confession is the person who is now
legally dead and, thanks to the liberation in Christ Jesus and
the power of the Spirit, even effectively dead (see Rom. 7:1-6;
8:9-11 and cf. Gal. 2:19-20). Yet, even those who have received
the Spirit still groan, as they wait for the redemption of the
body (Rom. 8:23). We have no evidence to prove that confession
of sin before God was practiced in the Pauline communities, as
it was, more or less regularly, at Qumran, in the Synagogue
liturgy and, apparently, in some early Christian circles (see 1
John 1:9). It is hard to say whether or not an argument from
silence would be conclusive. In any case, Paul does not in Rom.
7 use the "I" form in order to give biographical information,
to set forth anthropological doctrines, or to give an abstract
interpretation of pre-Christian existence under the Law. He
wants to engage his readers, so that they concur both in the
conclusion that the Law is good and in the thanksgiving for the
liberation in Christ and, thus, let the Spirit, not the flesh,
direct their lives.

CHAPTER VI

THE DOCTRINE OF JUSTIFICATION:
ITS SOCIAL FUNCTION AND IMPLICATIONS

By the doctrine of justification I mean the Pauline
doctrine outlined in Rom. 3:28: man is justified by faith apart
from works of the Law. This doctrine Paul develops in the letters
to the Romans and the Galatians. In the letter to the Galatians
the form is polemical and pointed whereas the letter to the Romans
gives a more comprehensive, positive account intended to ward
off misinterpretations. Brief statements of the doctrine can
also be found in other Pauline letters (2. Cor. 5:21; Phil. 3:7ff.;
cf. Titus 3:5-7; Acts 13:38f.). Words such as righteous, righteousness and justify can also appear outside the context of the doctrine
of justification, and the substance of the doctrine can be present
even where the technical terminology of the doctrine is missing.[1]

I presuppose common knowledge of the content of the
doctrine and shall neither try to penetrate its theological depths
nor take a stand with regard to the contested parts of its interpretation. A close discussion of exegetical details in the central
texts would exceed the limits of my essay. My question is simpler
and pertains to Paul's use of the doctrine of justification. The
phrase "social function and implications" indicates that I see
the doctrine as something more than a dogmatic doctrine or an
answer to the question of how the individual is to find a gracious
God. In this study, I want to point out that this doctrine not
only concerns the individual and his relation to God but is also
of importance for the common life of Christians. This is no new

---

[1]The substance of this paper has, in various versions,
been given as a lecture at several theological schools in the
United States and at a pastors' institute sponsored by the
Theological Faculty at the University of Oslo.

insight but is an aspect which has only infrequently received due
attention in treatments of Paul's doctrine.

Before we turn to Paul's specific doctrine, I shall make
some remarks about the teaching about God's righteousness and
his justification of man in Judaism and early Christianity. Here
I use the common term "pre-Pauline" Christianity to refer to
teachings which Paul is likely to have had in common with other
early Christian teachers and preachers. We shall next turn to
Paul's special doctrine of justification by faith, as we find
it in Romans and Galatians, and conclude with some remarks about
analogies in other New Testament writings and about the use of
Paul's doctrine in the later history of the church.

*1. Righteousness and Justification:
    Early Christianity and Qumran*

The question of the background and origin of the terminology
which Paul uses in his doctrine of justification has, usually,
been answered in one of two ways. Many scholars have assumed
that Paul made an antithetical use of rabbinic terminology.
Whereas the Jewish theologians taught that man became righteous
and guiltless before God by observing the commandments, Paul
maintains that it is through faith and not through works of the
Law that we become righteous in God's judgment.[2] Others have
assumed that Paul drew upon the usage in the Old Testament, perhaps
mediated by the Septuagint. Especially in the Psalms and in Second
Isaiah, God's "righteousness" means his saving righteousness, his
vindication of himself and of his convenant people. Being faithful,
he sets things right for the poor and oppressed.[3]

The choice between these two possibilities has certain
consequences for the understanding of the term *dikaiosynē theou*
(righteousness of God). Interpreted as antithetical to rabbinic
doctrine, Pauline *dikaiosynē theou* means the righteousness from

---

[2]Especially in older literature, the rabbinic doctrine was
presented as a direct contrast to Paul's view and thus caricatured.
For more recent and balanced accounts, see e.g. A. Oepke, *"Dikaiosynē
Theou* bei Paulus in neuer Beleuchtung," *TLZ* 78 (1953) 257-63;
H. Ljungmann, *Pistis* (Lund: Gleerup, 1964) 24-28.
    [3]See esp. C. H. Dodd, *The Epistle to the Romans* (MNTC;
London: Hodder & Stoughton, 1932), 9-12. More recently, E. Käsemann
has tried to interpret "God's righteousness" against an apocalyptic
background, see *New Testament Questions of Today*, 168-182. The
same approach is followed by P. Stuhlmacher, *Gerechtigkeit Gottes
bei Paulus* (Göttingen: Vandenhoeck & Ruprecht, 1966).

God, the righteousness which God imputes and gives to the believers. If Paul's use of the term is derived from the Septuagint's usage, it is more natural to understand the genitive as a subjective genitive: God demonstrates his saving righteousness when he, as an act of grace, acquits or pardons sinners. This understanding informs the translation of Rom. 1:17 in *The New English Bible*: "Here is revealed God's way of righting wrong."[4]

It is not necessary to make an exclusive choice between the two possible explanations. Combinations or compromise solutions are also possible. Some scholars suppose that in different contexts Paul assigns somewhat different meanings to the term.[5] But the alternative, polemical or biblical terminology, is out of date today. Like many other problems, the question of the terminology of justification must be reconsidered in the light of the Dead Sea Scrolls. Some of the Scrolls from Qumran speak of the sin of man and of God's righteousness in a manner that sounds strikingly Pauline, not to say Lutheran. Especially some of the hymns stress that all men are sinners, the members of the sect and the "I" who prays not excepted: "And when he is judged, who will be just before Thee?" (1QH 7:28; cf. 9:14f.; 12:19; 16:11). "It is by Thy goodness alone that a man is justified and by the immensity of Thy mercy" (13:16f.). The praying person-- is it the Teacher of Righteousness himself?--elaborates at length his own misery. He is made of clay, kneaded with water, conceived in uncleanness and sin, "a spirit of straying, and perverse" (1QH 1:21f.). He leans on God's acts of grace and his rich mercy, because God in his righteousness wipes out sins and cleanses away guilt (1QH 11:30f.): "For I leaned on Thy favors and on the greatness of Thy mercy. For Thou pardonest iniquity and clean[sest m]an of sin by Thy righteousness" (1QH 4:37).

The confession of redemption through the righteousness of God alone is most clearly expressed in the hymnic conclusion of The Scroll of the Rule: "But to God I will say, My righteousness" (1QS 10:11).

> For to God belongs my justification,
> and the perfection of my way,
> and the uprightness of my heart
> are in His hand:

---

[4]On the most recent discussion, see G. Klein, "Righteousness in the NT, "*IDBSup* 750-752; M. T. Bauch, "Perspectives on 'God's righteousness' in recent German discussion," in Sanders, 523-542, Appendix.

[5]This opinion was held by several of the older commentators (e.g. Lietzmann) and has been restated by Sanders, 491-495.

by His righteousness are my rebellions blotted out. (11:2f.)

\- \- \-

and from the fount of His Righteousness comes my justifi-
                                                cation.
From His wondrous Mysteries is the light in my heart . . .
                                        (11:5)

\- \- \-

As for me, I belong to wicked humanity,
to the assembly of perverse flesh. (11:9)

\- \- \-

No, men cannot establish their steps
for their justification belongs to God,
and from His hand comes perfection of way.
By His undersatanding all things are brought into being,
by His thought every being established,
and without Him nothing is made.
And I, if I stagger,
God's mercies are my salvation for ever;
and if I stumble because of the sin of the flesh,
my justification is in the righteousness of God
which exists for ever.

\- \- \-

He has caused me to approach by His Mercy
and by His favors He will bring my justification.
He has justified me by His true justice
and by His immense goodness He will pardon all my iniquities.
And by His justice He will cleanse me of the defilement of man
and of the sin of the sons of men,
that I may acknowledge His righteousness unto God
and His majesty unto the Most High. (11:10-12, 13-15)[6]

The translation of this part of the Rule is beset with
several difficulties. It is sometimes hard to know how to render
a word, e.g., the plural of *heṣed* (mercy or acts of grace?).
Punctuation and tense cause other problems. For our topic it is
the interpretation of the noun *mišpāṭ* which is the most difficult
and most important problem. If one consistently translates it,
as Dupont-Sommer does, with "justification," the text sounds
considerably more Pauline than if one renders it with "right" or
"righteousness."   There are good arguments for abandoning the

---

[6]The translation is taken from A. Dupont-Sommer, *The Essene
Writings from Qumran*, tr. G. Vermes (Cleveland/New York: World,
1962).

attempt to find a single translation; the word *mišpaṭ* shifts
nuance: right, legal rule or decision, righteousness, etc. Even
in these quotations we must take into account the interaction of
several nuances. The concept must not be one-sidedly rendered
as either "imputed righteousness" or ethical righteousness as
a human quality; the meaning is more comprehensive. The right,
justice and righteousness of the praying person depends through
and through upon God. By his own strength he can neither do the
right thing nor obtain righteousness. God alone, in his righteousness, can forgive sin and acquit him, and only God can make his
life right.

Without any detailed exegesis of the texts we may state
that the beliefs voiced by members of the Qumran community
correspond to a number of the classical formulations of the
doctrine of justification. The ungodly is righteous only through
grace. A man is saved not by his own righteouness but by God's
saving righteousness. Man is at the same time sinful and righteous.
Thus: *justificatio impii - sola gratia - justitia salutifera -
justitia aliena - simul justus et peccator!* Expressions like these
would not have the meaning they acquire in Lutheran dogmatics if
applied to what is taught in the Qumran community. Nevertheless,
the parallels are striking and raise both historical and theological
questions. Where is the difference between Essene and Pauline
doctrine to be located? Does a direct or indirect connection
exist?[7]

One must be careful not to draw conclusions which are too
rash. Père Benoit and other sensible scholars have, with good
reason, called for caution. What the Qumran texts really prove
is that the Old Testament idea of God's righteousness was alive
in Judaism at the time of the New Testament, at least in certain
circles and in some connections: God's *ṣedaka* is not a revenging or
distributive justice but the saving righteousness he shows in
his treatment of his chosen ones. It is not necessary to suppose
that the Pauline terminology is directly taken over from circles
in Qumran or related groups. At the same time, however, it is
obvious that we no longer stand before the alternative that the
terminology of justification is either shaped in opposition to the
Pharisaic doctrine or taken over from the Septuagint: it has a

---

[7]On this question, see e.g. S. Schultz, "Zur Rechtfertigung
aus Gnaden in Qumran und bei Paulus," *ZTK* 56 (1959) 155-185;
W. Grundmann, "Der Lehrer der Gerechtigkeit von Qumran und die
Frage nach der Glaubensgerechtigkeit in der Theologie des Apostels
Paulus," *RevQ* 2 (1960) 231-254. For more recent literature, cf.
note 3 above.

positive connection to a religious language still existing in
Judaism. It is also important to point out that what we find
in the Qumran texts is not merely the use of Old Testament terms
like "God's righteousness": these expressions appear in a new
context marked by a deep sense of the sinfulness of man, a mood
of penance and practice of piety, and, moreover, a personal hope
for salvation, all of this within a special group of chosen ones.
The similarity with Paul's doctrine of justification through the
saving righteousness of God is truly remarkable.

At this point I would like to refer to an observation
made by David Flusser, professor at the Hebrew University in
Jerusalem. The closest parallels in the New Testament to the
Dead Sea Scrolls are, by and large, not to be found in thoughts
and formulations which are especially characteristic of any one
of the authors of the New Testament. They appear in terminology
or phraseology which is common to Paul, John, the letter to Hebrews,
and, to a certain extent, 1 Peter and other works.[8] This means
that they are found in the layer of tradition which Bultmann
presents in his *Theology of the New Testament* under the title
"The kerygma of the Hellenistic church aside from Paul." This
observation should be linked with the conclusion which a number
of scholars have drawn from completely different observations.
Paul has in his doctrine of justification made use of a terminology
already current among the Christian congregations. Not only the
noun *dikaiosynē* (righteousness) but also the verb *dikaioun* (justify)
occur in the New Testament outside the context of Paul's special
doctrine of justification, sometimes in a way which is rather
close to the technical use of the terms. It is sufficient to
mention the tax collector who "went down to his house justified"
(Luke 18:14; cf. also Rom. 6:7; 1 Cor. 4:4). Especially remarkable are a few Pauline texts which seem to reflect traditional
early Christian language and doctrine and at the same time have
close parallels in the Qumran Scrolls.

Concerning the unrepentant, the Scroll of the Rule says:
"When he dissembles the stubbornness of his heart he shall not
be justified (*lô yisḏāḳ*), . . . he shall not be absolved (*lô
yizzākeh*) by atonement nor purified by lustral waters, not sanctified
by seas and rivers, nor cleansed by all the waters of washing.
Unclean, unclean shall he be for as long as he scorns the ordinance
of God" (1QS 3:3-6). Whether the verbal forms are to be viewed

---

[8]D. Flusser, "The Dead Sea Sect and Pre-Pauline Christianity,"
Scripta Hierosolymitana, 4 (1958) 215-266.

as passive or reflexive is open to some question. In either case, the thought is probably that the unrepentant is not to be admitted to the purifying rites of the community and that these rites would have no effect without conversion of the heart and adherence to a way of life in accordance with the Law as it was interpreted in Qumran.

With this statement in the Scroll of the Rule one must contrast and compare what is said in 1 Cor. 6:11: "But you were washed, you were sanctified, you were justified in the name of the Lord Jesus Christ and in the Spirit of our God." In these two texts the words for washing, sanctifying and justifying are used in close, nearly synonymous, parallelism; in the Scroll, in connnection with the cleansing rites of the sect, in 1 Cor., in connection with Christian baptism. The negative formulation of the words in the text from Qumran does not, by and large, make any significant difference: the presupposition is obviously that anyone who is really converted is justified and guiltless, purified and sanctified through the cultic means of expiation and purification.

In 1 Cor. 6:11 Paul stresses something he regards as well-known. Among scholars today there is widespread agreement that the formulation does not express a specific Pauline doctrine. Justification is here linked to the name of Jesus and to the Spirit in a way not typical of passages where Paul develops his doctrine of justification through faith. Paul has here formulated his words in conformity with common teaching about baptism in the pre-Pauline congregations.

In other cases, too, one suspects that Paul has used more or less fixed formulations. The words in Rom. 4:25, "who was put to death for our trespasses and raised for our justification," seem to reflect confessional language. The formal parallelism, the elevated style and the unusual connection of the resurrection of Jesus with our justification indicate that the words are a loose quotation. Furthermore, it seems that a kind of confessional formulation forms the background for the well-known text in Rom. 3:24-26. Here too the style is elevated and several words occur which are unusual for Paul (e.g., *hilastērion* and *paresis*). In this case it is hardly a direct quotation but rather a free paraphrastic use of the given confession. The inserted *dia pisteōs* (by faith) in v. 25 is likely to be a Pauline comment. One can assume, however, that the pre-Pauline fragment spoke about the righteousness of God. Among the traditional formulations we can perhaps also include Rom. 8:29f., which may reflect baptismal

theology, and Rom. 8:33, the introduction to the closing hymn in
Rom. 8. Finally, we may mention the relative clause in 1 Cor.
1:30: "He is the source of your life in Christ Jesus, whom God
made our wisdom, our righteousness and sanctification and
redemption."[9] Characteristic for all these passages, and probably
for pre-Pauline doctrine as a whole, is that words like *dikaioun*
and *dikaiosynē* are used together with other more or less synonymous
terms and that the statements do not have any polemical intent.
Justification is linked to the death and resurrection of Jesus
and to the name of Jesus and the Spirit of God active at baptism.
One should perhaps note that according to Titus 3:5-7 it is "by
the washing of regeneration," baptism, that we are "justified by
his grace."

It would be hard to prove that in such early Christian
texts terms like justify and God's righteousness have a meaning
different from that which they possess in the Qumran texts. At
least, a very subtle analysis would be necessary to prove any
significant difference in the nuance of the words. What is said
in the texts from the New Testament and in the Dead Sea Scrolls
is nevertheless not the same. The difference, however, is due
to the context and to the purpose of the statements rather than
to word usage per se.

The Qumran texts, mostly hymns and prayers, refer to God's
justifying righteousness. The praying subject expresses his
confidence that God in his grace, faithfulness and righteousness
will forgive the sins which are due to the weakness of the flesh.
The members of the sect, who in the last days of wickedness live
according to the right interpretation of the Law, can trust in
God's righteousness and goodness. Prayers and hymns are not to
be interpreted merely as personal confessions: they also give
prototypical expressions of the right attitude toward God and
thus contain a didactic element. The person who becomes a member
of the sect must learn to trust God's mercy alone, but at the same
time he must convert with his heart and adhere to the Law. Nowhere, however, do we find in the Qumran texts anything like the
statement, "you have been justified."

---

[9]On Paul's use of current terminology in passages like Rom.
3:24-26; 4:25; 1 Cor. 6:11, see E. Lohse, "Die Gerechtigkeit Gottes
in der paulinischen Theologie" and "Taufe und Rechtfertigung bei
Paulus," in *Die Einheit des Neuen Testaments* (Göttingen: Vandenhoeck
& Ruprecht, 1973) esp. 218-223, 240-244. On Rom. 3:24-26, see
also Käsemann's commentary and my *The Crucified Messiah*, 155f.
with note 43 on p. 187. On Rom. 8:29f., see J. Jervell, *Imago Dei*
(FRLANT 76, Göttingen: Vandenhoeck & Ruprecht, 1960) 271ff.

The contrast between "once" and "now" is much more sharply expressed in early Christianity than in the Essene sect.[10]   It is not difficult to understand why this is the case. For the Qumran sectaries the revelation of God's saving righteousness and his justification of sinners is never linked with any event in history comparable to the death and resurrection of Christ. Accordingly, the initiation and purification ceremonies did not make the same kind of difference in the life of the members as baptism in the name of Jesus did for Christians. Christian baptism is important because it makes the believer participate in the grace of God as it was manifested in a saving event which occurred once and for all.

So far we have dealt with passages which relate justification to the death and resurrection of Jesus and to baptism in his name. Such baptismal reminders are rather common in the New Testament epistles. Those baptized are called to remember what they once were and what they now are, to realize the greatness of God's mercy and promise, and to understand what consequences it all must have for their behavior in the church and in the world. Paul constantly calls the congregation back to its beginnings: the first preaching of the Gospel, the foundation of a local congregation and the admission of individuals into the church.[11]

The terminology used in such reminders varies. One form indicates that the Christians have been justified. To the Christians in Corinth the apostle writes that they were unrighteous and committed all kinds of sins, but now they are purified, sanctified and justified. How can they then continue to do wrong, to make demands and to insist on their rights against Christian brothers, and to go to worldly courts for help in making these claims valid (1 Cor. 6:1-11)?[12] The reminder of baptism sounds paradoxical here. In spite of their injustice and wrongdoing they are nevertheless justified in Christ. But this in no way

[10]I assume that the Qumran convenanters were among those whom Pliny, Philo and Josephus describe as "Essenes." On the contrast between "once" and "now", see *Jesus in the Memory of the Early Church*, 33-34; P. Tachau, *'Einst' und 'Jetzt' im Neuen Testament* (Göttingen: Vandenhoeck & Ruprecht, 1972).

[11]See Chapters III and V, and also "Form-Critical Observations on Early Christian Preaching," in *Jesus in the Memory of the Early Church*, 30-36. (By a mistake it was not indicated that this essay had originally appeared in German in W. Eltester, ed. *Neutestamentliche Studien für Rudolf Bultmann* (Tübingen: Mohr, 1954) 3-9.

[12]On this passage, see E. Dinkler, "Zum Problem der Ethik bei Paulus," *ZTK* 49 (1952) 167-200 (= *Signum Crucis*, Tübingen: Mohr, 1967, 204-240).

means that they may complacently assume that the Christian is
simultaneously righteous in the sight of God and sinful in his
moral conduct. On the contrary, Paul stresses with great emphasis
that those who have been justified are not to go on with their
wrongdoings. Rightly understood, justification has very practical
consequences, even for conduct in legal and economic matters.
In the Qumran sect the Mosaic Law and the many rules of conduct
remain obligatory in spite of the believer's knowledge that it is
solely through God's grace that he can become guiltless and learn
to do right. To an even greater extent, for early Christianity
as well as for Paul, justification by grace was the very foundation
and motivation for a new way of life--whether or not the word
justification is used.

These remarks have shed some light on historical conditions.
There is no reason to assume that Paul took over the terminology
of justification directly from Essene circles. It is not the
specific Pauline formulation of the doctrine but rather pre-Pauline
theology which coincides in many respects with what we find in
the Qumran texts. The possibility of a direct link between certain
early Christian circles and the Qumran sect remains open, but
one cannot exclude the possibility that the similarity reflect
a common tradition interpreted by groups with a certain structural
resemblance and not direct influence. It was not only in Qumran
that the Old Testament concept of God's saving righteousness was
alive in Judaism.[13] Both in Qumran and in early Christianity, personal
certainty of salvation was connected with membership in a religious
sect, a new covenantal congregation. This assurance may have
generated in both groups, independently, a renewal of the Old
Testament concept that God's righteousness proves itself in his
salvation and justification of those who belong to the covenant.
The nature of the new covenant is the determining factor for the
meaning of justification. Thus, justification meant something very
different to the Qumran covenanters, who had vowed to observe
strictly the Torah as their community interpreted it, from what
it meant to the early Christians, who were members of the community
of the covenant in the blood of Jesus.

It is now possible to give a preliminary answer to the
question of the function of the doctrine of justification in early
Christianity. It is not merely a word of consolation to troubled
consciences. Neither is it simply a polemical doctrine developed

---

[13]Cf. Stuhlmacher, *Gerechtigkeit Gottes*, 166-173. There
is, however, no evidence that "God's righteousness" was an
apocalyptic term.

in controversies with the Jews. In what appears to be the more traditional early Christian usage, the references to justification serve to remind all members of the congregation of what God has done for them and with them in Jesus Christ. In this general, not specifically Pauline, form the doctrine of justification has its setting (*Sitz-im-Leben*) in Christian teaching, perhaps especially in teaching addressed to the newly baptized. It is possible that the terminology of justification was also used in missionary preaching or in formal liturgical language, but as far as I can see, the sources do not permit more definite conclusions.

2. *The Doctrine of Paul*

When Paul simply reminds Christians that they are justified through Christ he is probably applying current terms and teachings of a commonly accepted doctrine. However, the Pauline doctrine of justification through faith, not through works of the Law, further develops the terminology. In its specifically Pauline form, the doctrine has a polemical purpose. The words "justify" and "justification," receive a stress that makes it difficult to substitute synonyms. Such substitution is all the more difficult because of the closeness of the doctrine of justification in this narrower sense to scriptural exegesis.

The more common use of the terminology of justification has its background in the language of the Old Testament, a background which it shares with the equivalent expressions in the Qumran documents. Paul's more theologically developed doctrine depends on quotation of, and comments upon, specific Old Testament passages. To interpret these texts, Paul uses exegetical methods common to the Judaism of his day. Nevertheless, he achieves results which directly contradict those which Jewish and Judaizing exegetes obtained. The reason for this is his presupposition that these passages agree with his understanding of God's act and revelation in Jesus Christ. That does not mean that Paul simply finds scriptural prooftexts to undergird his theological position. Paul's scriptural exegesis has a more constitutive significance; it makes it possible for him to articulate his theological convictions.

One of the texts on which Paul builds is Psalm 143:2 (LXX 142:2): "For no man living (*pas zōn*) is righteous before thee." For Paul this means: "For no human being (*pasa sarx*) will be justified in his sight by works of the Law" (i.e., before

God's court; Rom. 3:20; Gal. 2:16). Paul knows that there is
justification in God's sight, but its foundation is different
from works of the Law.[14]

     Paul found a positive counterpart to the Psalm's negative
statement in Hab. 2:4: "The righteous shall live by his faith"
(LXX, "by my faithfulness"), or as Paul quotes it: "He who
through faith is righteous shall live" (Rom. 1:17; Gal. 3:11).
For Paul, this verse means that only through faith in Jesus
Christ shall the righteous man receive life--and that only by
faith is he righteous. Paul's understanding of Hab. 2:4 is
analogous to the interpretation we find in the Qumran commentary
on Habakkuk: "God will deliver them from the House of Judgment
because of their affliction and their faith in the Teacher of
Righteousness" (1QpHab. 8:2f.). The difference between them is,
however, more striking than the similarity. The Qumran document
stresses trust in the Teacher of Righteousness and faithfulness
to his interpretation of the Law. Faith in the Teacher is in no
way opposed to adherence to the Law but is the presupposition for
its right observation, and therefore also for obtaining life.
The interpretation of Hab. 2:4 is not related to the praise of
God's saving righteousness, even though this concept occurs in
hymnic texts from Qumran. In Rom. 1:17, by contrast, Paul quotes
Hab. 2:4 to support his statement that the gospel reveals God's
righteousness and, for that reason, is the power of God for
salvation. Identifying the faith of Hab. 2:4 with faith in the
crucified and risen Christ, Paul even draws the conclusion that
the quotation proves that nobody is justified by the Law, since
righteousness and life are given to those who have faith (Gal.
3:11).

     For Paul, the quotation that the righteous shall live by
faith contradicts the statement of the Mosaic Law that the one
who keeps the Law's commandments and ordinances shall live by
them (Gal. 3:12; Rom. 10:5). Paul's entire exegesis depends on
the presupposition that faith and works of the Law exclude each
other, that the Mosaic Law and faith in Christ cannot simultaneously
express the proper way for man to relate to God. At the same
time, Paul takes for granted that the Mosaic Law was from God,
that it was good and holy. To extricate himself from the dilemma
that these two views taken together create, Paul asserts that God
never intended the Law to last forever. It was a temporary measure,

---

     [14]For the hermeneutical principle that warrants the
apparently arbitrary addition of "by works of the Law," see Chapter
IX, "Contradictions in Scripture."

valid only until the coming of Christ made faith in him possible.
Paul finds in the Law itself evidence that its function was only
provisional, preparatory: the story of Abraham.[15]

The most important quotation is Gen. 15:6 (LXX): "And
Abraham believed God, and it was reckoned to him as righteousness."
Paul combines this quotation with Psalm 31(32):1f. (LXX):
"Blessed are those whose iniquities are forgiven, whose sins are
covered. Blessed is the man against whom the Lord will not
reckon his sin" (Rom. 4:3-8; cf. Gal. 3:6). Thus, Paul equates
reckoning faith as righteousness with not reckoning sin; this is
justification. Abraham is a model of the sinner who receives
justification by faith without having earned it. Paul associates
Gen. 15:6 with the promises which Genesis records, that Abraham
would be the father of a multitude of nations and that in him
would all the nations of the earth be blessed. Abraham's faith
is for Paul faith that God would do as he had promised and, with
an allusion to the birth of Isaac, faith in the God who brings
the dead to life, the same God who raised Jesus from the dead.
Vital to Paul's argument is that God promised and Abraham believed
before Abraham's circumcision; circumcision cannot therefore be
a condition for the fulfillment of the promise. The Law was not
proclaimed on Mt. Sinai until long afterward, so the fulfillment
of God's promises cannot depend on adherence to the Law any more
than it can on circumcision (Rom. 4:9-16; Gal. 3:15-18). If
obeying the Law was a condition for the fulfillment of God's
promises, those promises would in fact have become invalid (Rom.
4:13-15; Gal. 3:18-23). Accordingly, the Law is simply an
interim measure, which serves to identify sin as sin and thereby
increases it, so as to emphasize the essence of grace: it is
completely underserved (Rom. 5:20-21).

Paul deduces from all this that Jews and Gentiles are
justified in the same way, by faith alone. Those who believe in
Christ, men and women of every nation, are the true children of
Abraham, heirs according to promise. Paul uses other scriptural
quotations as well to advance his argument (e.g., Rom. 10:6-17;
Gal. 4:21-31). To the scriptural argument he adds an argument
from experience: it is by the proclamation of faith that God
has given the Holy Spirit to Gentiles as well as to Jews, as a
down payment on, and guarantee of, their inheritance. In this

---

[15]For Paul's interpretation of the story of Abraham,
see B. Schein, *Our Father Abraham* (Diss., Yale, 1973), and cf.
note 19 to Chapter V.

way the Gentiles have come to share in the promises God made to
Abraham (Gal. 3:1-5, 14; 4:6f.; cf. Rom. 8:15-17; etc.).

For our purposes it is neither possible nor necessary to
follow Paul's argument in detail. It is enough to emphasize how
Paul has refined the doctrine of justification which he held in
common with others:

1) Paul bases his doctrine on specific quotations from the
Old Testament and expresses it as a pointed theological thesis;

2) Paul stresses that justification occurs specifically
through faith, not just, more generally, in Christ and through
baptism. There is no contradiction here; for Paul, as for the
early church generally, baptism and faith belong together. When,
however, Paul uses Gen. 15:6, Hab. 2:4 and other scriptural
quotations to emphasize faith, he understands that faith as faith
in Christ; the preaching of the gospel produces justifying faith;

3) Paul asserts that faith excludes works of the Law as
a condition for justification and salvation; he expresses this
view in an extreme form when he refers to God as the God who
justifies the ungodly (Rom. 4:5);

4) Paul emphasizes the universal dimension of justification.
As all men have sinned, Jews and Gentiles alike, so are all men
justified only through faith: there is no distinction between
Jews and Gentiles.

The Pauline formulation of the doctrine of justification
has a clear social relevance; it implies an understanding of what
Christian community is, and it provides guidelines to show the
members of that community how they ought to relate to one another.
In Galatians, Paul presents the doctrine in the context of his
polemic against the requirement that Gentile believers in Christ
be circumcised and obey at least some of the ceremonial commandments and ordinances of the Mosaic Law. He completely rejects that
demand; if Christ makes justification and salvation available at
all, he makes them available to those who have faith; there is no
other requirement. The doctrine of justification proves that
Christian Gentiles need not and should not become Jews, not even
in part, in order to become full members of the church, true
children of Abraham and legitimate heirs to all that God has
promised. As Christians, Gentiles should remain part of the ethnic
group from which they came, Greek, Galatian or whatever. Without
rejecting the validity of the Old Testament, Paul can, with the

help of his theologically formulated doctrine, assert uncompromisingly the universality of the gospel and of the church. That
assertion had historical and social consequences that we cannot
overlook.

It is not by accident that we find the quotation: "There
is neither Jew nor Greek, there is neither slave nor free, there
is neither male nor female; for you are all one in Christ Jesus"
(Gal. 3:28; cf. 5:6; 6:15; Rom. 3:29f.; 10:12f.) in the context
of a discussion of the doctrine of justification. Of course,
Paul does not claim that there are no differences among individuals
in sex, nationality, or social position. The codes of household
duties are not the only evidence that this is not what Paul means.
But if it would be a mistake to attribute to the Apostle a modern
humanistic ideal of equality, it would be just as wrong to suppose
that he is making an abstract theological statement about unity
and equity before God which does not have social implications.
The doctrine of justification which Paul so emphatically asserts
has practical social consequences.

The most obvious example is the episode at Antioch which
Paul describes in Gal. 2:11ff. Paul does not criticize Peter's
theology; he presupposes that Peter's theology is essentially the
same as his. If Peter did hold certain views which would later
on have been classified as--let us say--crypto-semipelagian, I
suspect that Paul would have passed over them in silence. Paul
himself is not always as careful in his choice of theological
formulations as strict Augustinians and orthodox Lutherans might
wish. But the issue in Antioch was not theological clarity and
precision. Peter, considering the problems of Christian Jews,
thought it wise and prudent to withdraw from table fellowship
with Gentile Christians. For Paul, the behavior of Peter and
Barnabas constitutes their rejection of the doctrine of justification by faith. To preserve Christian unity at the Lord's table,
Gentile Christians would have to "judaize"; in practice, the
commandments of the Mosaic Law would regain their validity. But
if the Law remained valid, then Christ had died to no purpose.
Then--and only then--those who had sought their justification in
Christ and not in works of the Law would be shown to be lawbreakers.
Paul could be tolerant about differences in formulating doctrine.
But when the unity of the church, as it was realized in fellowship at the common table, is at stake, Paul becomes adamant,
forceful, uncompromising. For him, justification by faith and
the truth of the gospel message are in danger, and he springs to
their defense.

As Paul formulates the doctrine of justification, it has
a polemical application.[16] Nevertheless, it would be wrong to
understand it as purely polemical. In his letter to the Christians ·
at Rome, Paul introduces himself and the gospel which he preaches,
in order to win the Romans' support for his projected work in
the West. At the same time--and I consider this one of his most
important reasons for writing--Paul asks the Roman Christians to
support him and his congregations in Macedonia and Achaia with
their prayers, that the gift which Paul's Gentile congregations
offer might prove acceptable to the saints in Jerusalem (Rom.
15:15-22). With this request in sight, Paul develops his doctrine
of justification, attempting as he goes along to guard against
misunderstandings, to avoid providing a pretext for Christians
continuing to sin and to safeguard the holiness of the Law. Paul
insists that he has not turned his back on his own people; on the
contrary, salvation for Israel is the ultimate goal toward which
he is working as an apostle to the Gentiles. In other words, the
doctrine of justification appears in Romans as an essential and
decisive component of a comprehensive theology of mission.[17]

Justification does not simply involve the individual
and his salvation. Paul's perspective includes history and
eschatology: Adam, mankind and Christ, the promise to Abraham
and the Law given to Moses on Sinai, the gospel preached to Jews
and to Gentiles, God's work in the past and in the future, the
Apostle's own work in the present, the first fruits among the
Gentiles and the remnant of Israel, the unity of Jews and Gentiles
in the local congregation and in the worldwide church, Christ's
dominion over principalities and powers, and the all-encompassing
ultimate goal of God's plan for his creation. Obviously, the
doctrine of justification is not primarily social; it is theological
and soteriological. But the framework which Paul uses to locate
the doctrine is social and historical rather than psychological
and individualistic.

This does not give us any reason to doubt that the doctrine
of justification is closely connected to Paul's personal experience

---

[16]The characterization of the doctrine as a *Kampfeslehre*
(polemical doctrine) goes back to W. Wrede, *Paul* (1904, ET 1907,
tr. E. Lummis; repr. Lexington, Ky.: American Theological Library
Association, 1962).

A. Schweitzer and, most recently, E. P. Sanders have also
expressed the opinion that the doctrine is part of Paul's polemics
and not at the center of his theology. E. Käsemann agrees that
the doctrine is polemical but stresses that it is constitutive
for the gospel, see *An die Römer*, 24, 94f.; cf. Chapter X below.

[17]Cf. Chapter V.

and convictions. A confession like the one in Phil. 3:3-11 is
enough to prove this connection (cf. also Gal. 2:15-21). But
Paul's description in Philippians makes it clear that his road
to the doctrine of justification was different from Luther's.
Paul's life as a Pharisee was, by the Law's standards, "blameless";
his zeal for the Law made him a persecutor of the church. He
rejected everything in which he had once hoped, he accepted a
status equivalent to that of pagan sinners, in order to obtain
a righteousness which was not his own but a gift from God.

   Paul knows that as an apostle he is nothing more than a
sinner who has received God's grace and who now works as its
instrument. But the sin that comes to his mind is always that
he once persecuted the church of God. Paul knows that he is not
perfect and that God will judge him (Phil. 3:12; 1 Cor. 4:4), but
it is extremely difficult to find in Paul's letters any allusion
to sins committed during his life as a Christian or in his work
as an apostle. The person and the office are inseparable: what
Paul is, he is as an ambassador of Christ. Paul's remarks in
Romans 7 about the differences between intention and action do
not disprove this assertion. In context, Romans 7 proves that
it is sin in the flesh and not the Law itself which causes the
Law to bring men to death rather than to life. The end of the
chapter stresses the sinner's terrible plight more than is necessary
to establish the holiness of the Law, but only to emphasize that
the Christian's new life is not his own achievement, that it is
the work of God and of his Spirit (Rom. 8). Romans 7 is not
introspective religious autobiography.[18]

   Justification really is the merciful acquittal of sinful
men; Paul emphasizes that both Jews and Gentiles are without excuse
for their sinfulness. He discusses with stark realism the sin
and injustice present in his own congregations. Yet, nothing
indicates that interior feelings of sin and guilt afflicted the
Galatians and the Romans to whom Paul wrote. If they were troubled,
it was for more obvious reasons: their fear that their uncircumcision
made them second-class Christians; the doubt about the status of
their relationship to God which their difficulties and sufferings
prompted; the anxiety which different beliefs and practices within
the congregation caused, especially in a congregation where "the
weak" were inclined to judge and "the strong" to despise their
brethren. Confronting such attitudes, Paul emphasizes that we are

_____

[18]See Stendahl, esp. 78-96; cf. Chapter V, Appendix III.

justified by faith; he interprets the tension between suffering and glory, weakness and power, as a necessary element of Christian existence in this world; he warns against boasting of one's religious accomplishments and against unwarranted self-confidence, and he reminds his readers that it is God who will judge. Even though many aspects of the congregation's life are not as they should be, Paul retains a striking, steadfast conviction: "He who began a good work in you (those who believe), will bring it to completion at the day of Jesus Christ"(Phil. 1:6).

Even where Paul does not use the terminology of justification, he can still express the underlying idea. At the root of the divisions within the church at Corinth Paul finds a fundamental misunderstanding of the gospel: the Corinthians distort the wisdom of God, the foolishness of the cross, into mere worldly wisdom. From this distortion flows boasting about the superiority of one's favorite teacher, self-complacency, and dissension, at the expense of unity in Christ (1 Cor. 1-4).[19]

The Colossian heresy was obviously an example of an encratitic, mystical piety: as Christ had put aside the earthly and had been elevated above the principalities and powers, so the Christian too had to free himself from the material by pious ascetic practices, in order to enter the heavenly sanctuary and to join the angels in their worship of God.[20] The letter to the Colossians denounces these attitudes as "human tradition." In Christ, as the gospel proclaims him, the believers already have everything they need for salvation. In baptism they died, were buried and have been raised with Christ, and when Christ, their life, appears, they will also appear with him in glory. Most important is that they continue in the faith which was preached to them. It is by day-to-day compassion, love and thanksgiving that a Christian puts to death what is earthly and seeks the things that are above. God gives salvation and liberation completely, unreservedly, through Christ's work of reconciliation--*sola fide*. For this very reason, "household instructions" have a fundamental theological importance, contrary to encratitic observances and mystical experiences.

---

[19]Cf. Chapter III above.
[20]See F. O. Francis, "Humility and Angelic Worship in Col. 2:18," in Francis and Meeks, *Conflict at Colossae*, (SBLSBS 4, Missoula: Scholars Press, 1973), 163-195.

Throughout his letters, Paul emphasizes that the believers neither obtained nor continue to possess justification, holiness, wisdom, power and life through their own efforts. They received everything because as members of his church they belong to Christ. An individualistic interpretation of Paul's ethic will almost inevitably lead to perfectionism, an attitude alien to the Apostle.[21] When Paul mentions growth toward Christian maturity and perfection, he means a growth within the congregation, serving one's brothers on the foundation which Christ laid once and for all. The Christian virtues (to use a word which some mistakenly avoid) are the fruit of the Spirit, but that does not mean that good works and righteous living automatically follow faith. Speaking in tongues is the only gift of the Holy Spirit which does not activate man's will and understanding. The Spirit provides the discernment that is necessary for knowing what is good and the power to do it. Christians must strive to realize what they have become, due to God's grace, in order to understand what God wills in situations which demand moral decisions and social action. Their judgments and their behavior will show whether or not they have understood what justifying faith means.

In his requests and exhortations, Paul puts heavy stress on Christians' relationships with one another. The commandment to love one's neighbor is interpreted to be a commandment to love one's brothers within the community (Rom. 13:8-10; Gal. 5: 14-15). In the life according to the Spirit which Christians live and in their mutual love, they fulfill the real requirements of the Law, on the basis of justification (Rom. 8:4). That God is Judge and that the gospel is for all men determines the Christian's relationship to those outside the community, but Paul underlines that Christian brotherly love fulfills the Law as he clarifies the relationship between Christ and the Law, between faith and works, in the doctrine of justification.

3. *Analogies in Other Writings*

In the non-Pauline writings of the New Testament we find different conceptions which correspond more or less exactly to Paul's doctrine of justification. The Johannine writings, especially 1 John, provide the most interesting basis for comparison.

---

[21]This point was stressed by A. Fridrichsen in an article on "Helgelse och fullkomlighet hos Paulus," (Sanctification and Perfection in Paul), *Den nya kyrkosynen* (Uppsala, 1946) 62-91.

Thus, 1 John 1:8-2:2 describes how Christians repeatedly sin and
receive forgiveness for Christ's sake.

Seemingly contradictory statements appear next to one
another in 1 John. The author writes: "If we say we have no sin,
we deceive ourselves, and the truth is not in us" (1:8) and also:
"No one born of God commits sin; for God's nature (*sperma*, seed)
abides in him, and he cannot sin because he is born of God" (3:9).
We can resolve this tension if we assume that both statements
polemicize against the teachings of docetic-gnostic heretics.
They appear to have believed that the pneumatic's inner, "real"
self was of divine origin and substance, and was for this reason
without sin. The pneumatic's self-awareness made it possible for
him to do things without guilt that would have been sinful for
others. The freedom from sin that they imagine they possess leads
to the illusion that there is no danger in committing sinful acts.
Against this background, the meaning of the contradictory
formulations in 1 John is clear: the sins of the baptized are
real sins; sin is never a matter of indifference, so the Christian
must always avoid it. But for those who confess their sins,
there is forgiveness.

The Reformation view that the baptized constantly need
forgiveness has a firmer foundation in 1 John than in Paul. 1
John is the New Testament book which most closely approximates
the paradoxical formulation, "*simul peccator, simul justus*."
Especially important from the perspective of this article is that
1 John emphasizes that Christian community and brotherly love
are the identifying marks of God's children (1:6f.; 2:7-11; 3:16-18;
4:7-21; 5:1-3). The Gospel of John also stresses the believers'
common life. It is not simple affection that we encounter in
John; it is a "juridical mysticism" which includes the ideas both
of community and of mission. Unfortunately, it would carry us
too far afield to pursue further the Johannine correspondences to
the Pauline doctrine of justification.[22]

In general, only if one includes the social aspect of the
doctrine of justification can one assert that the doctrine is
central, that it sums up the message of Scripture. The Old Testament testifies that God in his undeserved love has chosen and
preserved a people, a people unworthy of his goodness. Revealing
his saving righteousness, God gives his people victory, salvation
and peace. He has pity on the wretched and guards the rights of

---

[22]See Théo Preiss, "Justification in Johannine Thought,"
Life in Christ (tr. H. Knight; SBT 13; Naperville: Allenson, 1954)
9-31. Cf. also my *Jesus in the Memory of the Early Church*, 115-117.

the oppressed. Those whom he justifies receive the status and
position reserved for the righteous. It is impossible to separate
the religious from the social even when faith expects God's future
intervention to show forth his righteousness and to bestow
salvation on the faithful.

Jesus speaks rarely, if ever, of justification. But if
we think of his beatitudes of the poor, his miraculous help to
the disturbed and his solidarity with outcasts, we can be sure
that his work was a "justification of the ungodly." He did not
come to call the righteous, but sinners to repentance. The
Pharisees could certainly be aware of their sins. Thanksgivings
and confessions of sin had their place both in the communal
worship of the synagogue and in the prayers of the individual.
Jesus associated with notorious sinners, people whom the Law
condemned as unclean, who were excluded from the community of the
righteous. In some of his parables, Jesus explained that it was
just such people whom God loved. The joy which marked the meals
Jesus shared with tax collectors and sinners corresponds to the
joy in heaven over a sinner who repents.

To come to the point, what Paul stated systematically,
Jesus had already lived, in his attitudes and in his activities.
The correspondence between them becomes clearer when we realize
that Paul does not present the doctrine of justification as a
dogmatic abstraction. As Jesus' work destroyed the significance
of the distinction between sinners and the righteous in Israel,
so Paul's fidelity to the truth of the gospel had to forbid
discriminating within the church between Jews and Gentiles.

4. Paul and His Interpreters

Many have wondered why the Pauline doctrine of justification
seems not to have played an important role for Christians in the
period after Paul. This impression depends on a number of factors.
Protestant scholars have often been unjust in their evaluation
of the Apostolic Fathers, the Apologists, and other early Christian
authors. Viewed with an Augustinian or Lutheran understanding of
Paul, they may seem superficial, with a tendency to interpret
the gospel as a new law. But for them as for Paul it is of
fundamental importance that God in his grace has established a new
covenant and created a new people, a people reborn and sanctified
in the baptismal bath. The questions which the Pauline doctrine
of justification answered directly were no longer of interest to

a church composed principally of Gentile Christians, who took
for granted that the ritual commandments of the Mosaic Law did
not apply to them. As time went on, other questions became more
pressing. The change from the darkness of paganism to the light
of Christ was not a personal experience to the same extent for
later generations as it had been for the Pauline mission congregations. Christian sinfulness became a problem which could not
be easily solved simply by recalling the beginning of one's life
as a Christian, what one was because of the change worked by the
gospel, faith and baptism. The question of the possibility of
a second repentance arose, especially for Christians guilty of
apostasy or of other serious sins. A Christian penitential
practice developed, and it does not seem that anyone saw Paul's
doctrine of justification as a possible answer to the problems
with which that practice dealt. Even where one finds phrases
reminiscent of the Pauline doctrine, it is doubtful that the
doctrine of justification had much social relevance in the ancient
church before Augustine.

Augustine was the first Christian thinker after Paul to
assign central significance to the doctrine of justification.
According to Augustine, God's grace was at work not only in
baptism and at the beginning of the Christian life, but also in
the sanctification which continued throughout that life and in
the final perfection which would be its culmination. It would
be wrong to suggest any direct incompatibility between Augustine's
view and Paul's. But the context and the emphasis have shifted.
Paul develops an eschatological theology of mission, while Augustine
reflects theologically on human and divine activity in those
justified by baptism. The author of the *Confessions* was also far
more religiously introspective than the Apostle to the Gentiles
or than the men of antiquity in general. It is not without reason
that Augustine is sometimes called the first modern man.

Augustine's ideas about the *Civitas Dei* were probably more
important in molding medieval society than his doctrine of grace.
From his time onward, however, the struggle between Augustinianism
and Pelagianism, the problem of relating the divine and human
roles in salvation, remains a central concern for Western theology.
This controversy has profoundly shaped Christianity in the West,
whereas the Eastern church has never shown much interest in it.

The Augustinian monk Martin Luther stands in this Augustinian
tradition. The Reformation presupposes, both in a positive and
a negative way, the late Middle Ages, with its practice of penance,
its scholasticism and its mysticism. It was in this context that

Luther rediscovered the Pauline doctrine of justification, which gave him the answer to the question of how to find a gracious God. From the severity of the commandments of the Law and from God's wrath, the troubled conscience could flee again and again to the God revealed in Christ, who justifies by grace for Christ's sake, through faith.

The relationship between Paul and Luther has been very much discussed.[23] Not only Catholic scholars or radical Protestants like W. Wrede and A. Schweitzer, but even conservative theologians like A. Schlatter and Paul Althaus have maintained that Luther's interpretation of Paul is one-sided or even misleading. Others have shown how much Paul and Luther have in common. The question is complicated. If my view is right, they differ because they asked different questions, not because they gave different answers to the same questions. For this reason, it is not enough to list differences to prove fundamental disagreement any more than it is enough to list similarities to prove fundamental agreement. To use a musical image, we might say that the melody is the same, but that the harmony and the key are different. Or rather, Luther here furnishes a classic example of the inadequacy of the mere restatement of biblical themes; in order for these themes to have their full effect, they must be completely refashioned to fit the conditions and presuppositions of a different age. Yet, no transformation avoids the danger of one-sidedness.

I am not going to address here all the questions at issue. Certainly, what Paul had to say about the Mosaic Law and circumcision, about feasts and sabbaths, gained new currency when Luther applied it to the Catholic practices of penances and indulgences, to the piety of monastic life and to church ceremonies. The doctrine of justification, as it emerged from the new Lutheran exegesis, had social consequences which are impossible to ignore. For Luther and for the Lutheran confessions, the doctrine of justification by faith is not simply one doctrine among many; it determines the whole understanding of Christianity in a way that revolutionized the structure of the church and of society. It accomplished this negatively by abolishing monastic life and church hierarchy, by breaking away from canon law and from the papacy,

---

[23]To my knowledge, the best works on Paul and Luther are those of W. Joest, esp. *Gesetz und Freiheit* (Göttingen: Vandenhoeck & Ruprecht, [1951] 3.ed. 1963) and "Paulus und das lutherische *Simul Justus et Peccator,*" *KD,* I (1955) 269-320. Cf. also O. Modalsli, *Das Gericht nach den Werken: Ein Beitrag zu Luthers Lehre vom Gesetz* (Göttingen: Vandenhoeck & Ruprecht, 1963). For the discussion within the Lutheran World Federation Commission, 1958-1963, cf. the report by J. Rothermundt and other items in *Justification Today: Studies and Reports* (Lutheran World, Supplement to No. 1, 1965).

and positively by giving enhanced religious meaning to service in secular vocations, in the family and in society.

Taking his stand on the doctrine of justification, Luther aimed at a reformation of the whole catholic church. The historical result was the establishment of different Reformation churches with the doctrine of justification by faith alone as their confessional mark. Confessional controversies and struggle led to ever more precise dogmatic formulations.

Even during the orthodox period the doctrine of justification by grace through faith was more than a theological abstraction. The doctrine served as a foundation for life in Lutheran and Reformed countries. But a certain narrowing also occurred, not only in relation to Paul but even in relation to Luther. The focus of the doctrine became the individual's relationship to God; justification became a decisive step on the road to salvation, a part of the *ordo salutis*. The pattern could vary somewhat, but generally followed these lines: first, awakening through the Law, then rebirth through faith, and with it justification, the acquitting judgment in the heavenly court, after that sanctification, and so on. Justification lost its all-encompassing character.

This last statement applies especially to pietism, even to those branches of the movement that gave a central place to the doctrine of justification. For the last several centuries it has been mainly pietists (or evangelicals) who have meaningfully retained the doctrine of justification as the essential element of the religious life, rather than merely clinging to a confessional standard which preserved denominational identity.

We should not overlook that even in its pietistic form, the doctrine of justification appears socially relevant. I am thinking especially of the revivalist and missionary movements. Of course, these are immensely complicated historical phenomena. One essential impetus was no doubt the personal experience of sin and grace, and concern for the salvation of every individual scattered around the world. This made preaching the gospel of salvation by faith for Christ's sake to the whole world a necessity. As one factor which prompted the growth of the world mission, the doctrine of justification has in recent centuries been a power at work, with other factors, breaking down old societies and creating something new in their place, contributing to sweeping changes both in the churches and in the world at large.

The revivalist movement and the evangelical world mission provide obvious examples that the doctrine of justification can

have far-reaching social consequences, even as the result of
strictly religious movements which do not have those consequences
in view. But it is hard to deny, precisely on the basis of the
experience of the missionary churches, that a Christianity which
limits the doctrine of justification to personal religious
experience and salvation is insufficient. Young Asian, African
and Indian Christians today ask for guidance to overcome the
problems which their societies and their churches confront. Like
many Westerners, they have trouble finding the answers in pietistic-
evangelical religiosity. Missionaries brought not only the
justifying gospel, but also Western patterns of behavior and a
"ceremonial law" enacted by the traditions of the different
churches. The questions are complicated. One example is polygamy.
"The missionaries preach salvation by grace alone," said one
African pastor, "but in practice that turns out to mean salvation
by only one wife." What can we answer?

Because of this feeling of inadequacy which a one-sided
view of the doctrine of justification sometimes prompts, it often
happens, even among Lutherans, that some, more or less consciously,
move the doctrine of justification into the background in order
to bring other aspects of Christianity into the foreground, e.g.,
sanctification, social responsibility, the idea of the church,
etc. But it is a mistake to attempt to redress a distortion in
the presentation of the doctrine of justification by emphasizing
other doctrines. The urgent task is rather to rediscover the
social relevance and implications of the doctrine of justification.
That does not mean a project in systematic theology, to deduce a
social ethic from the doctrine of justification. The task is
paradoxically both more limited and more comprehensive. We can
formulate the question in this way: to what extent does the
current practice of the church deny *de facto* the doctrine of
justification, because it excludes certain groups of people from
free access to God's grace in his church?

Racial discrimination provides an obvious and painful
example. This problem is not something outside the task of
preaching the gospel, something the church might attack as an
addition to her central responsibilities. It belongs to the heart
of the gospel message that God shows no partiality, and that for
this reason neither can the congregations which gather in his
name, wherever they may be. If the Christian churches in the
United States, or elsewhere, had been able to resolve this problem
in their midst, it would have meant far more than countless pious
appeals for tolerance, far more than demonstrations; it would also

have made it easier to find political solutions to the problems of racial discrimination.

The social implications of the doctrine of justification mean that believers must visibly express their unity in the fellowship of the Lord's table, as Paul so forcefully insists. Even Lutheran churches have continued in practice to disavow their confession that true preaching of the gospel and right administration of the sacraments are sufficient grounds for the unity of the church. Has the message of the doctrine of justification: "There is no distinction," had any impact on the social structure of the churches? Today, does not full acceptance into a suburban congregation presuppose a certain social standard and certain patterns of behavior? Do I go too far to suggest that middle class social standards and stereotyped forms of conversion experience and of religious expression have become the ceremonial and ritual law of our time?

I must rest content with raising questions of this sort to suggest points at which the doctrine of justification could have practical, tangible social consequences today. It would go far beyond the limits of an article and of my ability to attempt to sketch what the results would be if we really rediscovered the doctrine of justification, what the consequences would be if it really shaped church practice and Christian life styles. That could be the task of a whole generation of theologians, not that biblical and systematic theology could solve the problem. No: here everything depends on what Christ's ministers preach from their pulpits and on how the faithful respond.

CHAPTER VII

PROMISE AND FULFILLMENT

Both in edifying language and in theological usage, it is
common to talk about the fulfillment of promises. Therefore, it
may come as something of a surprise to learn that this is not
common biblical language.

The Pauline letters, Luke-Acts and Hebrews use the Greek
word "promise" to signify God's commitment or pledge, but only
Acts 13:33 uses the expression that God has "fulfilled" his
promise. In the biblical perspective, God confirms his promises
or he does what he has promised (Rom. 15:8; 4:21). We find the
word "fulfillment" in other contexts: the fulfillment of the Law
and the fulfillment of the Scriptures. A prophet's oracle can be
fulfilled, and so also time. The words for promise and for
fulfillment occur in similar contexts, but normally not in direct
association with one another.

This observation becomes less striking when we consider
ordinary usage in everyday conversation. We say that a prediction
is fulfilled, but that a man keeps his promise, or that he does
what he has promised. A promise is not a prediction. A prediction
that two persons will marry is fulfilled when they have married.
But an engagement, the promise to enter into a marriage, is only
confirmed at the wedding. The promise made in an engagement is
kept only by living the married life. Using the terminology of
modern semantics, a promise is a "performative utterance," a self-
involving statement, or to use another phrase, a "self-obligating
pledge." I commit myself to do all in my power to accomplish
what I have promised, to move what I have pledged from the realm
of possibility to that of reality. The person who makes a prediction which is not fulfilled has made a mistake. The person who
breaks a promise is either untrustworthy or powerless.

We can make promises without using any specialized
vocabulary. We can say quite simply: "I shall do that," or "I
give you my word." To say: "He kept his promise," is to say no
more than: "He kept his word." The Old Testament generally
refers to God's promises as "the word of the Lord." Not even
prophecies are understood simply as descriptive statements about
future events; they are words of the Lord, with God's trustworthiness and power as guarantees, whether they threaten punishment or promise salvation. What we call a promise is a personal
pledge rather than an objective statement. But it ought to be
obvious that the personal self-involving character of a promise
does not exclude an objective content. A person may commit
himself to another by promising to do something for him or to give
him something. The story of Abraham serves as a good example:
God not only commits himself to Abraham, but he promises to give
him the land.

We can apply this preliminary analysis of the promise
concept to Paul's use of *epaggelia*, as the summary at the end of
Romans makes clear: "For I tell you that Christ became a servant
to the circumcised to show God's truthfulness, in order to confirm
(*bebaiōsai*) the promises given to the Patriarchs, and in order
that the Gentiles might glorify God for his mercy. As it is
written, . . ." (Rom. 15:8-9). This statement introduces a series
of quotations about praise and rejoicing among the Gentiles who
shall hope in the root of Jesse.[1] The promises to which Paul
refers are those which God made to the Patriarchs, Abraham,
Isaac and Jacob, and to their descendants, the sons of Israel;
these promises are a prominent feature of the book of Genesis.
The promises are part of Israel's patrimony, as Paul writes in Rom.
9:4. By sending Christ as a servant to Israel, God has reaffirmed
his commitment to do what he had promised; his fidelity to his
promises proved his truthfulness. In Paul, promise clearly means
more than mere prophetic prediction. Prophecy and fulfillment
may be understood to mean that there is an exact correspondence
between what is predicted and what actually happens. Christians
have for centuries sought in this way to prove that Jesus was the
Messiah predicted in Scripture. Such a view permitted Christians
to restrict the role of Israel after the period during which the
Old Testament was composed to transmitting the Scriptures which
contain the messianic promises. When those promises had been

---

[1]The passages quoted are Ps. 18(17):49; Deut. 32:43 LXX;
Ps. 117(116):1; Isa. 11:10 LXX.

fulfilled, Israel's unique role had run its course. This perspective has been common among Christians since the time of Justin Martyr.[2] Paul's view of promise is different: by making promises, God has involved himself, he has committed himself to those to whom he gave his word.

The Greek perfect which Paul uses in Rom. 15:8 implies that Christ remains a servant to the circumcised. His work as a servant demonstrates that God has confirmed his promises to the fathers. Consequently, Paul does not believe that Jesus' earthly ministry fulfilled God's promises. On the contrary, Jesus' work reaffirmed the commitment of the God who is faithful. This does not mean that Christ's work has significance only for Israel. But Paul does not say that God has proved his trustworthiness to the Gentiles by confirming a promise made earlier. Rather, God has shown them mercy, and for that the Gentiles will praise his name. True, Scripture did foretell that the Gentiles would praise God, but God had not given them his promises. Israel receives the confirmation of prior promises; God shows mercy to the Gentiles "according to the Scriptures," but in a broader sense.

One would go too far to claim that Paul always maintains the distinction between confirmation of promise and the more general idea that events happen according to the Scriptures. In another context he can stress that the promise to Abraham is valid for believing Gentiles: "That is why it depends on faith, in order that the promise may rest on grace and be guaranteed (*einai bebaian*) to all his descendants--not only to the adherents of the Law but also to those who share the faith of Abraham" (Rom. 4:16). We might paraphrase Paul by saying that God gave his promises to the Jewish Patriarchs and to their descendants, but that they do include blessings for the Gentiles. Indeed, Christians live in the age of fulfillment, and whatever has been written has been written for them (cf. Rom. 4:23; 15:4; 1 Cor. 10-11). For this reason, we ought not to attempt to define too precisely our title: "Promise and fulfillment" in Paul. Rather, we consider the title a catchphrase which draws together an extensive and complex group of issues. Explicit statements about God's promises must of course receive greatest attention, but Paul's varied use of Scripture makes it impossible to set definite limits for our study.

---

[2]An earlier version of this model is already present in Luke-Acts, see W. Kurz, *The Christological Proof from Prophecy in the Writings of Luke and Justin Martyr* (Diss., Yale, 1976). For the lexical data, see *TDNT* II, 576-586.(Schniewind-Friedrich).

Paul is a biblical theologian. Judged by the standards
of modern scientific exegesis, his exegesis often seems arbitrary.
Exegetes tend to regard Paul's quotations from and allusions to
Scripture as embellishments which support his thought without
being integral to it. But Paul is not a systematic theologian.
He is more like a good preacher, who can vary his use of the
texts depending on the situation and purpose of the sermon. If
the preacher is well prepared, then he has an exegetical basis
to support his use of the text, even though he would make that
basis explicit only when he has special reasons to do so. Paul
has done his homework well. If we study his use of Scripture
against the background of the hermeneutics of his day, we shall
soon see both method and meaning emerge.

This does not imply that Paul uses some special exegetical
method. The concept of promise and confirmation is important
and has its own special function. But it constitutes only one
of several possible models; we find patterns like prophecy and
fulfillment, thematic statement and scriptural proof, typology
and allegory. It is neither possible nor necessary to go into
detail here. But we must make clear that Paul does not know the
modern distinction between the meaning of a text as an ancient
document within its original context and the meaning of a text
for contemporary conditions and questions. For Paul, the Holy
Scriptures are the words of God, of a God who through them speaks
directly to the present. Conversely, present experience and
events of the recent past belong within the Scriptural sphere.
For Paul, there is an ongoing interplay between interpretation
of Scripture and Christian existence in the present. Scripture
helps to interpret events and experiences, and events and
experiences help to reinterpret Scripture.[3]

At this point we should remark that our emphasis on Paul
as biblical theologian does not mean that we should view him only
against his Old Testament and Jewish background, ignoring his
Hellenistic environment. "Jewish" by no means excludes "Hellenistic."
By Paul's times, Hellenistic culture had influenced Judaism for
centuries, both by making positive impressions and by causing
negative reactions. The Old Testament is not simply one element
of the historical background like others, but has a special status:
it functions as Holy Scripture. The histories both of Judaism

---

[3]In this respect, Paul's use of Scripture agrees with
Jewish Midrash. See J. Goldin's introduction to Shalom Spiegel,
The Last Trial (New York: Pantheon Books, 1967) and cf. *The
Crucified Messiah*, 144, 159f.

and of Christianity demonstrate that scriptural interpretation,
like other cultural phenomena, is open to the influence of
environment, including that of changing spiritual climate. Time
and place, the world in which one lives, help determine the
questions addressed to Scripture, the method and presuppositions
used for interpretation and, finally, the results of the exegesis
itself. Theologians who make conscious use of contemporary
science and philosophy still seek to establish a scriptural basis
for that use. We could name as classic examples both Philo in
Alexandria and Bultmann in Marburg. Contemporary thought and
current problems influence less philosophical exegetes more
unconsciously.

Paul uses heremeutical techniques both from contemporary
Hellenism and from Jewish and early Christian tradition. This
is true even when his exegesis itself is novel and revolutionary.
Paul's exegesis is original because interpretation of Scripture
has become an integral part of his ministry as the apostle of
Jesus Christ among the Gentiles.

2 Corinthians 1:20 states succinctly Paul's view on how
God had acted to keep the promises he had made: "For all the
promises of God find their Yes in him (Christ). That is why we
utter the Amen through him, to the glory of God." As in Rom.
15:8, the theme is the ratification of his promises which God
accomplishes in Christ. There is, however, a change of context
from one discussion to the other. In Rom. 15:8, the context is
Jesus' earthly ministry among his countrymen; in 2 Cor. 1:20,
the context is the apostolic proclamation that Jesus is Lord.

In 2 Corinthians, one accusation among others which Paul
tries to refute is that he vacillates; his Corinthians opponents
used Paul's changed travel plans as an example of his unreliability.
Paul answers by assuring the Corinthians that he has been honest
and open in his dealings with them, motivated only by his concern
for their well-being.[4] Paul wastes little time discussing the
particulars of the case against him; in a transition characteristic
of Paul which must have exasperated his opponents, he changes
topics. From justifying his travel decisions he moves to a solemn
affirmation of the truth of the gospel which he preaches. He
emphatically rejects the charge that he hesitates between saying
yes or no and offers in evidence the following statement: "For

---

[4]See 2 Cor. 1:12,15-18; 1:23-2:11; 2:17; 4:1-6; 5:11-13.
For a fuller analysis of 2 Cor. 1:15-22 and the context in 2
Cor. 1-7, see S. Olson, (Chapter IV, Appendix II.2, p. 39 above),
Chapter 3, esp. 121-136.

the Son of God, Jesus Christ, whom we preached among you, Silvanus
and Timothy and I, was not Yes or No; but in him it is always
Yes" (2 Cor. 1:19). The statement quoted above, that Christ is
God's Yes to all his promises, follows immediately.

The section 2 Cor. 1:19-22 refers to what the Corinthians
have themselves experienced. The apostle and his co-workers had
preached Christ as the confirmation of God's promises: those who
accepted the proclaimed Christ gained a share in those promises.
Those who were being baptized responded with their confession of
faith, their "Amen!" The concrete situation was perhaps their
response to questions of faith put to them before they received
the sacrament itself. With their "Amen!" they have said "Yes!"
to Christ, and thereby confessed their belief that God remains
faithful to his promises. Christ, whom they received when they
accepted Paul's preaching, is himself the agent of God to whom
the Corinthians make this confession. God has confirmed the
apostolic preaching and the Corinthian confession by sealing
the Corinthians with the Holy Spirit, a gift which guarantees
that God will fulfill all his promises. Clearly, Paul is not an
observer who asserts that God's promises have already been fulfilled.
Rather, he views his own work as an apostle of Christ as part of
the process by which Christ ratifies that his promises are valid
for those who believe in him.

In 2 Cor. 3:1-4:6 Paul discusses another aspect of his
role. As minister of the new covenant, Paul parallels Moses,
though Paul's ministry is of a higher order. The preaching of
the gospel is not simply a report about the new covenant, as
performative speech it effectively mediates the covenant promises.
The existence of the church at Corinth not only testifies to the
success of Paul's work, like a letter of recommendation; it even
certifies the validity of the new covenant, as the stone tablets
of the Law confirmed the validity of the old. The Spirit of the
living God is the inscription on the Corinthians' hearts.[5] In
2 Corinthians 3 Paul speaks about the glory of the new covenant,
and not directly about God's promises. But it is evident that
here as in 2 Cor. 1:19-22 Paul views the preaching of the gospel

---

[5] 2 Cor. 3:3 with allusions to Exod. 34:1; Jer. 31:33;
Ezek. 36:26, etc. In his treatment of the ministry of the new
covenant (2 Cor. 3:4-4:16), Paul draws not only upon Exod. 34
but also upon other passages, esp. Num. 12:7-8; Jer. 31:31-34;
Gen. 1:26-27 and 1:3. For the exegetical traditions used, see
now esp. M. R. D'Angelo, *Moses in Hebrews* (Diss., Yale, 1976).
On 2 Cor. 3:1-3, see W. G. Baird, "Letters of Recommendation:
A Study of II Cor. 3:1-3," *JBL* 80 (1961) 166-172.

as a mediation of God's promises, not as a logical demonstration
that they have already been fulfilled.

2 Cor. 7:1 mentions God's promises explicitly: "Since
we have these promises, beloved, let us cleanse ourselves from
every defilement of body and spirit, and make holiness perfect
in the fear of God." The promises to which Paul refers, he
enumerates in the immediately preceding section, which consists
of loose quotations of Old Testament passages. Paul begins the
catena with the covenant promise: "I will live in them and
move among them, and I will be their God and they shall be my
people,"[6] and he concludes with a "democratized" form of the
promise to David contained in Nathan's oracle: "And I will be
a father to you, and you shall be my sons and daughters."[7]

2 Cor. 6:14-7:1 is a self-contained unit, whose content
and form strikingly resemble material found in Jewish sectarian
literature. But the pericope also makes sense in its present
context. Other passages in 2 Corinthians show that Paul regards
rejection of his gospel, and of himself, its proclaimer, as
Satan's work: the devil hardens the hearts of the unbelievers
(2 Cor. 4:3f.; cf. 11:3). In 2 Cor. 6:13-7:2 Paul has transformed
a warning against social intercourse with outsiders into a warning
against making common cause with unbelievers by adopting their
attitude toward Paul and his gospel.[8] The promises call for
sincere purity and sanctity, to be demonstrated in the mutual
relations between the Apostle and his beloved Corinthians.

In his letter to the Romans, Paul introduces himself as:
"A servant of Jesus Christ, called to be an apostle, set apart
for the gospel of God which he promised beforehand through his
prophets in the holy scriptures" (Rom. 1:1-2). Paul's special
task is to preach to the Gentiles the saving message which God
had promised to Israel (cf. Rom. 1:1-6). Here too Paul includes
a reference to his own work when he speaks about the gospel and
about God's promises. In Rom. 1:1-3 Paul states explicitly that
it is the gospel itself, "the gospel of God, . . . the gospel
concerning his Son," which God has promised. Paul continues
in vv. 3-4 with a christological formula which summarizes the
content of the gospel. The summary itself is based on a specific
promise, the promise to David in Nathan's oracle in 2 Sam. 7:12-14,

---

[6]The quotation in 2 Cor. 6:16 conflates Ezek. 37:27 with
Lev. 26:11., cf. Jer. 21:34f. etc. 2 Cor. 6:17 is based upon
Isa. 52:11.

[7]2 Cor. 6:18, cf. 2 Sam. 7:14. Generalized ("democratized")
versions of the same promise occur also in Jubil. 1:24-25; 2:19-20;
and in Rev. 21:7.

[8]On 2 Cor. 6:14-7:1 see also Chapter IV above.

interpreted as referring to Christ. Jesus, descended from David
according to the flesh, is the Messiah whom God promised David.
In accordance with the spirit of holiness, he was designated Son
of God at his resurrection from the dead, just as it was promised:
"I shall be his father, and he shall be my son." It is quite
likely that the christological formula in Rom. 1:3-4 results
from primitive Christian exegesis of 2 Sam. 7.[9] Paul wants to
assure the Romans that the gospel he was called to preach is
the gospel which God had promised beforehand, the same gospel
in which the Romans themselves have believed.

Paul refers to the gospel about Christ, as briefly summarized
in the letter's opening statements, when he writes: "For I am not
ashamed of the gospel: it is the power of God to salvation to
every one who has faith, to the Jew first and also to the Greek.
For in it the righteousness of God is revealed through faith for
faith" (Rom. 1:16-17). Paul takes this thematic statement up
again in Rom. 3:21: "But now the righteousness of God has been
manifested apart from Law, although the Law and the prophets bear
witness to it. The reference to the Law and the prophets[10] implies
general scriptural attestation, but the specific concept of God's
fidelity to his promises may be implicit in what follows.
According to Rom. 3:26, God put Christ Jesus forward as an
expiation by his blood in order "to prove at the present time that
he himself is righteous and that he justifies him who has faith
in Jesus."

The expression "God's righteousness" (*dikaiosynē theou*)
includes both the righteousness by which God himself is righteous
and the righteousness by which God makes the believer righteous.
That God shows himself righteous means in this context that he has
kept his promise and thereby confirmed his fidelity. Neh. 9:8

---

[9]See e.g. D. C. Duling, "The Promises to David and their
Entry into Christianity," *NTS* 20 (1973/74) 55-77, esp. 72f. Cf.
also my article "The Messiahship of Jesus in Paul," in *The Crucified
Messiah*, 37-47. In Rom. 1:3-4 the phrases *kata sarka* (according
to the flesh) and *kata pneuma hagiosynēs* (according to the Spirit
of holiness) have been taken to refer to two natures or aspects
of the person of Jesus. Most recent interpreters prefer to think
of two contrasting spheres of existence (cf. 1 Tim. 3:16; 1 Pet.
3:18). But it may be better to interpret the phrases in analogy
with Gal. 4:21ff. There the contrast *kata sarka/kata pneuma* is
equivalent to the other contrast *kata sarka* and *di'epaggelias*
(Gal. 4:29 and 4:23). In Rom. 1:3-4 Jesus is a descendant of
David by virtue of his biological ancestry; he is the Son of God
in accordance with the promise (cf. 2 Sam. 7:14) or, as Paul
writes, "according to the Spirit of holiness." The Spirit of
God inspired the prophets; it is also the life-giving Spirit of
God who raised Jesus from the dead (cf. Rom. 8:11; 15:8-10).
[10]Cf. Rom. 1:2, 17; 4:1-25; 9:32-33; 10:6ff.; 15:8-12.

expresses the same idea: "Thou hast fulfilled thy promise
(*debarēka: thy words*), for thou art righteous." The statement
in Rom. 3:5: "Our wickedness serves to show the justice of God,"
paraphrases Psalm 51:4: "(Against thee, thee only, have I
sinned, . . .)so that thou art justified in thy sentence and
blameless in thy judgment." The verse means that God keeps his
word, and that he is vindicated. Rom. 3:25-26 probably has the
same meaning. The passage is difficult to interpret for several
reasons, among them the uncertainty about the meaning of the
unusual word *paresis*. Several translations presuppose that it
means tolerance; e.g., the RSV translates: "Because he had passed
over former sins." Some interpreters believe that *paresis* is
synonymous with the more common *aphesis* and means forgiveness.
There is another possiblity. The word *paresis* may refer to the
dismissal of a criminal charge.[11] This last meaning fits the
context of Rom. 3:25 well. The passage would then mean that God
let Christ die to expiate the sins of men, so that he could justly
dismiss the case against men, and thereby dispense with the just
condemnation that men's sins had warranted. In this way God
preserves his own righteousness, for justice prevails; he remains
faithful to his word by declaring the person righteous who has
faith in Jesus Christ (*ton ek pisteōs Iēsou*).

Paul develops more fully his thesis that a man is justified
by faith apart from works of the Law in his discussion of the
faith of Abraham (Rom. 4). Arguing from Gen. 15:6: "And he
(Abraham) believed the Lord; and he reckoned it to him as
righteousness," Paul presents Abraham as the father of and model
for all believers. We cannot pause here to consider this passage
at length, but it is worthwhile for our purposes to make a few
observations. Using Abraham as an example, Paul is able to portray
justifying faith as belief in God's promises. Even though he
did have good reason to doubt, Abraham was firmly convinced
that God had both the power and the will to do what he had
promised (Rom. 4:17-22). Abraham believed in the God who gives
life to the dead; Christians believe in the God who has raised
the Lord Jesus from the dead (4:17, 24). Though they live in the
time of fulfillment, Christians too believe in God's promises;
they share Abraham's conviction that God remains faithful to his
word. Paul interpreted the promise of the land (Gen. 15:7, 18,
etc.) to mean that Abraham and his descendants would inherit the
entire world (Rom. 4:13). At this point, Paul endorses an

---

[11]Dionysius of Halicarnassus (VII, 37) distinguishes
between dismissing a case (*paresis*)and temporarily delaying it.
On Rom. 3:24-26, cf. also *The Crucified Messiah*, 154-157.

exegetical tradition from Jewish eschatology. But unlike his
Jewish predecessors, Paul does not hope for political power in an
earthly kingdom. For Paul, the promise guarantees participation
in Christ's universal sovereignty. If the believers suffer with
Christ, they will also be glorified with him and become heirs
together with him (cf. Rom. 8:17-30).

Finally, Paul stresses that Abraham's faith was reckoned
to him as righteousness before he was circumcised; therefore the
promise is not dependent on the Law. Paul maintains that if
fulfillment of the Law is the condition for participation in the
promise, then faith is nullified and the promise void (cf. esp.
Rom. 4:14-15). Paul further spells out the relationship between
Law and promise in Galatians; his statements there will serve us
as a basis for futher discussion.

Paul's conviction that the crucified Jesus is the Messiah
underlies his understanding of God's promises, faith and the Law.
At Damascus, Paul came to believe that God had raised Jesus from
the dead, thereby vindicating his status as Messiah. In Romans,
the concept of the messiahship of Jesus appears in texts like
1:2-4 and 15:8-12. In Galatians, a series of scriptural testimonies
about Jesus the Messiah forms a partially concealed substructure
for the whole argument concerning the promise and the Law.

In Gal. 3:16, Paul emphasizes that the scriptural promise
to Abraham uses the singular form "his offspring" (*tō spermati
autou*) rather than the plural form "thine offsprings" (*tois
spermasin*). From this observation, he concludes that "thine
offspring" refers to Christ and not to the Jewish people as a
whole. His argument completely ignores the collective significance
that both the Greek and Hebrew terms for seed, descendants or
offspring (*sperma, zeraʿ*) have. Scholars have often adduced this
text as an example of Paul's use of arbitrary rabbinic exegesis.
It is true that Paul's exegesis conforms to rabbinic hermeneutics
both in method and in terminology. But the exegesis is not
arbitrary. It depends on an exegetical inference by analogy.
Just as "thine offspring" in the promise to David refers to the
Messiah, so does "thine offspring" in the promise to Abraham.[12]

_____

[12]The messianic interpretation of "your offspring" in 2
Sam. 7:12ff. goes back to pre-Christian Judaism, see "Florilegium"
from Qumran (4QFlor 1.10-11). A paraphrase of Gen. 49:10 combines
this text with 2 Sam. 7:10 (4QPatrBl). Probably by analogy with
2 Sam. 7:12, rabbinic exegesis could also interpret Gen. 4:25
(*zēra ʾaher*, RSV "another child") and Gen. 19:32 (*zeraʿ*, "Offspring") messianically. The Messiah descends from Seth and,
through Moab (Gen. Rab. 51:8; Ruth Rab. 7:15). Already the
Septuagint seems to have taken the words about the woman's offspring
in Gen. 3:15 to refer to the Messiah, since it uses the masculine

Paul's allusion in Gal. 3:19 to Gen. 49:10, the Shiloh oracle,
another text which tradition interpreted messianically, reinforces this assertion. The enigmatic *s l h* was vocalized *šĕ lô*,
which made it possible to take the clause to mean "until the
Messiah comes." Paul's paraphrase is freer still: "Till the
offspring should come to whom the promise had been made."[13]

Gal. 3:14a already presupposes the messianic interpretation of "the offspring of Abraham": "that in Christ Jesus the
blessing of Abraham might come upon the Gentiles." The text
which underlies this verse is Gen. 22:18 (LXX), part of the report
about God's oath to Abraham after he had proved faithful to God
by demonstrating his willingness to sacrifice Isaac: "and in
your offspring shall all the nations of the earth be blessed,
because you have obeyed my voice." In Paul's paraphrase, the
expression "the blessing of Abraham," derives from Gen. 28:4,
and "in Christ Jesus" replaces "in your offspring."

It is possible that the promise in Gen. 22:18 is more
generally the background for the Pauline expression "in Christ
Jesus," especially when we find it in contexts like "the redemption
which is in Christ Jesus" (Rom. 3:24),or "who has blessed us in
Christ" (Eph. 1:3). In any case, it is clear that Gal. 3:14 refers
to Gen. 22:18; further, it is likely that all of Gen. 22 underlies
Paul's statements in Gal. 3:13-14 about Christ's vicarious death.
Paul writes: "Christ redeemed us from the curse of the law,
having become a curse for us," and then adds a free quotation
of Deut. 21:23: "Cursed be everyone who hangs on a tree." This
text perhaps served in early Jewish polemics as an argument
against Christianity. Since Jesus died by hanging on the cross,
he was cursed under the Law and could not possibly be the Messiah.
According to Acts, the Jewish leaders handed Jesus over to the
Gentiles who hanged him on a tree. Thus Jesus was apparently
under the curse of Deuteronomy, but God vindicated him, raising

---

form of the personal pronoun (*autos*). On Jewish and early Christian
use of the Nathan oracle, see Duling (note 9) and D. Juel, *The
Messiah and the Temple* (SBLDS 31, Missoula: Scholars Press, 1977),
Chapter IX; M. R. D'Angelo (note 9), Chapter II (on Heb. 1:5 and
3:1-6).

[13]Gal. 3:19. In the translation of Dupont-Sommer,Vermes,
the comment on Gen. 49:10 in 4QPatrBl reads: "Until the Messiah
of Righteousness comes, the branch of David; for to him and to
his seed has been given the covenant of the kingship of his people
for everlasting generations." The Fragment Targum paraphrases:
"Until the king Messiah comes, for the kingdom belongs to him."
Targum Neofit has: "Until the time king Messiah shall come, whose
is the kingship; to him shall all the kingdoms be subject" (tr.
M. McNamara - M. Maher).

him from the dead (Acts 5:30f.; 10:39f.).

In Gal. 3:13f. we encounter a more profound answer to the
objection: Jesus did fall under the curse, when he suffered,
though innocent, in the place of the guilty. This interpretation
may depend on a combination of Deut. 21:23: "For a hanged man
is accursed by God," with Gen. 22:13: "And behold, behind him
was a ram, caught in a thicket by his horns." Both later texts
and Christian art show the ram bound to a tree. As the ram was
offered as a sacrificial victim in place of Isaac, so Christ was
hanged on a tree, incurring the curse of Deut. 21, in place of
Israel which had incurred the curse of Deut. 27:26 by failing to
observe the Law. Christ thus redeemed Israel, saving them from
the condemnation which the curse entailed. This interpretation
overcomes the offense of the crucified Messiah by assigning a
positive significance to his death on the cross. Jesus is the
Messiah (the Redeemer), not despite his humiliating death on a
cross, but because of it. The redemption granted Israel in
Christ means that the blessing of Abraham will come to the Gentiles,
according to God's promise in Gen. 22:16-18.

The division in Gal. 3:13-14 between "us" and "the Gentiles"
shows that Paul uses an early tradition, which must have had its
origin in internal Jewish debate about the messiahship of Jesus.
In the observation which concludes verse 14, Paul lets fall the
distinction between Jews and Gentiles; he identifies the promised
blessing with the Spirit, which "we" (now all Christians) have
received through faith. In good rabbinic fashion, Paul applies
existing exegetical traditions to new situations. In Gal. 3, Paul
uses the exegetical argument that Jesus is Abraham's messianic
offspring against the Judaizers in Galatia, who argued that the
Law retained its validity even for Gentiles who came to believe
in Christ.

Affirmations about the Spirit which the Galatians received
when they came to believe constitute the framework of Paul's
discussion of the promise to Abraham (Gal. 3:1-5; 4:6-7). Structure
and content form a single whole, not two independent arguments
for the Pauline doctrine of justification, one from experience
and one from scripture. The exegetical argument proves the validity
of what the Galatians experienced when they heard the gospel
preached and received the Spirit, a gospel which imposed neither
circumcision nor any of the other observances prescribed in the
Law of Moses. With an emphatic "thus" (*kathōs*, just as) Paul
emphasizes the analogy between what the Galatians have experienced
and what Scripture says of Abraham, that he believed God and it

was reckoned to him as righteousness (Gal. 3:6; Gen. 15:6).
Using this analogy, Paul concludes that believers are the sons
of Abraham (Gal. 3:7). That this is true not only for Jews
but also for Gentiles, Paul deduces from the promise to Abraham:
"In you shall all the nations be blessed" (Gal. 3:8-9; cf. Gen.
12:3, etc.).

The argument in Gal. 3:6-9 relates closely to the image
of Abraham as the father of and model for believers which we
find in Rom. 4. According to the exegetical tradition which
underlies Gal. 3:13-19, however, it is Jesus alone who is the
promised messianic offspring of Abraham. In Gal. 3:26-29 Paul
weaves together these two strands of thought. In this passage,
Paul interprets baptism with reference to Gen. 1:27; Christ, as
the image of God, is the prototype of redeemed mankind: "There
is neither Jew nor Greek, there is neither slave nor free, there
is no 'male and female'[14]; for you are all one in Christ Jesus"
(Gal. 3:28). Since in baptism the Gentiles have put on Christ,
the offspring promised to Abraham, they too have become "Abraham's
offspring, heirs according to promise." Returning to the beginning
of his argument in 3:1-5, Paul is able to add an additional proof.
God has accepted those to whom he has given the Spirit of his
Son as sons and heirs (Gal. 4:6-7).

Thus, the Galatians' reception of the Spirit, and their
experience of its work among them, proves that God has justified
them, given them a share in the blessing of Abraham and made
them his sons and heirs. Justification and the gift of the
Spirit are inseparable from one another. Paul makes no distinction between the forensic and the pneumatic. The gift of the
Spirit is evidentiary proof of God's acceptance. Paul views the
Spirit which the believers have received as the first fruits of
the glory which is coming, as a pledge, a down payment on the
inheritance which God has promised.[15] He can therefore in Gal.
3:14b, 22 identify the content of the promise with the Holy Spirit.

In Galatians, the interpretation of the promises to
Abraham as referring to Christ and to the Spirit serves to prove
that Gentile believers are no longer under the Law. At this
point, Paul goes beyond the early Christian tradition of which he
has made use. If we read Gal. 3:13-14a in isolation, we learn
that Christ, by his vicarious death, has redeemed Israel from the

---

[14]I have translated "no 'male and female'" rather than
"neither male nor female" in order to make the allusion to Gen.
1:27 clearer.
[15]Cf. Rom. 8:23; 2 Cor. 1:22; 5:5; Eph. 1:13-14; 4:30.

curse which had come upon them because they had transgressed
the Law.[16] In its present context, however, the passage states
that freedom from the curse is actually freedom from the Law
itself. Paul asserts emphatically that because the righteous
man obtains life through faith (Hab. 2:4), he cannot do so on
the basis of works of the Law. As a consequence, no one is
accepted as righteous "in the Law." Indeed, all those who rely
on works of the Law stand under the curse on those who transgress
the Law (Gal. 3:10-12). Furthermore, Paul affirms that the
promises which were solemnly ratified at the "covenant between
the pieces" (Gen. 15) have a validity which is wholly independent
of the Law which, according to rabbinic chronology, was given
430 years later. The Law is not a codicil which states conditions
for the validity of the covenant. If it were, the promise would
have been rendered void. But the covenant with Abraham was
unconditional, given in the form of a gracious promise (Gal.
3:15-18).

Paul's insistence that the promise is independent of
the Law does not lead him to compromise the integrity of the Law
as a part of Scripture. As an interpreter of Scripture he must
therefore uphold the Law; he must make its purpose clear. Paul's
answer is that the Law was never intended to be more than a
temporary expedient, valid only for the period from Moses to the
Messiah (Gal. 3:19-20).[17] God did not give the Law to enable men
to live justly and thereby to attain salvation, but rather to
multiply sins and to make sin into transgression liable to punishment. Understood as serving this negative, merely preparatory
function the Law does not stand in opposition to the promise but
aims at its fulfillment in Christ (Gal. 3:21-29; cf. Rom. 5:20-21;
7:7-8:4). Any attempt to prolong the validity of Law, to extend
into the period after Christ its use as a moral code which governs
the fellowship of Jews and Gentiles within the church implies
for Paul both a denial of faith and a misunderstanding of the
Law (cf. Gal. 2:11-21).

Paul's doctrine of the Law deviates radically from the
common Jewish view. Jewish scholars have properly emphasized
that using Paul's statements about the Law to describe Pharisaic
Judaism produces a completely misleading caricature. Many of
them have often also asserted that Paul cannot have been familiar

---

[16]Cf. Dan. 9:11; Deut. 27:15-26; 28:15-68. See also
Chapter IX, esp. note 19.

[17]On Gal. 3:20, see Chapter IX note 21.

with the classical Jewish doctrine that the Torah is God's life-
giving revelation.[18] This simply does not follow. Paul knows
very well that Jews rejoice at their possession of the Law (Rom.
2:17-20). But he explicitly denies that the Law was able to make
alive (Gal. 3:21). He does not give a historical, objective
description of the Jewish view of the Law; that was clearly not
his intention. On the contrary, in Gal. 3 and elsewhere he
constructs a specifically Christian view of the Law and of its
function as a part of Scripture. Methodologically, the argument
agrees well with Jewish hermeneutic, but it persuades only when
approached with specific Christian assumptions.

Paul's discussion of the relation between promise and Law
centers on the presupposition that the crucified Jesus is the
promised Messiah. It ought to be obvious that belief in a
crucified Messiah was not a detail which could be inserted into
the structure of Pharisaic Judaism without profoundly changing
the structure itself. Zeal for the Law had made Paul a persecutor
of the church. Belief in the crucified Messiah, hanged on a tree
under the curse of the Law, must have appeared to Paul to be a
shocking and offensive denial of the Law's validity. The appearance of the Risen Christ to him totally reversed his religious
perspective and attitudes (cf. Phil. 3:4-11). Paul's Christian
understanding of the Law's function differs from the Jewish view
no more radically than his faith in the crucified and risen Jesus
Christ differed from traditional Jewish messianic expectations.
Both for the apostle and the persecutor, the Law and faith in
Christ mutually exclude one another as ways to attain life.

As a Christian, Paul identifies the faith about which
Scripture speaks with faith in Christ. While for the pious Jew
faith and works of the Law were two sides of the same coin, for
Paul the statement in Hab. 2:4: "The righteous shall live by
his faith," excluded the statement in Lev. 18:5: "You shall
therefore keep my statutes and my ordinances, by doing which a
man shall live; I am the Lord." If the Law really had been able
to make alive, then this contradiction would have been insoluble.
Then Scripture would contain two incompatible doctrines of
justification. By maintaining that the Law was not meant to
give life, but to increase sin and the awareness of sin and by

---

[18]See e.g. H. J. Schoeps, 213-218 etc. At this point I
am in basic agreement with E. P. Sanders: "It is the Gentile
question and the exclusivism of Paul's soteriology which dethrone
the law, not a misunderstanding of it or a view predetermined by
his background" (497).

so doing to make grace pure grace, Paul manages to resolve the
contradiction. In this way he can uncompromisingly maintain his
Christian view of promise and yet retain the Law as a part of
Scripture which had a legitimate, but limited, validity. Those
who possess the Spirit are free of the Law, but at the same time
it is precisely they who are able to fulfill the Law, in love
and in freedom (Gal. 5:13-23; cf. Rom. 8:4-13; 13:8-10).

According to Paul, God has shown, by sending Jesus Christ
and by his death and resurrection, that he remains faithful to
his promises even though men have broken his Law. God has not
yet fulfilled his promises, but he has confirmed that he will
fulfill them. The believers have received a guarantee that they
are God's children and coheirs with Christ, but they have not
yet taken possession of their inheritance. The whole created
order still groans in travail, Christians still suffer. The
tension between God's promises and empirical reality, a serious
theological problem for Jews, remains. The belief in God's promises
is still a belief that God has the power to do what he has promised.
But the Christian view of present suffering and future hope has
a very different character from that of Judaism. In the midst
of suffering Christians experience not only the Spirit's helping
presence but also union with the crucified Christ (cf. esp. Rom.
8:18-39). The future hope is first of all a hope to participate
in the glory of the Risen Christ; little remains of the Jewish
eschatological expectation that God will gather the dispersed
sons of Israel, that he will reestablish them in the land, free
from foreign domination. Although Paul has, by the standards of
Jewish expectations, dissipated the promise's objective content,
he nevertheless remains committed to the view that by his promises
to the fathers God obligated himself to Israel. By his act in
Christ Jesus, the servant to the circumcised, God confirmed his
promises rather than voided them.   This conviction leads naturally
to the question of Paul's view of the future of Israel.

CHAPTER VIII

THE FUTURE OF ISRAEL

In only one of the Pauline letters which have come down
to us does Paul discuss thematically the future of Israel--in
Romans 9-11, especially at the end of chapter 11. Two other
texts, both difficult to interpret, may also deal with the topic,
1 Thess. 2:14-16 and 2 Cor. 3:16. 1 Thess. 2:14-16 contains one
of the strongest anti-Jewish statements in the New Testament.
After describing the Jews as persecutors, Paul continues: "But
God's wrath has come upon them at last." Some have tried to
reconcile this statement with the different view which Paul
expresses in Romans 11 by assuming that the wrath of which Paul
speaks in 1 Thessalonians is only provisional, that at the end
God will show the Jews mercy. This interpretation is, however,
syntactically implausible. Still, Paul can hardly mean that
God's wrath has come upon the Jews forever; such a statement
would completely contradict the carefully developed argument in
Romans 11. Most likely is that in 1 Thess. 2:16 Paul is not
discussing the future of Israel at all, but only a punishment
which God has already meted out to the Jews.[1]

Some translations and some commentators make 2 Cor. 3:16
a general statement which refers to Israel: "But when a man turns
to the Lord, the veil is removed."[2] It is more likely that here

---

[1]The relationship between 1 Thess. 2:14-16 and Rom. 11:24-
26 has often been discussed. It was treated at length by N. Månsson,
Paulus och Judarna (Stockholm: Diakonistyrelsen, 1947). B. A. Pearson
has argued that the passage in 1 Thessalonians is an interpolation,
dating from the time after the destruction of Jerusalem, in "1
Thessalonians 2:13-16: A Deutero-Pauline Interpolation," *HTR* 64
(1971) 79-94.

[2]Recent Norwegian translations use the plural: "When they
turn..." The French *Traduction oecumenique* is even more paraphrastic:
"C'est seulement par la conversion au Seigneur que le voile tombe."

Paul is referring to Moses: "But when he turns to the Lord the
veil is removed." In 2 Cor. 3:16 Paul freely quotes Exod. 34:34,
then in 2 Cor. 3:17-18 he both comments on the verse and applies
it.[3] The whole section attempts to relate the ministries of
the Old and New Covenants. Only in the light of Romans 11 can
one find expressed in 2 Corinthians 3 hope for the conversion of
Israel. Thus, we are free to concentrate on Romans 11 to develop
Paul's view of the future of Israel.

Paul's statements about the future of Israel in Romans
are well known. The literal sense is fairly clear. There ought
to be no doubt that the statement in Romans 11:25, that all Israel
will be saved, applies to the people of Israel, not to the church
as a new Israel. The details of Paul's view about the future
of Israel remain unclear; scholarly exegesis has made only limited
progress in bringing them to light. For this reason I have chosen
to concentrate on the question: what place does Paul's view of
the future of Israel have in the composition of Romans and in
the theology of Paul?

Many commentaries, monographs and articles discuss the
interpretation of Romans 9-11.[4] In spite of the vastness of the
literature, two aspects of these chapters have not received enough
attention. Scholars rarely consider Paul seriously as an interpreter of Scripture. We still have no detailed investigation of
Paul's use of the Old Testament in Romans 9-11, comparing it to
other Christian and Jewish interpretations of the passages quoted,
and examining their wording in textual tradition and in translations. The other aspect which scholars have neglected is a
formal analysis of the composition and style of Romans 9-11.
Here I hope to make a few useful suggestions.

The discussion of the place which chapters 9-11 occupy
in the composition of the letter as a whole has oscillated between
two poles. Some scholars regard Romans 9-11 as nothing more than
a postscript to Paul's doctrinal presentation in chapters 1-8.

---

[3]The *NEB* makes this explicit: "However, as Scripture says
of Moses, 'whenever he turns to the Lord the veil is removed.'"
The formal analogy with 2 Cor. 3:13-15 favors this interpretation:
    A. Text: "Moses put a cover over his face" (2 Cor. 3:13a,
       cf. Exod. 34:33 (35));
    B. Comments (2 Cor. 3:13b-15).
    A'. Text: "Whenever he turned to the Lord" etc. (2 Cor.
       3:16, cf. Ex. 34:34);
    B'. Comments (2 Cor. 3:17-18).
    Thus, in 2 Cor. 3:16-18 Moses is seen as a type for all who
behold (or reflect ?) the glory of the Lord with an uncovered face.
[4]Two examples may suffice: J. Munck, *Christ and Israel*, and
Chr. Müller, *Gottes Gerechtigkeit und Gottes Volk* (Göttingen:
Vandenhoeck & Ruprucht, 1964). See also Käsemann, *An die Römer*.

Others completely reverse this view; they regard chapters 1-8 as a prelude to chapters 9-11. Only in these chapters does Paul state what he wanted most of all to make clear to the Christians of Rome. Strong arguments support both positions.

Although Romans 9-11 constitutes an internal unity, with its own beginning and conclusion, without any direct connection to the immediately preceding (6-8) or succeeding (12-13) sections, it nevertheless belongs to the development of the theme of the letter stated in 1:16: "I am not ashamed of the gospel: it is the power of God for salvation to every one who has faith, to the Jew first and also to the Greek." Paul discusses the relation between Jews and Gentiles in Romans 1-4, but only in chapters 9-11 does he make clear what he means by "to the Jew first." It is also true that the concluding sections of the letter presuppose what Paul has said in chapters 9-11 (cf. Rom. 15:7-13, 25-33). Thus, there is no need to choose between the two extreme points of view.

It is important to note that the argument in Romans does not move steadily forward in a straight line.[5] The best way to grasp the outline of the letter is to observe that a number of thematic formulations introduce various segments of the letter. Several times Paul introduces a theme and appears to leave it undeveloped only to take it up again later in the letter.[6] He raises objections to his own arguments and discusses them in sections which seem to interrupt the main line of argumentation but which enrich and deepen it. Thus, in the midst of Paul's description of the revelation of God's righteousness and of the salvation which results from it, we find discussions of the Christians' relation to sin, to the Law, and to the trials which beset them.[7] In chapters 9-11 Paul answers the questions he asked but did not answer in 3:1-5: What advantage has the Jew? Will God be faithful to his promises to Israel? The peculiar construction explains why the letter has no fewer than three climactic conclusions, praising God for the completion of the work of salvation (Rom. 5:1-11; 8:31-39; 11:28-36; cf. also 15:7-13).

The doctrinal exposition of Romans is inserted into an epistolary framework. Most scholars, however, have failed to notice that epistolary style is somewhat more evident in chapters

---

[5]See Chapter V.
[6]See e.g. Rom. 3:1-8; 4:15-16; 5:20a.
[7]Sin and the flesh: 6:1-7:6; 8:1-17; cf. 3:7-8; the Law: 7:5-8:4; cf. 3:20,31; 4:13-15; 5:20-21; tribulations, 8:17-39; cf. 5:3-4. See also Chapter V, Appendix I.

9-11 than in 1:17-8:39. In Rom. 9:1 Paul addresses the recipients
in very personal terms, asserting that he speaks the truth in
Christ, that he does not lie.[8] The reference to the testimony
of his conscience in the Holy Spirit corresponds to oath-like
assurances in other sections where the epistolary character is
clearer.[9] In 9:1-3 Paul tells the Romans what he feels, his
sorrow for Israel, and in 10:1 he speaks of his intercession on
behalf of the Israelites. In general, Paul confines his assurances
to his recipients of his thanksgiving, his intercession and his
joy to the opening sections of a letter.[10] In Romans 9:1ff. and
10:1ff. Paul's assertions concern a third party, his kinsmen
by race, Israel.[11] The phrase in 10:2, "I bear them witness,"
is a common recommendation of a third party.[12] The same is true
of the style in 9:4-5, where the characterization, "who are
Israelites," is followed by three other relative clauses. Paul
uses parallel, attributival relative clauses with the same antecedent
much more frequently in recommendations than in other contexts.[13]

     In large parts of Romans 9-11 we find the same argumentative
style as in some earlier sections of the letter, with thematic
formulations, rhetorical questions and dialog with an imaginary
discussion partner, scriptural quotations, etc.[14] But Paul also
addresses his audience as "brethren".[15] When he discloses the
mystery of Israel's salvation, he uses a conventional epistolary
introduction to important information: *ou gar thelō hymas agnoein,
adelphoi* (I want you to understand, brethren).[16] In 11:13 he

----

[8]Cf. 2 Cor. 11:10; Gal. 1:20.
[9]Cf. Rom. 1:8; 2 Cor. 1:12,23; Phil. 1:8.
[10]See e.g. 1 Cor. 1:4-9; Phil. 1:3-11; Philemon 4-7. Even
within the main body or at the conclusion of letters, such assertions occur in epistolary contexts, cultivating the good relations
between sender and recipients of the letter, e.g. 2 Cor. 1:23-24;
7:4,16; Phil. 4:10,14,19; 1 Thess. 3:9-13.
[11]The nearest analogy to this would be Col. 2:1-2. Except
for Rom. 9:3, the expression "my kinsmen" (*syggeneis*) appears only
in greetings; Rom. 16:7,11,21.
[12]Cf. 2 Cor. 8:3; Col. 4:13.
[13]See Rom. 16:3-4; 1 Cor. 4:17; Phil. 4:3; Philemon 9-13.
I owe this observation to the complete survey of Pauline relative
clauses by H. H. Lester, *Relative Clauses in the Pauline Homologoumena
and Antilegomena* (Diss., Yale, 1973), Appendix I, 331-337. Passages
like Rom. 4:16-18; 1 Cor. 15:1; 2 Cor. 1:10 are not fully analogous.
[14]See Rom. 9:6-33; 10:4-21; 11:1-7, 11-12, 19-24; cf.
2:1-3:9; 3:27-31, etc.
[15]Thus in the opening and closing sections of the letter,
1:13,15; 15:14, 30; 16:17; also in the request in 12:1 and in 7:1,4
and 8:12, but not in the more essay-like parts of the letter.
[16]Cf. Rom. 1:13; 1 Cor. 10:1; 12:1; 2 Cor. 1:8; 1 Thess.
4:13. On this and similar disclosure formulas, see J. L. White,
"Body-opening formulae in the Pauline Letter," *JBL* 89 (1970) esp.
91-92, and T. Y. Mullins, "Disclosure: A Literary Form in the
New Testament," *NovT* 7 (1964) 44-50, and "Formulas in the New
Testament Epistles," *JBL* 91 (1972) 380-390.

addresses one part, probably the majority of his audience: "Now
I am speaking to you, Gentiles." He continues by writing about
his own vocation, as he otherwise does only in the epistolary
opening and conclusion of the letter.[17] His praise of his own
ministry recalls the thematic statement in 1:16 that he is not
ashamed of the gospel.[18]

Attention to such details shows that in Romans 9-11 Paul
not only unfolds the theological theme of the letter as a whole,
but also addresses the epistolary situation more directly than
in most parts of Romans 1-8. The content confirms that this
is the case. Paul's statements in Romans 9-11 are closely
related to what he says in Romans 15 about his approaching journey
to Jerusalem. In chapter 11 Paul describes the Christians in
Israel as the chosen remnant, and the Gentiles as wild branches
grafted on to the cultivated olive tree; in chapter 15 Paul tells
the Gentile Christians that they are indebted to the saints in
Jerusalem because they have come to share in their spiritual
blessings.[19] It is only in the light of Romans 9-11 that we are
able to understand why Paul had worked so hard for the collection,
and why it is so important to him that the Christians in Rome
should support him with their intercessory prayers.[20]

The epistolary situation also explains the differences
between Romans and Galatians, differences which are very obvious
in Romans 9-11.[21] The tendency of the two letters at some points
runs in opposite directions, contrary to one another. In Galatians
Paul reacts passionately to opponents who claimed that his good
reputation among the apostles and churches in Judea proved that
in special circumstances Paul himself "preached circumcision,"
and that it was due to a missionary tactic of adaptation that he

---

[17]See Rom. 1:1-6, 9-15; 15:15-21. In Rom. 10:15,17 and
15:21 Paul applies passages from Isa. 52:7; 53:1 and 52:15 to
the preachers of the gospel, including himself.

[18]See Rom. 11:13f., and cf. also the concluding praise
of Paul's ministry in 15:15-21. The concluding doxology in Rom.
11:33-36 corresponds to the opening thanksgiving in 1:8ff., and
is followed by a request, introduced by *parakalō* (I appeal).
For analogies, see 1 Cor. 1:9; 2 Cor. 9:15; Eph. 3:20-21; 1 Thess.
3:11-13.

[19]See Rom. 11:5-6, 15-24 and 15:27. For a somewhat
similar view, cf. Eph. 2:11-22.

[20]See Rom. 15:22-31.

[21]The differences are especially clear in the treatment
of Abraham and his offspring in Rom. 4 and 9:5,6-16 on the one
hand and Gal. 3 and 4:21-31 on the other. There is also a striking
difference between the whole tenor of the two letters and between
the conclusion in Gal. 6:11-17 and Rom. 11:25-36 and 15:25-33.
See my article "Der Name Israel: I. Zur Auslegung von Gal. 6,16,"
Judaica 6 (1950) 161-170.

had refrained from telling the Galatians to observe the Law.
Paul answers by maintaining that through a revelation of his Son,
God himself had commissioned Paul to preach to the Gentiles and
that Paul had everywhere and under all circumstances defended the
gospel which he preached in Galatia, without any compromise.[22]

In Romans, by contrast, one of the purposes is to refute
false rumors that Paul had rejected the Law and his own people.
In this letter it is important for him to prove that he is
neither an antinomian nor an apostate from Judaism. Paul may
have had a special reason to stress this. In A.D. 49 a decree
of the Emperor Claudius expelled Jews from Rome, Christian Jews
among them. Many of them returned when Claudius was succeeded
by Nero in 54, and shortly afterwards Paul wrote his letter to
Rome.[23]

For many centuries, Romans 9-11 has been read as a Pauline
theodicy. Since Augustine, the problem of predestination and
free will has been at the center of discussion in the Western
part of Christendom. The preoccupation with these problems has
often obscured the realization that in Romans 9-11 Paul is dealing
with God's faithfulness to his people Israel. The section does
indeed contain statements that raise the issue of predestination
and its relation to human responsibility; still, that issue is
not Paul's principal concern. Only neglect of the formal composition and of the historical setting has allowed that issue to
dominate the discussion of Romans 9-11.

Even interpreters who have recognized that the theme
of Romans 9-11 is God's dealings with Israel in the past, the
present, and the future have often failed to liberate themselves
from the common dogmatic approach. As a result, the analysis
of the composition is dominated by questions about God's election
and Israel's responsibility. The following summary sketches
the most common outline of Paul's argument, which a number of
commentaries reproduce with minor variations:

> I. The failure of Israel is not incompatible with God's
>   promises because in his absolute sovereignty God is
>   free to elect and to reject whomever he wills. (Romans
>   9)

----

[22]I presented an interpretation of Galatians along these lines
in a paper, "Paul's letter to the Galatians: Epistolary Genre,
Content, and Structure," delivered at the SBL Seminar on Paul,
1973. I hope some day to be able to return to the topic and to
revise the paper for publication.
[23]Several scholars have made this suggestion, see, e.g.,
G. Harder, "Der konkrete Anlass des Römerbriefes," *Theologia
Viatorum* 6 (1954-58) 13-24.

II. The 'hardening of the hearts' is due to the Jews' own guilt; their lack of faith is at fault. (Romans 10, or 9:30-10:21).[24]

III. The current situation, the Jewish rejection of Christ, will not last forever; at the end, God will show mercy and save all Israel (Romans 11).

According to an analysis of this type, Paul in Romans 9-11 gives three relatively independent answers to the problem raised by the Jews' negative reaction to Christ. The further question then is how the three answers relate to one another; are they really independent, or are they complementary to one another? Is Paul's argumentation an early example of theological dialectics, or has he committed the logical error of proving too much? Such questions have been discussed for a long time and many answers have been proposed. But, at least on the surface, Paul's argumentation is more straightforward than most of his commentators have assumed.[25] The argument appears to be more complicated than it really is, because Paul at various points in Romans 9-11, as in 1-8, refutes objections, clarifies presuppositions, or takes up special problems.

In Rom. 9:1-5 Paul affirms his own sorrow and the privileges of the Israelites. But at this point he does not explicitly state what the reason for his sorrow and anguish was. He immediately proceeds to formulate his thesis: "But it is not as though the word of God has failed" (Rom. 9:6). Paul has in mind God's promise to Israel; it is still valid. This is the sum and substance of what Paul wants to say in Romans 9-11. He begins his exposition of the theme with two subordinate theses: "For not all who are descended from Israel belong to Israel," and "Not all are children of Abraham because they are his descendants" (Rom. 9:6b, 7a). Paul proves the second thesis by citing scriptural statements contrasting Isaac with Ishmael and Jacob with Esau. From these examples Paul deduces that God's promise and election matter, and not ancestry or merit. The

---

[24]Many commentators, including Käsemann, connect 9:30-33 with chapter 10 rather than with chapter 9. It is true that the passage introduces the 'theme' of chapter 10, but it is in itself a conclusion and transition. In 10:1 Paul makes a new start.

[25]J. Munck, *Christ and Israel*, is one of the few exegetes who have succeeded in liberating themselves from the common way of treating the composition and the problems of Romans 9-11. His own interpretation could not carry conviction because of the strained effort to prove that Rom. 9:30-10:4 dealt with "The unbelief of the Jews toward Christ during his life on earth" (79-84), whereas chapter 10 shows "that God has not ceased to call Israel" (85) but "has done everything in order that the Jews may believe" (89ff.), as the preaching of the apostles has reached them everywhere (95-96).

specific application which Paul intends in the context is clear:
even in the present God's word and promise stand firm; the
relation between the chosen remnant and the rest of Israel is
analogous to the relation between Isaac and Ishmael, Jacob and
Esau   (cf. Rom. 9:27-29; 11:1-6).

In the course of his argument, Paul develops the first
of his sub-theses, that not all who are descended from Israel
are "Israel" in the strict sense of the word. In Rom. 9:14, however, he inserts an objection: "Is there injustice on God's
part?" The objection is caused by Paul's comment that the
difference between Jacob and Esau was not due to anything they
had done but merely to the call of God who chose one and rejected
the other. A quotation from Mal. 1:2-3 supports this notion of
God's selective choice: "Jacob I loved, but Esau I hated." For
Paul, Scripture not only poses the problem but provides the
solution, for God said to Moses: "I will have mercy on whom I
will have mercy and will have compassion on whom I have compassion,"
and to Pharaoh: "For this purpose have I raised you up, for the
very purpose of showing my power in you, so that my name may be
proclaimed in all the earth"(Exod. 33:19; 9:16). Paul deduces
from these verses that salvation does not depend on human will
or effort but on the mercy of God, who has mercy upon whom he
will and who hardens the heart of whom he will. We should not,
however, overlook the context of the Exodus narrative. The
hardening of Pharaoh's heart and his destruction served God's
purpose, the liberation of Israel, a liberation which resulted
in the proclamation of God's name to all the earth.

Paul's observations raise still other problems: "Why
does he still find fault? Who can resist his will?" Paul answers
with counter-questions based upon the biblical image of the potter
and the clay.[26] Paul's reply does not even attempt a rational
explanation. It simply recalls that God is God and man is a sinner
who has no right to make complaints against his Creator.

In Rom. 9:21ff. Paul returns to his main theme. He applies
the image of the potter and his products to the situation of his
own time.[27] The syntax of verses 22-23 poses some problems. There
is a conditional clause without any independent clause. The point
becomes clear when we observe that Paul has modeled these verses

---

[26]See esp. Isa. 29:16; 45:9; Jer. 18:1-6.
[27]The Greek word *skeuos* is used for all kinds of utensils
or tools, not only for hollow vessels. In Jer. 27:25 LXX (= 50:25
TM), *ta skeuē orgēs autou* refers to the tools or weapons (*RSV*) of
God's wrath. Cf. also Isa. 10:5: "Ah, Assyria, the rod of my
anger," and Isa. 13:5 (Hebrew and Symmachus).

after God's statement to Pharaoh quoted in verse 17. The schematic diagram below makes the correspondences clear.

Rom. 9:17	Rom. 9:22-24
For the very purpose of showing my power in you,	What if God, desiring to show his wrath and to make known his power,
I have raised you up	has endured with much patience the vessels[28] of wrath made for destruction,
so that my name may be proclaimed	in order to make known the riches of his glory for the vessels of mercy, which he has prepared beforehand for glory,
in all the earth	even us whom he has called not from the Jews only but also from the Gentiles?

Paul puts the non-believing Jews of his time on the same level not only with Ishmael and Esau, but also with Pharaoh and with Babylon (Jer. 50:25), the last-named a symbol for a world power hostile to God. The expression "the vessels of wrath" probably implies both that they are targets of God's wrath and that they are instruments of it. According to Paul, even though vessels of wrath are destined for destruction, they have a teleological function. Pharaoh's destruction not only demonstrated God's power, but also freed Israel, an act which made God's name known all over the earth. In the same way, Paul thinks, the hardening of the heart of a part of Israel will both show God's power and wrath and also demonstrate God's abundant goodness toward the vessels or tools of his mercy.

In an appended relative clause, Paul identifies the vessels of mercy with us, those whom God has called, "not from the Jews only, but also from the Gentiles." He adds passages from Hosea: "Those who were not my people I will call 'my people,' and her who was not beloved I will call 'my beloved.' And in the very place where it was said to them, 'You are not my people,' they will be called 'sons of the living God.'"[29] Paul understands these

---

[28]Here the "vessels of wrath" seem to be instruments used by God, even if they are themselves under his wrath. The verb *ēnegken*, translated "has endured," can also mean "has carried forth." It probably alludes to Jer. 27(50):25 LXX: "The Lord has brought forth the tools of his anger." It corresponds to the phrase "I have raised you up" (*exēgeira se*) which Paul has himself introduced in the quotation from Exod. 9:16 in Rom. 9:17.

[29]Rom. 9:25-26, cf. Hos. 2:23; 2:1 and 1:10 (= 2:25; 2:1 and 1:10 TM).

quotations as scriptural proof that the Gentiles also are to be
called and to become God's people; yet it is not likely that he
has overlooked that in Hosea the symbolic names refer to God's
mercy toward the rejected Israel. As a rule, Paul reserves the
designation "people of God" for Israel.[30] The relative clause
inserted in Rom. 9:24 is probably to be understood as a parenthesis.
The quotations from Hosea do not refer to the Gentiles alone, but
to all the vessels of mercy. The phrases "in the place" and "there"
(*ekei*) in 9:26 make better sense when we include the Israelites
among those to whom it was said: "You are not my people," but
who are to be called "sons of the living God." Possibly, Paul
has Jerusalem in mind.[31] Throughout the letter, Paul represents
God as the one who justifies the ungodly, who makes the dead to
live, who loves his enemies and who in his mercy accepts those
who are not his people as his people, indeed as his own children;
this applies to Jews and to Gentiles without distinction (cf.
Rom. 4:5, 17; 5:6-8; 11:15; 28-32).

The traditional interpretation of Romans 9:24-26 results
from reading the verses in the light of later thought of the
Gentile Christian church as God's new people. The context might
at first seem to support that view; the promises to those who
are to be called God's people precede quotations from Isaiah to
the effect that only a remnant of Israel will find salvation
(Isa. 10:22-23; 1:9). But the thought in 9:25-29 conforms to
the introductory section 9:6-11. The promises for the future in
Hosea correspond to the promises made at the births of Isaac and
Jacob; they confirm that God's promises remain valid. The
prophecies from Isaiah about the remnant agree with the thesis
that not everyone who descends from Israel is Israel. Not all
Israel will be saved, but only a remnant, those among Israel who
are vessels of mercy. Paul adds almost as an aside that there
are Gentiles among these vessels of mercy, a point he develops
later on (cf. 9:30-33; 10:18-20). Both the analogy to the Exodus
story and the quotations from Hosea point ahead to the statements

---

[30]See Rom. 11:1-2; 15:10. In the New Testament the term
"God's people" is much less frequently transferred to the Christian
church than one might assume from the reading of later Christian
writings and modern scholarly literature, including my own book
Das Volk Gottes. The transfer usually occurs in the form of
quotations of biblical passages, see 2 Cor. 6:16;   Heb. 4:9; 8:10;
1 Peter 2:9-10; Rev. 18:4; 21:3; cf. Titus 2:14.

[31]Munck, *Christ and Israel*, 72-73, thinks that 'there' (*ekei*)
refers to Jerusalem as the place where the Gentile nations will be
gathered and proclaimed the sons of the living God. On the basis
of this interpretation, Munck (12-13) assumes that Paul expected
his collection journey to open the way for Israel to the salvation
determined by God.

about the future of Israel in chapter 11. The hardening of hearts
and God's wrath are the negative factors in a design whose
principal purpose is the demonstration of God's mercy.

The question: "What are we then to say?" introduces a
provisional summary of Paul's view of the contemporary situation
(9:30). The Gentiles have embraced the righteousness that stems
from faith whereas Israel (here the majority of Israel which does
not belong to the remnant) has not reached the goal it pursued,
namely righteousness based on Law (9:31). Israel tripped over
the stumbing block, Christ. As in Galatians 3, traditional
scriptural testimonies to Jesus as Messiah, here Isa. 8:14 and
28:16, are interpreted in the context of the Pauline contrast
between faith and works. The crucified Messiah is a stumbling
block, an offense to those who want to gain righteouness by
their own efforts, while at the same time he is the cornerstone
about whom the prophet spoke: "He who believes in him will not
be put to shame."[32]

The summary in Rom. 9:30-33 functions as a transition to
the following section of the letter. Yet, Paul makes a new start
in 10:1-3, reaffirming his concern for his compatriots. Only
at this point does Paul explain what prompts the sorrow and
anguish about which he spoke in 9:1-3.[33] The Jews have a genuine
zeal for God, but they lack understanding. Their attempt to
establish their own righteousness has prevented them from subordinat-
ing themselves to the righteousness of God revealed in Christ.
Here Paul inserts a new, final explanation of the relation between
the Mosaic Law and Christ: "For Christ is the end (*telos*) of the
Law, that every one who has faith may be justified." Paul supports
this thesis by contrasting Lev. 18:5 with a quotation of Deut.
30:12-14 adapted and amplified by additions from other passages
(Deut. 9:4; Psalm 106 (107):26 LXX). In the context of Deuteronomy,
the word that is near is the commandment of the (deuteronomic)
Law (Deut. 30:11). Paul, however, attributes the quotation to the
personified righteousness by faith and takes it to refer to Christ
and to the "word of faith" which the apostles proclaim.

---

[32]Rom. 8:33 is a conflation of Isa. 8:14 and 28:16. The
same combination recurs in 1 Peter 2:6-8, where also Ps. 118:22
is alluded to. Paul is likely to draw on traditional testimonies
to the crucified Jesus as the Messiah. In Rom. 10:11-13 he uses
Isa. 28:16, in combination with Joel 2:32 (3:5 TM), to interpret
Deut. 30:14 and to prove that the promise pertains to all who
believe, without distinction between Jew and Greek.

[33]On epistolary expressions of joy, grief, and similar moods
(or dispositions), see R. D. Webber, *The Concept of Rejoicing in
Paul* (Diss., Yale, 1970) 96-156.

The reinterpretation is not quite as amazing as it appears
to be. In Judaism, the Torah was identified with Wisdom, and in
early Christianity statements about Wisdom were often applied to
Christ.[34] Paul is possibly drawing upon some traditional Christian
interpretation. But there is also another possibility. In order
to come to terms with what appeared to him as two contradictory
scriptural passages, Lev. 18:5 and Deut. 30:11ff., Paul introduces a distinction between two concepts of the Law. Lev. 18:5,
which states that the man who performs the commandments shall
live by them, represents the Law (*nomos*) in the narrow sense, the
commandments and prohibitions revealed at Sinai, in isolation
from the encompassing divine economy. The statement in Deuteronomy
about the commandment that is not too hard, not far off but near
by, Paul, by contrast, takes to refer to the entire Law, the Law
that together with the prophets bears witness to the righteousness
of God (cf. Rom. 3:21).

In any case, Rom. 10:4-17 provides an excellent example
of the process by which scriptural passages and present events
reciprocally influence one another's interpretation. Combining
Deut. 30:14 with quotations from Isa. 28:16 (already quoted in
Rom. 9:33b), Joel 3:5 (2:32) and Isa. 52:7 and 53:1, Paul draws
a picture of Christian preaching, faith, and confession; he also
finds a reference to the failure of some hearers to obey the gospel
they have heard. The whole section demonstrates how closely Paul's
view of Israel is interrelated with his doctrines of justification
and of the Law, with his Christology, with his conviction that
"there is no distinction between Jews and Greek," and with his
own mission and preaching of the gospel. But it is neither
possible nor necessary to elaborate on those themes here.

For our purpose it is important to recognize that Romans
10 is not a part of Paul's answer to the question of whether or
not God had repudiated his promises to Israel. The chapter is a
delayed explanation of the factors which caused him to raise that
question. From 10:4 onward Paul digresses from his main line of
argumentation, though at the conclusion of the section he returns
to it. At the end of chapter 10 Paul repeats the same point he
made at the end of chapter 9: the Gentiles have found the God
they did not seek, while Israel has proven to be a disobedient and
recalcitrant people. Paul proves this point with quotations from

---

[34]See esp. Prov. 8; Sir. 24; Baruch 3:24-4:4; and John
1:1ff.; Col. 1:15ff.; Heb. 1:2-3. Baruch 3:29-30, like Rom. 10:6ff.,
makes use of Deut. 30:12f. See e.g. J. Suggs, "The Word is near
to you," in Farmer, 289-312.

Deut. 32:21 and Isa. 65:1-2. Later on we shall see that the first
of these quotations has a special significance for Paul: "I will
make you jealous of those who are not a nation; with a foolish
nation I will make you angry."[35]

After this analysis of the existing state of affairs,
Paul returns in 11:1 to his main theme. The question implicit
from the beginning of chapter 9 emerges in a pointed form: "Has
God rejected his people?" Paul answers immediately with an
emphatic denial. He first mentions that he himself, the Apostle
to the Gentiles, is an Israelite, a descendant of Abraham, of
the tribe of Benjamin. Once more it becomes clear that Paul
does not interpret Scripture and history with scholarly detach-
ment; he is vitally involved in what he is writing about. In 11:2
Paul presents a new formulation of his main thesis that God's
word has not failed: "God has not rejected his people whom he
foreknew."[36] Referring to an analogous situation at the time of
Elijah, Paul points out that due to God's merciful choice and
not on the basis of works, a remnant of Israel remains faithful
(11:2-6).

Whereas in 9:27-29 Paul emphasized that only a remnant
remained, in 11:5-7 he stresses that a remnant does in fact remain.
Thus he has reached the conclusion of the line of argumentation
introduced in 9:6. As Isaac, not Ishmael, as Jacob, not Esau,
as the seven thousand at the time of Elijah, not the many who
bowed the knee to Baal, so the Jews who believe in Christ, not
the rest, are the children of the promise, chosen by grace. The
remnant that remains proves to Paul that God has not rejected his
people and that his word stands firm. At the same time it becomes
clear that the hardening of the hearts of the large part of the
people and their disobedience is not incompatible with God's
promises; on the contrary, the Scriptures themselves show that
the number of the faithful is small. Paul reinforces this point
in 11:8-10 by citing a series of quotations about the hardening

---

[35]See Rom. 10:19 and 11:11. Deut. 32:21 alludes to a
hostile nation; Paul takes the saying to refer to Christian Gentiles.
But both in Deut. 32 and in Romans 9-11 God's wrath and mercy
toward his disobedient people are at issue. Already Munck,
Christ and Israel, 90, stressed that "chapter 11 clearly resumes
the thread of 9:29," and that the intervening passage (9:30-10:21),
"is not some incidental parenthesis, but a necessary and basic
explanation." That is also my conclusion in spite of disagreements
with Munck's exegesis (see notes 25 and 31).
[36]Even here Paul alludes to scriptural passages, esp. Ps.
94:14 and 1 Sam. 12:22; cf. also Deut. 31:6; Josh. 1:5; Jer. 31:37.

of hearts.[37]

The question which remains concerns "the others," those who do not belong to the remnant: "Have they stumbled so as to fall?" (11:21). Again Paul responds with an emphatic denial: "By no means! But through their trespass salvation has come to the Gentiles, so as to make Israel jealous." Just as the hardening of Pharaoh's heart led to salvation for the Israelites, so the hardening of the hearts of the Israelites who rejected the gospel has led to salvation for the Gentiles. We should not overstress the correlation of cause and effect. We do not need to consider Jewish rejection of the gospel a necessary condition for its acceptance by the Gentiles. Paul interprets what has actually happened. The crucified Messiah became an offense to Jews but brought salvation to the Gentiles.[38] The Gentiles had become participants in the messianic salvation at a time and in a way contrary to all expectations, not as a consequence of the liberation of Israel, but before Israel had herself accepted her salvation. For Paul, however, this does not mean that God's promise of salvation is taken from Israel and given to the Gentiles, but only that the order of events has been reversed.

Using the quotation from Deut. 32:21 cited in 10:19, Paul argues that the purpose of what has happened is to make the Israelites jealous. He believes that when the Jews realize that through the gospel God has reconciled the Gentiles to himself they too will want to share in its richness. Paul goes so far as to interpret his own ministry to the Gentiles in the light of his hope for the Jews: "I magnify my ministry in order to make my fellow Jews (lit. "my flesh") jealous, and thus save some of them" (11:13-14). Paul's hope for the future of Israel (which he goes on to state with greater clarity) coincides with the aim of his own work.

The reference to Paul's ministry occurs between two analogous syllogisms (11:12, 15). The trespass of the Israelites was an evil which had positive consequences for the Gentiles; how much more must their complete obedience, their "full inclusion" (*plērōma*) have positive consequences! (v. 12). The conclusion from the minor is restated in verse 15: "For if their rejection meant reconciliation of the world, what will their acceptance mean

---

[37]The quotations in Rom. 11:8-10 are taken from Deut. 29:4 (29:3 TM) combined with Isa. 29:10 (cf. 6:9-10) and from Ps. 69:23-24. Both Psalm 69 and Isaiah 29 appear often in the New Testament, e.g. Matt. 15:8f.; 27:40; Rom. 9:20; 15:3.

[38]Rom. 9:30-33; 10:8-21; cf. 1 Cor. 1:23-25.

but life from the dead?" One can question the logical cogency of
these syllogisms, but one should recognize that Paul draws upon
well-established Jewish tradition when he asserts that Israel's
restoration will have worldwide consequences. Paul retains this
idea in a christianized form, and argues for it by appealing to
the positive consequences of the Jews' rejection of Christ. He
may also presuppose the idea that God's mercy has in general a
greater and more widespread effect than his judgment.[39]

Paul sees an alteration in Israel's relation to Christ as
more than a hypothetical possibility. He thinks that it will occur
eventually and says so, using figurative language: "If the dough
offered as first fruits is holy, so is the whole lump; and if the
root is holy, so are the branches" (11:16). The "lump" and the
"branches" must refer to Israel, including "the others" as well
as the chosen remnant. The argument presupposes that what is
holy, consecrated to God, cannot permanently remain opposed to
Christ or separated from him. It is less clear to what the
metaphors "first fruits" and "root" refer, to Israel's forefathers
or to the remnant. In the first case, the statement would say
much the same thing as Rom. 11:28f.: "They are beloved for the
sake of their forefathers. For the gifts and the call of God are
irrevocable." In the second case the statement would recall
the beginning of chapter 11: the presence of a remnant proves
that God has not rejected his people but remains committed to the
promise granted to the whole nation. This would correspond to
the view found both in the Old Testament and in Jewish tradition
that the remnant represents the whole people of Israel. It does
not make much difference which interpretation we choose. In
either case, God's election and promise is constitutive for the
holiness of Israel. Possibly Paul had both ideas in mind. The
metaphor of first fruits is more appropriate to the remnant,
those Jews who are already consecrated to Christ in faith. The
whole nation is consecrated through them, as the new harvest is
consecrated through the offering of the first loaves made from
the newly gathered wheat.[40] The metaphor of the root seems rather
to suggest the patriarchs, from whom all Israelites descend.

In the following section Paul elaborates the image of
the root and the branches (11:17-24). He portrays the remnant

---

[39]Cf. Exod. 20:5-6; 34:6-7, etc., and also Rom. 5:15, as
well as the rabbinic doctrine that the measure of mercy is greater
than the measure of judgment.
[40]Cf. the idea that the first converts are the first fruits
of their provinces, Rom. 16:5; 1 Cor. 16:5. The Law commanding
the offering of the first loaf appears in Num. 15:17-21.

as branches which the gardener left in place when he pruned the
olive tree and cut off other branches. The Gentiles are branches
from wild olive trees which God has grafted onto the domesticated
olive tree. Paul here uses the rhetorical technique of addressing
directly the individual Gentile Christian, whom he warns against
self-sufficiency and against boasting at the expense of the
unbelieving Jews. He turns God's impartiality and sovereign
freedom against Christians of Gentile origin. Though the language
is figurative, Paul obviously is speaking about Israel, Gentile
Christians, and Jews who have rejected Christ.[41] Paul portrays
unbelieving Jews as branches broken off, but he stresses that
their exclusion was a result of their lack of faith, that it was
not definitive: "God has the power to graft them in again" (11:23).
That means, in non-figurative terms, that God has given the
Israelites his promises and that he is able to do what he has said.
Paul even turns the warning addressed to Gentile Christians into
a supporting argument by drawing a conclusion from the greater to
the lesser: if God in Christ has accepted Gentiles, to whom he
had not committed himself, how much more will he welcome the
Jews, who received his promises (11:24).[42]

The question concerning "the others" raised in 11:11
receives its final answer in 11:25-26: "A hardening has come upon
part of Israel, until the full number of the Gentiles come in, and
so (*houtōs*, in this manner) all Israel will be saved." Paul
introduces this statement as the disclosure of a revealed mystery.
Yet the solution draws the conclusion of the preceding arguments.[43]
We should probably not think of a sudden, unmediated revelation
granted to Paul but rather of a mystery hidden in Scripture until
its explanation was unveiled.[44] It is easy to find biblical
passages which announce salvation for Israel.[45] The mystery which
Paul reveals is not Israel's ultimate salvation, but rather the
way in which Israel will achieve that ultimate salvation. Salvation will come to Israel indirectly, after a period during which

---

[41]Therefore, it does not matter whether or not grafting
of wild branches into the domesticated olive tree was ever practiced.
On Israel as an olive tree, see Isa. 11:16.

[42]Paul still uses metaphors, although branches that have
been pruned away are not grafted back onto the tree at a later
stage.

[43]See esp. 11:11-12, 15-16, 23-24.

[44]Thus, the term "mystery" seems to refer to a mystery that
is present in Scripture but only known by inspired interpreters.
The term is used in a similar way in Eph. 5:32 and in the Dead Sea
Scrolls. See e.g. R. E. Brown, *The Semitic Background of the Term
'Mystery' in the New Testament* (Philadelphia: Fortress, 1968).

[45]Cf. the rabbinic view that all Israel has a part in the
world to come, Mishnah Sanh. 10.

the hearts of many Israelites will be hardened. The Gentiles
will participate in this salvation first. Paul's view that Gentile
Christians will make the Israelites eager to participate in
Christ reemerges,[46] as his comment on the mystery he has just
revealed makes clear: "Just as you were once disobedient to God
but now have received mercy because of their disobedience, so they
have now been disobedient in order that by the mercy shown to you
they may also receive mercy" (Rom. 11:30-31).

The context makes clear that "all Israel" refers both to
the remnant and to "the others." Paul does not affirm that every
individual Israelite will attain salvation, but that God will
grant salvation to both parts of his people, to those who have
rejected Christ as well as to those who have believed in him.
To support his view Paul quotes the Septuagintal form of Isa.
59:20-21, adding a line, "When I shall have taken away their
sins," from Isa. 27:9.[47] In this way, Paul ties together God's
covenant with Israel in the last days with the remission of sin,
probably alluding to Jeremiah 31. Paul identifies the people's
disobedience with their rejection of Christ, and looks forward
to the disappearance of this disbelief, and to the forgiveness
which God will grant.

Even though the order in Paul's argument as a whole is
clear, it is hard to organize its component parts into a coherent
picture of the future. From the quotation in Rom. 11:26-27,
one could assume that Christ himself is going to save Israel
when he appears at the end of days, but no other passage suggests
such a view. Paul hopes that his own work among the Gentiles will
lead to the conversion of some Jews, and he connects salvation
for Israel with what he calls the coming in of "the full number
of the Gentiles." Unfortunately, what Paul means by this phrase
is far from clear. The word *plērōma* (fullness, "full number") has
a positive value but it can have various nuances of meaning. One
possible paraphrase of Rom. 11:25b would be: "Until the Gentiles
enter the kingdom of God in the full number that God has decreed
from the beginning." Another possibility is: "Until the salvation

---

[46]See the quotation from, and allusion to, Deut. 32:21 in
Rom. 10:19 and 11:11-14.

[47]In Rom. 11:26-27, Paul connects the first clause in Isa.
59:21 with the preceding verse. For Paul, Isa. 59:21 states that
the Deliverer will come from Zion, while the Septuagint has "for
the sake of Zion" and the Hebrew text "to Zion." Does Paul expect
that at his parousia Jesus will appear "from Zion"? Or does he
make use of a form of the text that had been adapted in order to
prove that Jesus, who was crucified in Jerusalem, is the Deliverer?

of the Gentiles occurs to its full extent."[48] However we translate
the clause, it seems clear that Paul believed that his mission
and that of others had succeeded in fulfilling its condition in
the Eastern provinces of the Roman Empire, from Jerusalem to the
shores of the Adriatic.[49] Paul's vision extended only to the lands
around the Mediterranean. What he actually had in mind in speaking
about the *plērōma* (fullness) of the Gentiles may therefore have
been the successful completion of his mission to Spain.[50]

It is even harder to specify what specific consequences
Paul expects to result from the "full inclusion" (*plērōma*) or the
"acceptance" (*proslēmpsis*) of the Israelites. In Rom. 11:12 he
speaks in general terms of "riches;" in 11:15 he states that the
result will be life from the dead. Does Paul expect that the
resurrection of the dead will follow upon God's acceptance of
Israel, or does he speak figuratively about new life for the whole
world? Since the entry of the "full number" of Gentiles is to
precede salvation for all Israel, it is unlikely that Paul looked
forward to a great missionary epoch in which the gospel message
would spread to new, unknown areas. It is somewhat more likely
that he expected the small congregations, which he and others
had founded, to expand to include the entire regions they represented,
just as the division between the faithful remnant and the rest of
Israel would be overcome. Probably, the contrast between the
"reconciliation of the world," that followed upon the (temporary)
rejection of those Jews who failed to believe in Christ and the
"life from the dead," which will follow upon their acceptance by
God, is qualitative rather than quantitative. Whatever else Paul
has in mind, he stresses that the enrichment of the whole world,
which is to follow upon the restoration of Israel, is going to be
an act of the God who makes the dead alive.

Paul does not draw an exact map of future events, neither
in Romans 9-11 nor elsewhere. Attempts to coordinate what Paul
writes in Romans 11 with other eschatological statements in the

---

[48]The latter translation, mainly based upon the analogy
with Rom. 11:12, means the "full inclusion" of the Israelites rather
than their "full number." Munck, *Christ and Israel*, 132, argues
for the translation: "until the fullness of the Gentiles begins."
His argument that Paul does not think in terms of predestination
of a specific number to be obtained is more convincing than the
proposed translation.
[49]See Rom. 15:19-23.
[50]This is argued in a forthcoming paper by Roger D. Aus,
on the basis of numerous passages in the Old Testament and rabbinic
writings which refer to Spain as the most distant land from which
Gentiles will make pilgrimage to Jerusalem. For the more general
idea, cf. Mark 13:10; Matt. 24:14.

Pauline letters do not succeed in constructing a unified Pauline
doctrine about the last things.[51] It is harder still to reconcile
Paul's view with that of other New Testament writings, e.g.
Revelation. Paul has no interest in giving a detailed description
of what is going to happen at the end of time. He does not speak
abstractly about the distant future but concretely about a course
of events already in progress, of which his own work as apostle
to the Gentiles is an important part. Certain aspects of Paul's
eschatology emerge clearly, but Paul does not integrate them into
any eschatological dogmatic. Like Paul's theology in general, his
statements about the eschatological future vary with the circumstances and the purpose of each letter. He writes to his congregations about the future in order to guide, to warn or to comfort
them. Nevertheless, Paul's fundamental theological outlook underlies these varying formulations.

The initial thesis in Rom. 9:6 formulates Paul's fundamental
conviction that God's word has not failed; that God has not rejected
his people. This conviction provides the basis for what Paul says
in Romans 9-11 about the future of Israel, about Christ, and
about the Gentiles. But to a higher degree than the text reveals
directly, what Paul says flows from his faith in Jesus Christ.
Paul says more clearly in other places that God's promises to
Israel concern Christ, but that presupposition underlies the
discussion in Romans 9-11 as well.[52] Paul applies scriptural
quotations about Israel's disobedience, the hardening of the
Israelites' hearts and their temporary rejection to their refusal
to accept Christ. He identifies the faithful remnant with those
Jews who do believe in Christ. That God in the last days will
again show mercy and restore his disobedient people to favor means
that he has promised that all Israel will share in the salvation
Christ alone makes available. Paul does not discuss what else the
future holds for Israel, because for him Israel's relation to
Christ is the decisive problem.

Paul does not spiritualize the Old Testament as radically
as some of his hellenistic Jewish contemporaries did. Although
Paul's Christology completely determines his scriptural interpretation and his view of Israel's future, he continues to insist

---

[51]Cf. J. G. Gager, Jr., "Functional Diversity in Paul's
Use of End-Time Language," *JBL* 89 (1970) 325-337. The 'functional
diversity' extends to passages like 1 Cor. 15:22-28 and 1 Thess.
4:13-5:11.

[52]Therefore, I cannot give as much weight as Stendahl (4)
does to the observation that Paul does not use the name of Jesus
Christ in Rom. 10:17-11:36. Cf. also his article "In No Other
Name," in *Christian Witness and the Jewish People* (Geneva: Lutheran
World Federation, 1976).

that the Scriptures *do* speak about Israel and about their future.
Paul knows from his own experience that the Gentiles have proved
more willing to accept the gospel than the Jews. This phenomenon
leads naturally to the question, has God rejected his people? An
affirmative answer is impossible for Paul, not only because he
is himself a Jew, but also because the Scriptures contain God's
pledge to Israel. Christ's work as a servant to Israel confirmed
God's promises, and God could not be God if he did not remain
faithful to his word.

Paul's scheme, which provides the framework for his exegesis,
follows the workings of God's mercy from Israel to the Gentiles,
and from the Gentiles back to Israel, for the ultimate good of
all. Paul, in a sense anticipating Hegel and Marx, sketches a
dialectic of history, with thesis, antithesis and synthesis.
But Paul is not interested in the orderly progression of history;
he seeks to come to grips with God's sovereign freedom, a freedom
which extends even to his treatment of those whom he has chosen.
For all, Jews and Gentiles alike, the salvation made available in
Christ comes as undeserved mercy, as clemency toward the disobedient,
as justification of the ungodly. We could say that Romans 9-11
illustrates Paul's doctrine of justification by faith. However,
we express ourselves more correctly when we say that from the
beginning Paul's view of the relation of Israel to the Gentiles
profoundly shaped his doctrine of justification. Only later,
especially in the thought of Augustine and of Luther, did the
doctrine of justification become fundamentally important apart
from the problem of Israel and the Gentiles.[53]

Paul completes his description of Israel's future with a
doxology which praises God's inscrutable wisdom (Rom. 11:33-36).
Paul largely models the style and the wording after Old Testament
prototypes.[54] But the closing declaration of God's omnipotence,
"For from him and through him and to him are all things," follows
Greek patterns. In philosophical contexts similar formulations
refer to the one "ground of being" or to nature. Paul strips
the formula of its pantheistic overtones. He applies it to God's
sovereign action in history, from the creation to the consummation,
to the omnipotence of God's love. The combination of Jewish and
Greek stylistic elements both here and elsewhere in Romans is not
accidental. Paul's faith in Christ has provided him with a new
answer to a question which inescapably confronted Judaism amidst

---

[53]See Chapter VI, the last section, pp. 115-120.
[54]See Isa. 41:3; Job 15:8; 41:3 (TM 41:3), etc.

the universalism of the Hellenistic world: how could the one God be at the same time the God of the whole world and the God of Israel? Paul's answer is that God is not God for the Jews only but for the Gentiles as well.[55] There is no difference; all have sinned, all have fallen short of the glory of God, and all are justified in the same way, by accepting the unmerited offer of salvation which God gives through faith in Jesus Christ. But Christ, though Lord of all, became incarnate as an Israelite; God, though God of all, chose Israel to be his people, and by his word committed himself to Israel. In the future, God will keep the promises he has made. God's ways are unsearchable, but he is absolutely trustworthy.

The doxology in Rom. 11:33-36 serves to conclude not only the discussion in Romans 9-11, but the exposition in chapters 1-11 as a whole, both in form and in content. It is not only God's way of dealing with Israel which is miraculous, which surpasses man's understanding. That no man holds God in his debt, so that what he receives from God is never merited, is a fundamental idea which underlies all of Romans. Hardest for men to understand is that God uses man's disobedience and sinfulness to further his ultimate purpose, to show mercy to those who do not deserve it.[56]

When Paul calls God's judgments unsearchable and his ways inscrutable, he does not mean to imply that man can know nothing about God's way of acting. Paul has himself sought to understand exactly how God has acted with Israel and with the Gentiles, and how he will act in the future. The thought is more simply that God's ways are not man's ways, nor his thoughts man's thoughts. The doxology further explains why Paul does not presume to give an exact description of the future; he must leave room for surprises and for riddles.

Today, nineteen hundred years later, we know that the future did not unfold as Paul hoped and expected. His journey to Jerusalem with the collection he had gathered did not excite the envy of his compatriots in the way he had hoped. Israel has not accepted Christ, the parousia has not yet occurred. What has happened was precisely what Paul warned against. Christian Gentiles made themselves great at the expense of Israel. Already Ephesians had to remind the Gentile Christians about the greatness of the mystery that has

---

[55]Rom. 3:29-30. See Chapter X.
[56]Rom. 11:30-32, cf. 1:18-3:26; 5:20-21.

given them access to Christ and to God's promises together with
Israel.[57] Gentile Christians soon came to believe that God had
rejected Israel, that, much to the advantage of the Gentiles, he
had gathered for himself a new people from among them; Jewish
Christians they treat as a special case.

The controversy over the messiahship of Jesus and over
exegesis of the scriptures began as a debate within Israel, between
Jews who believed in the crucified Messiah and those who did not.
When Paul writes, Gentile Christian churches have become a significant new element, but the Apostle is himself a Jew, and he knows
that in Christ God has confirmed his promises to Israel. Later
on, the ancient church read the Old Testament as a part of its
sacred Scriptures, often using them to support its anti-Jewish
polemic. When Christianity became the state religion of the Roman
Empire, the polemic between two minority groups developed into
active Christian discrimination against Jews. We know all too
well the sad history of persecutions and pogroms which followed.

Paul does not envision any mission among the Jews by
Christians of Gentile origins. This does not necessarily mean
that such a mission is wrong, even though it has more often been
pursued with zeal than with understanding. Paul thought that
when Jews saw the richness of the spiritual benefits which the
gospel had conferred on Gentiles, that they too would wish to
share the blessings God had made available in Christ. What Paul
hoped for has not happened, and no one can reproach the Jews
for that.

In America it is sometimes said about the race issue:
"It is not the black man's problem, but the white man's." In
the same way, we could say of the relation of Christianity to
Judaism: "There is no Jewish problem, but there is a Christian
problem."

---

[57]See esp. Eph. 2:11-22 and 3:4-10. The author of Ephesians
was a disciple of Paul who belonged to a younger generation but
was, possibly, himself a Jew.

CHAPTER IX

CONTRADICTIONS IN SCRIPTURE

The Bible is full of contradictions. This fact is often
used to discredit both the orthodox doctrine of inspiration and
more recent fundamentalism. For scholarship, however, recognition
of disagreement within and among the individual writings of the
Bible has another, more positive meaning: it is an aid in
establishing chronology and in discerning the use of sources or
the development of traditions, and through this an aid to historical reconstruction in general.

It also occupies an important place in the debate over
biblical hermeneutics. Rudolf Bultmann, for example, defends his
program of demythologization by observing that statements in the
New Testament would contradict themselves if they were objectified
and interpreted as literal truths about God and the world beyond;
therefore, they must be interpreted existentially. At the other
extreme, a book published in the United States a number of years
ago, suggestively titled *The Varieties of New Testament Religion*,
understood the contradictions in the New Testament as a basis for
confessional relativism and denominational pluralism.[1] Others
have asserted that contradictions are to be overcome by seeing
the canonical scriptures as part of the emergence of catholic
tradition, allowing for variation and organic development. In
opposition to this Ernst Käsemann has emphatically insisted that
the gospel is the center of the canon and has used it in relentless
critique of all which is opposed to it, however firm its place in
the canon.

---

[1]E. F. Scott, *The Varieties of New Testament Religion*
(New York: Scribners, 1944).

In view of the importance of the problem of contradictions
in the Bible, one might expect that its history would already
have been investigated. However, there is little literature on
this topic, although the question of contradictions in Scripture
has been discussed almost as long as the canon itself has existed.
At the time of the definitive fixing of the Jewish canon, rabbis
discussed, among other things, the possibility that Ezekiel
contradicted the Pentateuch and that contradictions existed in
Proverbs and Ecclesiastes. Marcion and others rejected the Old
Testament writings on the grounds that they were self-contradictory
and opposed to the gospel. Church fathers such as Irenaeus and
Tertullian energetically opposed him and sought to prove the inner
unity of the two testaments. A unique compromise is known from
the pseudo-Clementine homilies. They assert that Moses and Christ
are in complete agreement, but at the same time concede that
the Pentateuch contains contradictions and falsehoods. This they
explain by the theory that false pericopes came into the Law in
the course of its oral transmission.

The question of contradictions also plays a role in the
discussion about which New Testament writings were canonical.
Shortly after 200, the otherwise orthodox Roman, Gaius, rejected
the Gospel of John and the Book of Revelation on the grounds that
these writings stood in opposition to the other Gospels and to the
letters of Paul. To refute Gaius, Hippolytus wrote at least one
reply explaining the disagreements. Like many other theological
polemicists, Hippolytus seems to have misrepresented the position
of his opponent.[2]

The discussions about the extent of the canon show that
both Jews and Christians thought that the Holy Scriptures could
contain no irreconcilable contradictions. But the discussions

---

[2]According to Hippolytus, Gaius believed that it was the
heretic Cerinthus who wrote the Fourth Gospel and the Apocalypse.
This assertion of Hippolytus is constantly repeated. But from
a fragment preserved by Eusebius (*Hist. Eccl*. III, 28.2) it
seems probable that Gaius said only that Cerinthus lied when he
introduced the revelation in the Apocalypse as written by a great
apostle, and as given to him (the apostle) by angels. This is
confirmed by excerpts from Dionysius of Alexandria who was probably
also dependent on Gaius (*Ibid*. VII, 25.2). The fragments of
Gaius' writing which were preserved by Dionysius bar Salibi and,
without naming him, by Epiphanius, show that Gaius attacked the
apostolic and canonical character of John and Revelation. Cerinthus
was probably mentioned only incidentally; like the Montanists,
Cerinthus had cited the Apocalypse as support for his chiliastic
fantasies. A more detailed investigation is being prepared by
J. D. Smith.

also reveal that there was an awareness of contradictions and that attempts were made to deal with them. The assumption that an apparent contradiction requires explanation opened the way to creative exegetical endeavor. A classic example of this is the question, familiar from the Gospels, of how the Messiah could be David's son if David himself calls him Lord (Mark 12:35-37 par.). The answer is not made explicit but is clearly to be found in the identification of the Lord at the right hand of God with Jesus of Nazareth, who is of David's family. In several places Paul deals with contradictory passages in Scripture which refer to Israel and to Gentiles or to the promise and to the Law. My own interest in this problem and its history was awakened particularly by his argument in the third chapter of the epistle to the Galatians. Here Paul cites Hab. 2:4, "But the righteous shall live by his faith" (or as Paul understands, "He who through faith is righteous shall live"). To this he opposes Lev. 18:5 which says about the commandments of the Mosaic Law, "For the man who does these things will live through them...," i.e., he shall have life in them.

The Jewish scholar Hans Joachim Schoeps has recognized that Paul's discussion of these two passages must be understood against the background of the treatment of contradictory scriptural passages in contemporary Jewish hermeneutics.[3] But Schoeps neglects to investigate the latter closely enough, and consequently what he says about rabbinic hermeneutics in this connection is as unreliable as his exegesis of Paul. The pertinent hermeneutical rule is the last of R. Ishmael's 13 *middoth*, or hermeneutical principles. Schoeps renders it, paraphrasing freely, "If two verses contradict one another, one seeks a third to set aside the contradiction." This rendering relies upon a widespread traditional understanding of the rule which is untenable for two reasons.

First, as was already noted by Prof. Adolf Schwarz at the beginning of this century,[4] the rule thus interpreted is not in accord with the usual rabbinic practice. Normally an apparent contradiction is resolved by means of an exegetical distinction. It is assumed that the two contradictory statements refer to

---

[3]*Paul: The Theology of the Apostle in the Light of Jewish Religious History*, tr. by H. Knight, Philadelphia: Westminster, 1961, pp. 177f.

[4]A. Schwarz, *Die hermeneutische Antinomie,* Wien/Leipzig: A. Möller, 1913. Like other works of this scholar, this investigation has played only a small role in later discussion. This is understandable in view of Schwarz's inclination to uncertain, partly fantastic hypotheses. The correct conclusions were drawn from his data by V. Aptowitzer in a review in *MGWJ*, n.f. 24 (1916)

different things, or that they apply under different circumstances.
Only in exceptional cases is a third statement introduced to
resolve the conflict. Second, the traditional interpretation is
also unsupported by the text of the rule. Literally translated
the rule says, "Two scriptural passages which contradict one
another until a third passage comes and decides between them."
The formulation merely declares in what case the rule holds,
without describing how to resolve the conflict. An older, more
complete formulation known from the tannaitic midrashim, where
it is ascribed to R. Akiba, but which also occurs in the traditions
of the school of Ishmael makes clear how to deal with the two
biblical passages: "Two scriptural passages which correspond to
one another yet conflict with one another, should be upheld in
their place until a third passage comes and decides between them."[5]

Thus the basic rule is that the two scriptural passages
should be upheld, each in its place; i.e., they should be so
interpreted that they do not negate one another, but rather both
remain valid, each with a specific meaning within its own context.
The third passage is mentioned only in a subordinate clause
which adds a condition: the resolution of a conflict between
two scriptural passages on the basis of contextual exegesis must
be abandoned if it turns out that a third passage requires another
resolution of the conflict.

One of Hillel's famous antinomies best illustrates the
application of the basic rule and this condition.[6] Concerning
the Passover sacrifice, Exod. 12:5 states: "From the sheep and
the goats shall you take it." But Deut. 16:2 says, "And you
shall slaughter the Passover for the Lord your God, sheep and
cattle, in the place where the Lord will choose that his name
dwell." The narrative in 2 Chron. 35 seems to take both regulations into consideration since King Josiah gives 3000 lambs and
kids for the Passover sacrifice - in addition to cattle for holy
sacrifice, which were cooked and distributed to the poeple. But

---

[5]Mekilta, Pisha 4 (ed. Lauterbach, I, 32) on Exod. 12:5;
Sifre Num. 58 on Num. 7:89.

[6]Palestinian Talmud, Pesahim 6:1 (33a). The tradition
refers to three exegetical problems which caused Hillel to come
from Babylonia to Palestine. Another of the three problems was
an antinomy between Exod. 12:15 and Deut. 16:8, which Hillel
resolved by giving proof for the Pharisaic dating of the day when
the first sheaf of grain was offered and thus for Pentecost (Lev.
23:10-16). The third question concerned the interpretation of
Lev. 13:37: "He is clean and the priest shall pronounce him clean."
Such double statements in a single text were often discussed in
the same way as antinomies between two texts.

the parallel account in the apocryphal Greek book of Ezra differs
from this, making no explicit distinction between small cattle
and large (1 Esdras 1:6-13). A certain Ezekiel reworked the Exodus
narrative as a tragedy in Greek style and had God explicitly give
Moses the command that the Passover sacrifice should be both sheep
and cattle.[7] Thus here the two prescriptions are harmonized in
that the rule in Exodus is combined with the more encompassing
rule in Deuteronomy. This solution is rejected by Hillel. To our
knowledge he was the first to formulate with full consciousness
the exegetical problem of how one can uphold two texts which
differ from one another. He resolved the antinomy through a
distinction: Exod. 12 refers to the Passover lamb while Deut.
16, which also permits large cattle, does not refer to the Passover
lamb, but rather to the festal sacrifice for Passover (the Hagigah).

Hillel's solution was generally accepted. However, the
tannaim continued to discuss the problem on an academic level.
An obvious objection could be made to Hillel's solution. Exod.
12 contains a series of regulations which applied only to the
first Passover in Egypt, e.g., the command to paint blood on
the doorposts. If the two contradictory scriptural passages were
supposed to be interpreted in their own contexts, it could be
argued that the command to take a lamb or a kid applied only to
the first Passover in Egypt, while Deut. 16 contained the regulations for the Passover celebration in the following generations.

I assume that this line of argument was purely scholastic
in character, but it had to be refuted. A series of counter-
arguments was adduced, based either on the exact wording of Exod.
12:5 or on supporting texts. It is in this connection that R.
Akiba quotes in its full form the rule about two scriptural passages
which contradict one another.[8] He finds the decisive third passage
in Exod. 12:21: "Choose and take sheep for yourselves according
to your families and slaughter for the Passover." Thus the
clause, "Until a third passage comes and decides between them,"
is used when an antinomy admits to more than one solution. It
serves as legitimation for departing from a solution which

---

[7]Eusebius, *Praep. Ev.* IX, 29.13.
[8]Mekilta Pisḥa 4. Other arguments were attributed
to R. Ishmael and his pupils R. Josia and R. Jonathan, while two
different proofs were ascribed to R. Eliezer b. Hyrcanus (Lauterbach I, 30-32). In the interpretation of Deut. 16:12 two variants
occur. It is either assumed that the text as a whole concerns
the festal sacrifice, or that it speaks both about the Passover
lamb taken from the small cattle and about the festal sacrifice
taken from the large cattle. See J. Z. Lauterbach, *Mekilta de-
Rabbi Ishmael*, (Philadelphia: Jewish Publication Society, 1949)
I, 30-33.

contextual arguments could support.[9] The stipulation is probably
a later addition which presupposes learned discussions in the
rabbinic academies. The basic rule is that two scriptural
passages contradicting one another should be upheld with the help
of a distinction in the interpretation of the two contexts. In
this form - without the additional stipulation - the rule corresponds to Hillel's practice, and certain indications suggest that
Schwarz was right in his assumption that the formulation of the
basic rule also goes back to Hillel.[10]

In any case it is only the basic rule which can be
presumed to have been known and used at the time of Paul. Thus
the task which confronted an exegete when he encountered an
apparent contradiction in Scripture was not to find a third
passage which could resolve this conflict. It was necessary first
to establish which text contained the valid halakah, the correct
statement, or the fundamental teaching. Then it was requisite to
find a satisfactory explanation of the conflicting text to maintain
its validity. This is clear from the typical rabbinic formulation
of the problem: "One scriptural passage says..., but another
passage says, ... How are both of these passages to be upheld?"
It is also evident in controversies, e.g., between Pharisees and
Sadducees, where the participants take opposing positions and
both can adduce scriptural passages as the basis for their argument. The one who could show the probative force of his own text
and at the same time explain the text of his opponent prevailed
in the discussion. A good example of this is found in the
controversy between the Pharisees and Jesus about divorce -
especially as it is presented in Matt. 19:3-9. Jesus answers
the question about divorce by referring to the story of creation
(Gen. 1:27 and 2:24), but can also explain why Moses commanded
the writ of divorce (Deut. 24:1): it was on account of their
hardness of heart.

---

[9]See also Sifre Num. 58, Mekilta Bahodesh 9 on Exod. 20:
22, and Sifre Lev. 16:1 (Weiss 79b). No other references to a
third, deciding scriptural passage seem to occur in tannaitic
traditions.   The use of references to Scripture to support the
interpretation of one of the contradictory passages is something
different.
[10]According to Jewish scholars of the twelfth century
(Abraham b. David, Hillel b. Elyakim and the Karaite Judah
Hadassi) the fourth of Hillel's seven hermeneutical rules was
simply "two scriptural passages." This is probably right - and
other textual variants are corrupt. It makes far more sense that
Hillel's fourth rule be a rule for two contradictory texts, than
that it be a second rule for *Binyan ab;* according to the standard
texts, Hillel's third and fourth rules deal with the derivation
of an interpretation from one and from two scriptural passages
respectively.

In rabbinic literature there is a whole series of examples of the discussion of scriptural passages which contradict one another. Gradually, it became a kind of game to detect contradictions and to find explanations for them. This led to the discovery in Scripture of a series of legal rules, historical explanations and theological teachings which were not directly expressed; they had to be presupposed if seeming contradictions were to find a satisfactory explanation. In this way the study of contradictory statements in Scripture became an important factor in the steady growth of halakah and haggadah. Most of the rabbinic material dates from the second century after Christ or even later. However, it can be shown indirectly that the question of contradictions in Scripture must already have been discussed to a considerable extent at the time of Paul, as is evident even from the sparse traditions about Hillel and his immediate followers.

Harmonization of dissimilar religious traditions certainly took place at all times in the history of Israel. Only when the canon was defined and the text substantially fixed did the problem arise of how to maintain two scriptural passages which contradict one another. Even when the Pentateuch and eventually also other writings had achieved canonical status, the problem still did not arise immediately and everywhere. The exegetes of the Qumran sect, for example, seem not to have been interested in questions of this kind. Methodical discussion of contradictions in Scripture presupposes not only the existence of Holy Scriptures, but also contact with Greek philosophy and scientific method. The encounter with Hellenistic culture sharpened the problems and furnished the means of mastering them through logical distinctions and dialectic.

Biblical monotheism made a strong impression on many outsiders. Hellenistically educated Jews found support for their faith when they saw that the philosophers agreed with Moses, although they had not perceived the truth about the *one* God as clearly as he had. However, at the same time Moses could speak of God with anthropomorphic expressions and make use of mythopoetic language which agreed neither with reason nor with his own teaching. How could it be said, for example, that God descended on Mount Sinai when he is present everywhere? Or how can it be said that God rested on the seventh day since both nature and the Scriptures show that he is constantly active?

The first author known to have concerned himself with
questions of this sort was the Jewish philosopher Aristobulus,
who dedicated an apologetic work to Ptolemy VI Philometor (181-
146 BC).[11] Later, questions of this kind appear again and again
both in Philo and in the rabbis. According to the Letter of
Aristeas, the Alexandrian delegation in Jerusalem raised the
question of how, if creation is one, some animals could be
considered unclean and therefore not to be eaten or even touched.
The High Priest answered by explaining that the laws of ritual
purity served a pedagogical purpose. They served to keep Israel
separate and contained moral instruction in allegorical form.[12]

More than the rabbis, the Jewish exegetes in Alexandria
tended to explain contradictions in Scripture by means of
allegorical interpretation. In this respect the allegorical
interpretation of internal contradictions in Homer, as it was
practiced by Alexandrian scholars, served as a model. But the
contrast between Alexandrian allegorism and Palestinian literalism
should not be overstressed. It may be more important that both
Philo and his predecessors and Hillel and his successors deal
with the problem of conflicting scriptural passages, while this
problem is unknown to the Teacher of Righteousness and to other
exegetes in the Qumran community. Allegorical interpretation
was neither unknown in Palestine nor the sole order of the day
in Alexandria. Several times Philo mentions interpreters who
tried to explain all the disagreements in the laws without seeking
any deeper meaning in the text. These interpreters evidently
discussed problems like those which the Palestinian rabbis tried
to solve. Philo himself has little use for their sagacity. In
his systematic exposition of the laws he usually passes over legal
antinomies or tacitly harmonizes them.

There are two scriptural passages which Philo repeatedly
contrasts with one another in a formal antithesis: Num. 23:19
and Deut. 8:5. These are almost always cited in abbreviated form
so that the contrast emerges. sharply. The first passage says
"God is not like a man;" the second, on the contrary, says "like
a man (God educates his son)." Philo designates these two statements as the chief summaries (*kephalaia*) of Scripture.

---

[11]Cf. N. Walter, *Der Thoraausleger Aristobulos* (TU, 86),
Berlin: Akademieverlag, 1964. The most important fragments are
preserved in Eusebius, *Praep. Ev.* VIII, 10 and XIII, 12.
[12]Letter of Aristeas 129f.

He uses them as a hermeneutical key to the explantion of other contradictions in the laws.[13] The truth is that God is not like a man, and neither is he like the world or anything else. But it is only "friends of the soul" who are able to grasp this truth in its purity. Therefore God is portrayed in Scripture like a man: with hands and eyes, ascending and descending, and with human emotions like anger, envy and remorse. This portrayal is a pedagogical device, intended for those who cannot free themselves from the corporeal. They need elementary instruction about God in simple terms.

Philo is full of praise for the wisdom of Moses. As the best of lawgivers he cared for all for whom he legislated - both for those who could perceive the truth about God and for those who had need of elementary instruction and firm discipline. It was precisely with the latter in view that Moses portrayed God as a man who educates and disciplines his son. The verb *paideuein* can, as is well known, express both. Once Philo even uses the image of a doctor who must tell a lie in order to prevent his patients' being discouraged and thereby worsening their condition. The lie makes the patients willing to submit to a painful treatment.[14] This is a surprising image, implying as it does that there are lies in Scripture. I can understand it only as an apologetic argument directed against those Jews who asserted that the Law of Moses contained falsehoods and therefore rejected it, wholly or partly. Philo answers by agreeing that there are falsehoods in the laws, but he emphasizes that they are useful lies, fully justified in pedagogical and therapeutic terms.

A careful analysis shows that the idea of "white lies" is a secondary development of the image of the doctor who must cause his patients pain in order to heal them, just as a master must educate a bad slave with threats and punishment. This indicates that the resolution of the conflict between "God is not like a man" and "like a man" was not originally related to true and mythopoetic language about God; Philo has adapted the discussion of the summaries to bear on this problem, which was his particular concern. This is also indicated by his statement that the distinction between "like a man" and "not like a man" corresponds to the distinction between "fear of God" and "love for him." Further, it should be kept in mind that ordinarily the Ten

---

[13]The chief text is *Deus imm.* 51-73; cf. among others *QG* I 55; II 54; *Sacr.* 89-101; *Conf.* 96-101; *Somn.* I 233-237.
[14]*Deus imm.* 64-66.

Commandments are called "summaries" of the Law. The texts designated as the chief summaries must therefore stand in some
relation to the Ten Commandments; if so, however, they can
hardly refer primarily to the use or absence of anthropomorphisms.

The original idea underlying these chief summaries is
evident from the full text and context of the scriptural passages
in which they are found, more clearly in Hebrew than in Greek.
Num. 23:19 deals with God's gracious and unalterable purpose:
"God is not a man that he should lie, nor a son of man that he
should repent of anything." Deut. 8:5 speaks of his educative
discipline: "that the Lord your God educates you, as a man
educates his son." It is no accident that the fullest discussion
of the two summaries occurs in Philo's commentary on Gen. 6:6-8.
The judgment on the generation of the flood illustrates God's
educative discipline; the salvation of Noah and his family
illustrates his unalterable salvific purpose.

The Septuagint, which translates both Num. 23:19 and Gen.
6:6-7 in free paraphrase, avoids the statement that the Lord
regretted the creation of man. In spite of this, Philo explicitly
deals with the question: does God regret or change his mind?
This indicates that he is making use of a tradition which ultimately
goes back to a Hebrew midrash which dealt with the opposition
between Gen. 6:6-7 "The Lord regretted" and Num. 23:19 "God is
not a man that he should lie, nor a son of man that he should
regret anything."

In any case, there are indications which suggest that the
distinction between the two summaries, "God is not like a man"
and "like a man", was originally related to the distinction between
what Philo calls the two powers of God and the rabbis call his two
measures, namely kindness and punishment or mercy and judgment.[15]
Philo adapted the discussion of the two summaries, bringing them
to bear on the problems facing the Jews in Alexandria. But the
material which he has adapted forms an early stage of the discussion
among the rabbis about the relationship between judgment and mercy,
or fear and love.

---

[15]While the rabbis connected mercy with the Tetragrammaton
and judgment with the divine name *Elohim*, Philo presupposes a
tradition which said the opposite. In neither case could they be
separated absolutely, and in one sense that was the main point:
the gracious God is just, and the God who judges is merciful.
This was evident from the inconsistent use of the names for God
in Scripture. Greater use of the materials in Philo might have
confirmed the principal thesis of H. Ljungmann, *Guds barmhärtighet
och dom* (Lund: Gleerup, 1950).

With reference to Paul, the texts of Philo are especially interesting because they discuss problems in a literary fashion preserving the complexity of the arguments. The rabbinic traditions point out antithetical scriptural passages and give the exegetical solution to the conflict. And there is a pertinent similarity between Philo's exposition in "On the unchangeability of God" and Paul's in Galatians 3. The similarity is all the more interesting because there is no question of any historical connection between the two. In both cases, it is not merely isolated scriptural passages which stand in opposition to one another, but rather opposing principles, both of which have their place in Scripture, although only one of them contains the real teaching of Scripture. For Philo Num. 23:19 contains the truth, while Deut. 8:5 summarizes the pedagogical aspect of the Law. For Paul the truth lies in the Habakkuk passage "to live by faith," while Lev. 18:5 refers to the function of the Law as a guardian of children.

A formal similarity is especially notable; the important scriptural passages are summarized in short catch phrases, for Philo "not like a man" and "like a man," for Paul "by faith" (*ek pisteōs*) and "by works of the law" (*ex ergon nomou*). The Pauline formulas are best understood as abbreviations for "The righteous shall live by faith" and "He who does them shall live by them." This kind of abbreviation has a still closer analogy in the rabbis who applied the formulas "out of fear" and "out of love" to human acts depending on whether they conformed to the commandments to fear God or to love him.[16]

With respect to hermeneutical terminology and method, Paul is much closer to the rabbis than to Philo. This could be illustrated from many details of Gal. 3.[17] But what is most important is that the argument becomes clear and comprehensible when it is interpreted in the light of the treatment of conflicting scriptural passages in contemporary Jewish hermeneutics. The interpretation of Scripture is interspersed with expressions of

---

[16]Relevant material e.g. in R. Sander, *Furcht und Liebe im palästinischen Spätjudentum* (Stuttgart: Kohlhammer, 1935).

[17]Cf. for example the personification of Scripture in v.8 and v. 22, the formulation "it does not say..., but...," and the epexegetical "This is (the) Christ" in v. 16. In v. 17 Paul presupposes the usual rabbinic explanation for the contrast between Gen. 15:13 (400 years) and Exod. 12:41 (430 years). The first number, which applied to Abraham's offspring, is reckoned from the birth of Isaac; the other number is reckoned from the "covenant between the pieces" in Gen. 15. Paul has the latter in mind when he speaks of a legally valid covenant in Gal. 3:15-18.

dismay at the new direction taken by the Christians in Galatia,
combined with reminders of what they experienced when they first
came to faith (Gal. 3:1-5; 4:6-11). Paul's thesis is that those
who have heard the preaching of faith and received the Holy
Spirit no longer stand under the Law. What happened to them
corresponds exactly to what happened to Abraham: "Abraham
believed in God, and it was reckoned to him as righteousness"
(Gal. 3:6; cf. Gen. 15:6). From this Paul draws the conclusion
that those who are "of faith" are sons of Abraham. For Paul, the
promise that in Abraham all the nations shall be blessed proves
that this also holds true for Gentiles (Gal. 3:8-9; cf. Gen. 12:3
etc., as understood at the time of Paul).

Paul concludes *e contrario* that since only those who are
of faith (*ek pisteōs*) are blessed, those who rely on the works
of the Law stand under the condemnation of those who do not keep
all of it (Gal. 3:10; cf. Deut. 27:26). Thus, Paul presupposes
that those under the Law can only incur its curse; they cannot
receive its blessings (Deut. 28:1-14). For this view, he provides
another scriptural proof. According to Hab. 2:4, the righteous
shall live by faith; therefore, the opposite principle cannot
also be valid at the same time - and righteousness, life and
blessing cannot be dependent on doing all the things which the
Law prescribes (Lev. 18:5). The whole train of thought in Gal.
3:1-12 rests on the presupposition that Hab. 2:4 and Lev. 18:5
contradict one another, and that the two corresponding principles
"by faith" and "by (works of) the law" mutually exclude one
another as qualifications for justification and life.[18]

A pious Jew would see no contradiction here: for him,
keeping the commandments is part of genuine faith. This was
certainly also Paul's view in his Pharisaic past. But as a
Christian, he identified the faith spoken about in Scripture with
faith in the crucified Messiah, Jesus, who hung on the tree under
the curse of the Law. Because of this, the contradiction is
complete. The conviction that faith in the crucified Messiah is
incompatible with the enduring validity of the Law made Paul a
persecutor of Christians in his early life; and he held fast to
this conviction as an apostle.

---

[18]Like Gal. 2:16d, Gal. 3:11a is a paraphrase of Psalm
143:2. The apparent contradiction between this passage and Hab.
2:4 and Gen. 15:6 is resolved by means of an exegetical clarification: Psalm 143:2 is not to be taken absolutely, but means
that "by works of the Law" or "in the Law" no one is justified
before God. Cf. Rom. 1:17 and 3:20.

Paul is confronted by the problem that Hab. 2:4 and
Lev. 18:5 are analogous; both explain how a man shall live, i.e.,
partake of the real life which God gives to the one whom he regards
as justified.   But at the same time the two passages contradict
one another, for the one says "by faith" and the other says "who
keeps the commandments," i.e., "by works of the law." While the
one passage corresponds to the promise which was given to Abraham
who had faith, the other states the basic principle of the Law
given at Sinai.   Thus Paul must solve the problem of how it is
possible to uphold the two passages which contradict one another
so that each, promise and Law, can take the place which is due
it according to Scripture. In accordance with the usual method
of discussing contradictions between scriptural passages, Paul
begins by determining which is valid (Gal. 3:13-18), in order
that he may then explain how to resolve the apparent contradiction
(Gal. 3:19-25). Here I can only briefly present my interpretation
of these much debated verses.

The key to the understanding of vv. 13-14 lies in the
recognition that the words of 14a: "That the blessing of Abraham
might come upon the Gentiles in Christ Jesus," are a paraphrase
of God's oath to Abraham after the offering of his son Isaac:
"In your offspring shall all the peoples of the earth be blessed"
(Gen. 22:18). The expression "the blessing of Abraham" comes
from Gen. 28:4, and the words "in Christ Jesus" have been inserted
in place of "in your offspring."[19] The messianic interpretation
of "offspring" derives from an analogy with Nathan's promise to
David; in 2 Sam. 7:12 "your offspring" was understood as a
designation of the Messiah.

The statement in v. 13 that Christ was made a curse on our
behalf derives from a combination of the statement in Deut. 21:23
that the one who hangs on a tree is cursed with the report in
Gen. 22 about the ram that was caught in a shrub and offered in
place of Isaac. Here Paul makes use of an old Jewish Christian
midrash which understood the crucifixion in light of Genesis 22.
Paul's use of the midrash reveals his concern that the Law has
not been arbitrarily set aside. Through Christ's vicarious
bearing of the curse, a legal redemption has occurred. God's
promise to Abraham has been fulfilled. The Gentiles have partaken
of the blessing in Jesus Christ since they have received the

---

[19]Already in Gal. 3:14 Paul presupposes the messianic
interpretation of "Abraham's offspring" which he sets forth in
3:16. See chapter VIII note 12 and *The Crucified Messiah*, 153f.

Spirit through faith.[20]

In vv. 15-18 Paul asserts that the Law cannot make the
promise invalid. As proof he uses an analogy with the law governing inheritance and wills. If the Law were a codicil added to
God's covenant with Abraham, it would annul the validity of the
whole covenant, and that cannot have been its intent. The
analogy raises some legal questions, but it is clear that Paul
is asserting that the promise - and therefore also the words "by
faith" - have an unconditional validity which the Law does not
abrogate.

The real problem in discussing two contradictory scriptural
passages is explaining how to interpret the other, differing
statement. Paul addresses this problem when he asks: "Why then
the law?" (v. 19). The answer is that it was given on account
of transgressions, as a temporary provision "until the offspring
should come, to whom the promise applies." Here again Paul seems
to make use of a Jewish Christian messianic testimony. As was
the case in v. 16 and even in v. 14, "offspring" is understood
as a designation of the Messiah. The words *achris hou elthē...hō*
(until the one should come...to whom) come from the oracle
concerning Judah in Gen. 49:10, understood messianically, and
read *ʿad kî yābōʾ še-lô.*

In order to understand Paul's application of the phrase,
however, it is even more important to note that similar formulations
were used in connection with prescriptions and decrees which were
in principle only provisional. They would be valid only "until
a priest with Urim and Thummin should arrive" or "until a trustworthy prophet should arise" or "until the prophet and the anointed
ones of Aaron and Israel come."[21]

What is radical in Paul's argument is that he understands
the entire Law of Moses itself as such a provisional, interim

---

[20]By means of the appended clause in Gal. 3:14b, Paul
blurs the distinction between "us," the Israelites, and the
Gentile nations in 3:13-14a. He equates the blessing of Abraham
with the Spirit which even Gentiles have received (cf. 3:5-9) and
takes redemption from the curse of the Law to imply freedom from
the Law itself (cf. 3:10-21; 4:5-6). Paul's whole argumentation
in Galatians 3 is based upon two premises: 1. God's promises
to Abraham, including the oath in Gen. 22:18, pertain to the
crucified Christ, through whom Gentiles were made partakers of
the promised blessing. 2. For this reason, the statements in
Lev. 18:5 and Hab. 2:4 are mutually exclusive and must have
different functions. On the basis of these presuppositions, Paul
can draw the inference that only the covenantal curses, and not
the blessings, apply to those who are under the Law (Gal. 3:10).
[21]See Neh. 7:65 (Ezra 2:63); 1 Macc. 14:41; cf. 4:46;
1 QS 9:10f.; cf. CD 6:10f.; 12:23f.; 20:1.

arrangement, valid only for pre-messianic times. He further
develops this understanding in Gal. 3:23-25 and 4:1-6. Paul
stresses the provisional character of the Law when he says that
it was given by angels through a mediator (v. 19c). This indicates
that the Law was not an enduringly valid expression of God's
will. But the text is completely misunderstood when, as some
exegetes believe, the angels are thought to be hostile to God.
The logical subject of the passive construction is God; he gave
the Law.[22] Moses as mediator must take account of both parties -
both God and the people. But if both the promise and the Law
derive from the same God, then the idea that the Law is a provisional enactment does not give a satisfactory answer to the
problem of the contradiction in Scripture. Paul sharply formulates
this problem in the question: "Is the law then contrary to the
promises?" (v. 21a).

Paul emphatically rejects the possibility of a conflict
between the Law and the promises. He first inserts an explanatory
observation: "If a law had been given which would make alive,
then righteousness would indeed be from the law." In that case,
Scripture would have contained two incompatible teachings about
justification and life. But even as the Law cannot be understood
as a restrictive clause added to the promise (v. 15-18), neither
can it be understood as a provisional arrangement so that "by
faith" would be valid for Abraham and for the time of the Messiah,
while "by the Law" and therefore "by works of the Law" would be
valid for the time between Moses and Christ. The unity of the
will and purpose of the one God excludes such a duality.

Thus a real contradiction would have existed only if the
Law had been able to lead to justification and life. Paul asserts
that it was unable to do this and that this was never even God's
intention for it. The Law served another purpose: "Scripture

---

[22]The interpretation of Gal. 3:20 remains difficult, but
the context excludes interpretations that would make Paul deny
that God is the ultimate originator of the Law. In that I agree
with R. Bring, even if I am not able to follow the exegesis of
Galatians 3 which he has set forth in several works, including
Commentary on Galatians (Philadelphia: Muhlenberg, 1961) and
"Der Mittler und das Gesetz," *KD* 12 (1966) 292-302. On the
syntactical construction, see E. Bammel, "Gottes *diathēkē* (Gal.
III.15ff.) und das jüdische Rechtsdenken," *NTS* 6 (1960) 317,
n. 5; A. Giblin, "Three Monotheistic Texts in Paul," *CBQ* 37 (1975)
540-541. For a full survey of the discussion and a fresh proposal,
see T. D. Callan, *The Law and the Mediator* (Diss., Yale, 1976).
While Callan has not fully succeeded in solving the enigma, his
proposal may point in the right direction, see esp. p. 214: "Thus
Ga 3:20a is a parenthetical explicative comment on Moses' mediation
of the Law seen in terms of Ex 32-4."

consigned all things to sin, that what was promised to faith in
Jesus Christ might be given to those who believe" (v. 22). Thus
Paul finds no contradiction here. Rightly understood, the Law
is in harmony with the promises. It had a subordinate function
which contributed to the realization of the promises.

It is important to note that it is not the Law, but
rather Scripture which is the subject of the statement in v. 22.
The Law is not a self-contained entity but rather a part of
Scripture. It consigned all things to sin by ordaining the Law
and demanding works (Lev. 18:51). In Romans, Paul explains more
fully that the Law transformed sin into culpable transgression
and in this way increased it. In Galatians he emphasizes that
the function of the Law was subordinate to what was, according
to Scripture, God's real aim - that the promise should be fulfilled
and that those who belong to Christ should partake of it "by
faith." The idea that the Law had an interim, negative, preparatory function is expressed in the statement that it was a
paidagōgos eis Christon (custodian until Christ came); it is to
be compared to guardians and trustees who watch over the heir
until he come of age at some definite time. To assert the validity
of the Law after Christ has come is, for Paul, not to uphold the
Law, but rather to misuse it, to contradict the intention of the
lawgiver. Though Paul goes on to apply the argument to the
situation in Galatia (Gal. 3:23-4:6), I shall not follow the
Apostle further, but will draw a few conclusions concerning our
main problem.

Contradictions in Scripture are an old hermeneutical
problem - discussed by the rabbis since Hillel. This problem was
well known to Philo and to his predecessors, learned Jews of
Alexandria. Paul is certainly not the first Christian exegete
who concerned himself with it. But in connection with his doctrine
of justification through faith, the problem received special
emphasis. The argument in Gal. 3 follows in an independent way
the usual pattern for the discussion of two scriptural passages
which correspond to, yet contradict, one another. The promises
to Abraham and the statement in Scripture that it is faith by
which the righteous shall live are upheld uncurtailed. But the
Law and its basic principle - that those who keep the commandments
shall live by them - are also upheld. The Law was neither a
clause added to the promise, nor a temporary substitute for it.
In spite of the contradiction between the Law and the promise,
or rather precisely because of this contradiction, the Law

contributed to the fulfillment of the promise in Christ, "by
faith" and not "by works of the Law." Precisely the necessity
of preserving the freedom of the believer from the Law requires
Paul to explain its role in Scripture.[23]

In no other place does Paul deviate more from the views
of the rabbis. But in no other place is his style of argumentation
more similar to that of the rabbis than in Galatians 3. After all,
this follows logically; for if it is first proved that those who
have been baptized in Christ and have received the spirit no longer
stand under the Law, then the necessity for a halakic interpretation of individual commandments disappears.

Thus my investigation confirms Olof Linton's thesis that
Paul used legal arguments precisely to assert freedom from the
Law.[24] In recent years scholars, especially Germans, have
discussed whether Paul in Gal. 3 (and Romans 4) outlines "salvation
history" or gives an "existential interpretation" of the promise
to Abraham.[25] This modern statement of alternatives is false.
Paul is concerned not with a choice between objective salvation
history and the individual's understanding of his existence, but
rather with a correlation between the situation in a mission
congregation and the witness of Scripture. Events of the recent
past and of the present - the coming of Jesus, his death and
resurrection, the mission to the Gentiles and the outpouring of
the Holy Spirit - are explained on the basis of Scripture, and
Paul interprets Scripture in the light of these occurrences.

Since Paul as an apostle identifies the faith which is
proclaimed in Scripture with faith in the crucified Messiah,
Jesus Christ, he sees a contradiction between Christ and the Law,
between faith and works, between Hab. 2:4 and Lev. 18:5. Jewish
scholars especially have noted that in a passage like Gal. 3 Paul
makes use of an idea of "the Law" which sharply deviates from the
rabbinic understanding of the Torah as the life-giving revelation
of God. From this, however, these scholars draw the incorrect
conclusion that Paul cannot have been very familiar with the
Jewish understanding of Torah.

---

[23]The ideas in Galatians 3 are, consequently, supplemented by what Paul says in Gal. 5:13-14, 18 and 23; cf. Rom.
8:4; 13:8-10.

[24]"Paulus och juridiken," *STK* 21 (1945) 173-165. It
is unfortunate that this important article on "Paul and law"
(in the wide sense of the term) has never been made available
to an international public.

[25]On this problem see esp. G. Klein, "Individualgeschichte
und Weltgeschichte bei Paulus," *EvT* 24 (1964) 126-165.

Faith in the crucified Christ altered Paul's understanding
both of the Law and of the promises. Because Paul understood it
to be the antithesis to Christ and faith, the Law of Sinai was
isolated from promise and covenant and understood one-sidedly,
on the basis of Lev. 18:5, as saying that life is to be gained by
keeping the commandments. In this way Paul could maintain that
the Law, in spite of the contradiction between it and the fulfilled
promise, nevertheless had its legitimate place in Scripture.[26]

The argument in Gal. 3 addresses the greatest problems
faced by the early church in its mission, i.e., the relationship
between Jews and Gentiles and the validity of the Mosaic Law for
believers in Christ who were not of Jewish origin. These questions
were discussed in a series of writings, some within and others
outside the New Testament, and were resolved in various ways.
Nevertheless, considerable agreement on Christian practice prevailed among the writings which have been accepted into the canon:
believing Gentiles were acknowledged as brothers and full members
of the church. It was not demanded that they let themselves be
circumcised or that they keep the ritual laws. However, Israel's
Holy Scriptures remain the Bible of the church and insofar as
the Law is summarized in the commandment of love (or in the two
great commandments), it remains the valid expression of the will
of God. Disagreement in practical matters occurs only on particular
points, such as eating meat offered to idols. In great measure
the situation of the early church is similar to that which we
find among the rabbis when, e.g., they almost unanimously accept
Hillel's halaka concerning the paschal sacrifice, while they have
different ways of supporting this view exegetically.

This is not without relevance for contemporary discussion
of conflicts in Scripture and among the churches. It shows that
agreement in matters of practice is not necessarily dependent
on agreement about exegetical questions and hermeneutical principles.

---

[26]This must be kept in mind in interpretations of Rom.
10:4: "Christ is the end (*telos*) of the law." In Rom. 10:4ff.
Paul treats Lev. 18:5 and Deut. 30:12-14 as conflicting scriptural passages. He takes Lev. 18:5 to be a statement which Moses
wrote in reference to the righteousness which is based upon the
Law. The diverging statement in Deut. 30:12-14, that the word
is near, is attributed to the righteousness based upon faith,
and taken to refer to Christ who is proclaimed in "the word of
faith." Since Deut. 30:12-14, no less than Lev. 18:5, refers
to God's commandment, Paul would here seem to have made a
distinction within the Old Testament concept of the Law. A
similar distinction may, possibly, be presupposed in Rom. 3:27;
cf. Gal. 6:2 and the variant reading in Gal. 3:19 (P46 and G d).

With respect to the relationship between Jews and Gentiles in the church and to the freedom of Gentile Christians from the individual prescriptions of the Law, other early Christian theologians reached conclusions similar to Paul's but in different ways. What is characteristic of the teaching of Paul is that he comes to his interpretation through clarification of the relationship between promise and Law, so that justification by faith stands in contrast to the rule that he who keeps the commandments lives by them. Even if he has the concrete Law of Moses in view the whole time, he moves toward reduction of the Law to a principle of justification and life through works. Later Augustine and Luther moved further in this direction.[27]

For them the question of the validity of the Law of Moses was no longer so important. The question of the relationship between the demand for works and the promise of grace in Scripture related to the salvation of the individual Christian was primary. But their concentration on the contrast between Law and gospel as the main point in the interpretation of Scripture was an extension of Paul's approach.[28]

---

[27]The problem of contradiction in Scripture is also discussed in other contexts than that of law and gospel. Several Church Fathers are, like Philo and other hellenized Jews before them, concerned with the contrast between true knowledge of God and the anthropomorphic expressions in Scripture. It is noteworthy that this problem is hardly mentioned in the New Testament.

[28]In his essay, "Trosrättfärdighet och lagens fullgörande," *STK* 45 (1969) 101-115, R. Bring criticized the original version of this study and restated his own interpretation of Galatians 3. He disputes that Paul sees a contradiction between Hab. 2:4 and Lev. 18:5. Without going into exegetical details, I will simply note that my interpretation of Gal. 3:10-12 was not a result of, but rather the starting point for, my work on Jewish hermeneutics.

CHAPTER X

THE ONE GOD OF JEWS AND GENTILES
(ROMANS 3:29-30)

In his commentary on the Epistle to the Romans, Ernst
Käsemann has placed the short paragraph Rom. 3:27-31 under the
heading: "Polemische Zuspitzung" (Polemical sharpening).[1] The
formulation is typical for Käsemann, who has both provoked and
stimulated his students and colleagues by his polemical sharpening
of questions and opinions. His polemic has had two chief targets:
on the one hand, any softening of Paul's doctrine that God
justifies the ungodly, and on the other, a purely anthropological
interpretation of the doctrine of justification. In both respects,
Käsemann can draw support from the brief series of questions and
answers in Rom. 3:27-31. Yet, his interpretation of the verses
needs to be supplemented and corrected, mainly because Käsemann
has failed to do justice to the target of Paul's polemic, the
imagined spokesman of Judaism.

The formulation "Polemical Sharpening" summarizes the
content of Rom. 3:27-31 in a correct but one-sided way. At the
conclusion, Paul states that he does not abrogate but upholds the
Law by his doctrine of justification. Käsemann himself understands
this as a transition to Paul's interpretation of the story of
Abraham in Rom. 4.[2] But the thesis in 3:27, that there is no
longer room for boasting (*kauchēsis*), already points forward to
chapter 4, where the treatment of the story of Abraham develops
the theme. Abraham is also the chief example, whose story warrants
the thesis that God justifies circumcised Jews and uncircumcised
Gentiles in the same way, by faith. Just in doing so, God proves

---

[1]*An die Römer*, 94.
[2]*Ibid.*, 97.

that he is the sovereign Creator who makes the dead alive.

As to the form, the questions and answers in Rom. 3:27-31 serve a double function. They comment on the preceding exposition of Paul's main thesis and prepare for the supporting argument from Scripture that follows. Even so, the verses sharpen what Paul has already stated in 1:16-17 and 3:21-26 by giving a polemical twist to his theses. This also applies to the concluding statement in 3:31. If Paul's contention that a person is justified by faith without works of the Law does uphold the validity of the Law, it follows *e contrario* that works of the Law do not (see Rom. 9:31). Käsemann is also right when he makes the following comment on Rom. 3:29-30: "Here the Apostle attacks Judaism on its own premises."[3] The question is whether Käsemann has given a correct description of those premises or not. The answer depends mainly on the meaning of some rabbinic passages. But before we turn to them, it may be useful to give a short, highly generalized sketch of Greek and Jewish monotheism.

Greek and Jewish Monotheism

In insisting that God is one, the Christians were in agreement with many educated Greeks and Romans as well as with the Jews. According to James 2:19 even the demons would agree. The formulation *heis theos* (one God) is well attested by inscriptions as well as in philosophical and theological literature. Erik Peterson, a learned scholar and one of Käsemann's teachers, has demonstrated that the formula can be used as an acclamation, in which the numeral has an elative meaning. It was possible to acclaim a god as being "one," i.e. unique, singular, without any denial of the existence of other gods.[4] In the Greek tradition, *heis theos* could also express a conceptual monotheism. This philosophical tradition can, at least, be traced back to the famous saying of Xenophanes (ca. 500 B.C.): "One God, greatest among gods and humans, in no way similar to mortals in either body or mind."[5]

---

[3] *Ibid.*, 96: "Der Apostel schlägt das Judentum von seinen eigenen Voraussetzungen aus."

[4] E. Peterson, *HEIS THEOS:* Epigraphische, formgeschichtliche und religionisgeschichtliche Untersuchungen (Göttingen: Vandenhoeck & Ruprecht, 1926) esp. 216-221, 227-236, 304-305.

[5] Quoted by Clement of Alexandria, *Strom.* V 109, cf. VII 22; H. Diels - W. Kranz, *Die Fragmente der Vorsokratiker* (Berlin: Weidmann, 1959), I,55, fr. 23. English translation e.g. in J. M. Robinson, *An Introduction to Early Greek Philosophy* (Boston: Houghton Mifflin, 1968), 3.33 and 35. On monotheistic trends in

The theme of unity and multiplicity pervades Greek
philosophy from its beginnings. The one God, or the divine One,
could be identified with the universe that encompasses all its
parts, in some form of pantheism, or be identified with the hidden
source and goal of all things. But the divine unity could also
be contrasted with the diversity and the conflicts in the world
of matter and of human beings. Occasionally, philosophical
monotheism could have a polemical note, as when Xenophanes mocked
the Ethiopians who made their gods snubnosed and black, or the
Thracians who made theirs gray-eyed and red-haired, thus rejecting
all anthropomorphic concepts and images. In general, however,
philosophical monotheism was tolerant and coexisted with religious
pluralism, polytheism, and worship of images. The one God of
the philosophers left room for the many gods of civil religion
and of cult associations. The traditional names of the gods
could either be taken to refer to the one God, who had many names,
or they could be interpreted as mythopoetic designations of the
many powers, who were the agents of his rule. Commenting on the
disagreements between the theologians of his day, the rhetorician
Maximus of Tyre (2nd. cent. A.D.) states: "In all of this war-
fare and uproar and disagreement you can see on all the earth
one generally accepted law and doctrine (*logos*), that there is
one God, king and father, and many gods, children (*paides*) of
God and co-rulers with God."[6]

If we turn to the Old Testament, we find a very different
picture. The formulation "one God" is not in common use, even
though it does occur, see Mal. 2:10: "Has not one God created
us?" The classical statement of Jewish monotheism, the "Hear,
O Israel" or *Shema*, does not speak of one God but of *YHWH ehad*,
later read as "one Lord," in Greek *heis kyrios*. The original
meaning may well have been: "YHWH is our God, YHWH alone."[7]
The oneness of God is not an inference from the unity of the
world, as it was among the Greeks. What is at stake is, much
more, the exclusive sovereignty of YHWH, the God of Israel, who
is the only God of his people and of the entire creation, and
who does not tolerate that any other god is worshiped beside
himself (see e.g. Deut. 32:39; Isa. 44:6; 45:9). The tension

Greek philosophy and religion, see e.g. M. P. Nilsson, *Greek Piety*
(Oxford: Clarendon, 1948, H. J. Rose, tr.) 115-124; A. J. Festu-
gière, *La révélation d'Hermès Trismégiste*, II. *Le Dieu cosmique*
(Paris: Gabalda, 1949).
      [6]See *Maximi Tyrii Philosophoumena* (ed. H. Hobein, Leipzig:
Teubner, 1907), XI, 57b (p. 132, 2-6).
      [7]S. D. McBride, "The Yoke of the Kingdom: An Exposition
of Deuteronomy 6:4-5," *Interpretation* 27 (1973) 273-306.

between the monotheistic faith in God as the Creator of all mankind, and the specific, covenantal relationship between YHWH and
his people, was resolved by means of the doctrine of election,
which received its classical formulation in the book of Deuteronomy
and in the oracles of Second Isaiah.[8]

With few exceptions, post-biblical Judaism retained the
exclusive monotheism without any compromise. A syncretistic
identification of YHWH with other gods posed a threat at the
time of radical Hellenization during the reign of Antiochus IV
Epiphanes. After the crisis had been overcome, syncretistic
theocracy (mixture of deities) was hardly more than a tangential
phenomenon at the fringes of Judaism. Nonetheless, Greek and
Jewish ideas did converge. Thus, it was *heis theos*, and not the
kyrios heis of Deut. 6:4, that became the slogan of preaching,
apologetics, and propaganda among Greek-speaking Jews.[9] Some
Jewish writers, of whom only fragments have been preserved, quoted
Greek thinkers and poets in support of their monotheistic faith,
subjecting the sentences and verses to a Jewish interpretation.
Such quotations were frequently altered, and new ones were
produced.[10] The writings of Philo of Alexandria provide ample
evidence for the degree to which it was possible to interpret and
adapt the biblical concept of God to the presuppositions of Greek
philosophy. Under these circumstances, it is not strange that
the Jewish historian Josephus can claim that the doctrine of God
set forth in the laws of Moses is in full harmony with the teaching
of the wisest among the Greeks. He found the main difference to
be that only a tiny minority of the Greeks had reached the insights
that were common to all members of the Jewish people.[11]

As Greek monotheism is oriented toward the problem of
unity and plurality, it was intimately bound up with cosmology.
To Jews like Philo and Josephus it was also a matter of course
that the one God is the God of the whole universe and of all mankind. This does not mean that they have abandoned the idea that
the Jewish nation has a peculiar relationship to God and, as a
consequence, a unique role in the world. The idea of election is,

---

[8]Deut. 4:37ff.; 14:2; Isa. 41:8; 43:10; 44:1f. Cf. my
article "Election and the People of God," in P. D. Opsahl and
M. Tanenbaum, ed., *Speaking of God Today* (Philadelphia: Fortress,
1974) 31-38.
[9]P. Dalbert, *Die Theologie der hellenistisch-jüdischen
Missions-Literatur* (Hamburg-Volksdorf: H. Reich, 1954) 124-130.
[10]On this literature, cf. A. M. Denis, *Introduction aux
pseudépigraphes grecs d'Ancien Testament* (Leiden: Brill, 1970);
E. Schürer, *The Literature of the Jewish People in the Time of
Jesus*, ed. N. N. Glatzer, (New York: Schocken, 1972) 294-302.
[11]*Against Apion*, II. 169.

however, no longer the main means of mediating between universal
monotheism and Jewish particularism.   Philo and Josephus stress
much more that Moses was a wise lawgiver who made the true doctrine
of God the basis for his legislation.   Josephus used the term
"theocracy" to describe the Jewish constitution; possibly he
coined it himself.[12]   Philo stresses, again and again, that the
Mosaic legislation corresponds to the cosmic order after which
it was modeled.[13]   Common to both is the idea that a life conducted
according to the Jewish laws is in full harmony with the order of
the universe and the moral laws of nature.   Slogans like "one
law," "one temple," "one nation," which to the pagan world
appeared as signs of intolerant exclusivity, become symbols of
the universal oneness of God.[14]

Some Rabbinic Passages

In the Greco-Roman world, even the rabbis had to deal with
the question of how the God of the whole world could be in some
special sense the God of Israel.   Drawing upon Billerbeck's
collection of material, Käsemann in his commentary on Rom. 3:29
adduces a passage from the homiletic Midrash Exodus Rabba (29)
as an example of the predominant rabbinic doctrine of God: "I
am God for all who come into the world but I have associated
my name with you alone; I am not called the God of the nations
of the world but the God of Israel."[15]   This passage can indeed
give the impression that the rabbis affirmed what Paul in Rom.
3:29f. denies, that God is only the God of the Jews and not also
the God of the Gentiles.   But the rabbis would not make that

---

[12]*Against Apion*, II. 165.
[13]On Moses as the wise lawgiver in Philo and Josephus,
see T. D. Callan, *The Law and the Mediator* (Diss., Yale, 1976),
79-130.
[14]See e.g. Philo, *Spec. leg*. I 67: "As God is one, there
should only be one sanctuary;" *Sepc. leg*. IV 159: "The best
constitution (*politeia*) and the same law and one God." Josephus,
Against Apion II. 193: "One temple for one God, common to all for
the God common to all, for what is like is always dear to everyone." Cf. also Josephus, *Ant*. IV. 200f.; Syr. Baruch 48:24; 78:4;
85:14 and, from a later period, Origen, *Against Celsus* V. 44;
Hippolytus, *Refut*. IX. 18.1, and the Pseudo-Clementine letter
from Peter to James 1:5.   Contrast Eph. 4:4-6; 1 Clem. 46:6,
etc.   Cf. M. Dibelius, "Die Christianisierungeiner hellenistischen
Formel," *Botschaft und Geschichte* (Tübingen: Mohr, 1956) II,
14-29; Peterson, 254-256.
[15]*An die Römer*, 96.   Cf. (H. L. Strack &) P. Billerbeck,
Kommentar zum Neuen Testament aus Talmud und Midrash (München:
Beck, 1922-31) III, 185.

claim any more than Philo and Josephus did. Before we proceed,
it is necessary to interpret the passage quoted and analogous
statements on the presuppositions of rabbinic Judaism.

It is first of all necessary to observe that the rabbis
treat almost all theological questions as problems of the right
interpretation of Scripture. It was a basic presupposition that
Scripture could not contradict itself, so that all apparent
contradictions had some deeper meaning.[16] Especially within the
school of Akiba it was also assumed that no single word of
Scripture was superfluous but that even apparently negligible
particles and repetitions had a special meaning. For this reason,
scholars devoted a great deal of attention to phrases that seemed
to be pleonastic or tautological. The passage which Käsemann
adduced has a parallel in Ruth Rab. 1.1 and is ascribed to R.
Shimeon b. Yohai, one of Akiba's students. It is a comment on
the double name of God in Exod. 20:2: "I am YHWH your God"
(*'ānōkî YHWH 'ĕlōhêkā*).   The same explanation is also used to
explain Ps. 50:7. This passage is more striking than Exod. 20:2,
since the same word for God is here repeated twice (*'ĕlōhîm
'ĕlōhêkā 'ānōkî*). It would seem likely that the midrash was
originally designed to interpret Ps. 50:7. In any case, it
explains the double name of God by stating that God, who as such
is the God of all mankind (*'ĕlōhîm* or *YHWH*), is at the same time
called the God of Israel (*'ĕlōhêkā*),   because he has associated
his name with Israel alone or, better, with Israel in particular
(*b y w t r*).[17] The concluding statement, "I am not called the
God of the nations of the world but the God of Israel," does not
in any way deny the universalistic monotheism which remains
axiomatic. The point is that God has given his people a special
honor by letting himself be called the God of Israel (by Scripture).
As a matter of fact, the conclusion is lacking in earlier versions,
found in tannaitic midrashim. It may well be a later, polemical
addition, directed against Christians who claimed that the God
of the Bible was their God.

In the tannaitic midrashim, Mekilta, Kaspa 4, and Sifre

---

[16]See chapter IX above.
[17]The version in Ruth Rab. Proem 1 reads: "I have not
associated (*y y ḥ d t y*) My name but with my people Israel." In
rendering this and similar statements I have, in general, followed
the translation in the Soncino Midrash Rabba (ed. H. Freedman - M.
Simon, London 1939), see vol. VIII, *Ruth*, p. 3. For the tannaitic
midrashim, I have consulted other existing translations without
feeling bound by any one of them, as I have tried to render
stereotyped phrases with some consistency.

Deuteronomy § 31, the midrash on Ps. 50:7 is preceded by an
analogous discussion of Exod. 34:23 and Deut. 6:4, or vice versa.[18]
The problem in Exod. 34:23 is the apparently repetitious phrase:
"Before the Lord YHWH, the God of Israel." The problem in Deut.
6:4 is caused by what the interpreters read as two independent
nominal clauses: "YHWH is our God" and "YHWH is one," i.e. he is
the God of Israel and at the same time the one God of the whole
world. The Mekilta draws the conclusion which we have already
encountered: "I have associated my name with Israel especially."
The variant in Sifre has a slightly different wording: "His
name was made to rest upon us (or upon Israel, or upon you)
especially." This would seem to make the presence of God's name,
i.e. of the revealed God, in Israel, the reason why he is called
the God of Israel.

Sifre § 31 adds another explanation of the two parallel
clauses in the *Shema*: "'YHWH is our God,' i.e. for us. 'YHWH
is One,' i.e. for all who come into the world. 'YHWH is our God,'
i.e. in this age. 'YHWH is One,' i.e. in the age to come, as it
is written: 'On that day YHWH will be one and his name one' (Zech.
13:9)." This passage is of special interest in that it explicitly
takes the confession *YHWH* '*eḥād* to imply the universality as
well as the exclusive oneness of God. Eschatological hope resolves
the tension between the universal and the particular components
of Jewish monotheism.

Even the Mekilta parallel includes an addition, in this
case inserted between the exegesis of Deut. 6:4 and Psalm 50:7:

> "Therefore thus says YHWH, the God of Israel."
> (2 Kings 21:12, Jer. 23:2, etc.).[19] But has it not

---

[18] I have used J. Z. Lauterbach's edition of the Mekilta
(I-III [1933-35] Philadelphia: Jewish Publication Society, 1949)
and L. Finkelstein's edition of Sifre on Deuteronomy (1939,
repr. New York: Jewish Theological Seminary, 5729/1969) 53f.
The term translated with "especially" is *b y w t r*, which is
used adverbially to express a very high degree (of attachment).
Lauterbach, III, 184f., on Kaspa 4, translates: "I have conferred
my name particularly on my people Israel," but this translation
tends to obscure the correlation between the comment and the
designation "God of Israel" (or "your God"). In the Mekilta
passage the term *b y w t r* occurs twice, but it is absent from
the comment upon Ps. 50:7, as in Ruth Rab. 1.1.

[19] Lauterbach, III, 184 (on Kaspa 4) only gives the reference
to 2 Kings 21:12, but the stereotyped formula of introduction
occurs several times in the Hebrew Bible. Most likely, a passage
from Jeremiah is meant. The later version in Midrash ha-Gadol
on Deut. 6:4 reads: "Thus says YHWH Sabaoth the God of Israel."
See S. Schechter, *Aspects of Rabbinic Theology* (1909, repr. New
York: Schocken, 1961) 63 n. 2.

> also been said: "(I am YHWH,) the God of all
> flesh" (Jer. 32:27)? What, then, does Scripture
> teach by saying: "The God of Israel"? Simply this:
> He associated his name with Israel especially.

Here the problem is not simply caused by the use of a double
designation of God, as it was in the passages we have already
discussed. The form is, rather, that of a midrash upon two
apparently contradictory passages, one asserting that YHWH is the
God of Israel, the other that he is the God of all mankind. The
solution, however, is given in the stereotyped wording that is
used throughout the catena in Mekilta Kaspa 4.

The solution is somewhat different in another series of
apparently contradictory passages, discussed in Sifre Deuteronomy
§ 40 (p. 80) on Deut. 11:12:

> "A land which YHWH your God cares for." Does he
> really care for it alone? Does he not care for all
> the lands, as it is written: "To bring rain on a land
> where no man is, . . . to satisfy the waste and desolate
> land" (Job 38:26f.). What, then, does Scripture
> teach by saying: "A land which YHWH your God cares
> for"? That he does not care but for this one, but
> because of the care with which he cares for it, he
> cares for all the lands together with it. In the same
> way, you read: "Behold, he who keeps (guards) Israel
> will neither slumber nor sleep" (Psalm 121:4). Does
> he not keep the whole universe, as it is said: "In
> his hand is the life of every living thing and the
> breath of all mankind" (Job 12:12)? What does
> Scripture teach by saying: "He who keeps Israel"?
> That he does not keep but Israel, but because of the
> keeping with which he keeps them, he keeps the universe
> together with them.

The midrash continues by contrasting 1 Kings 9:3 with Zech. 4:10b
and Prov. 15:3. The solution is analogous to the other cases:
because God's eyes and heart are in his house, they are in every
place.

The book of Jeremiah does not only call YHWH "the God of
all mankind" (*'ĕlōhê kōl bāśār*, Jer. 32:27) but also "King of
the nations" *melaek ha-gôyim*, i.e. "King of the Gentiles,"
Jer. 10:7). This latter designation is discussed in two fairly
late midrashim, in both cases in the form of a short story. One
of them occurs in the Midrash on the Psalms (93:1):

> " Who would not fear thee, O king of the nations"?
> The Holy One, blessed be he, said to Jeremiah: "You
> call me King of the nations? But am I not their
> (Israel's) king"? He said to Him: "Because thou hast
> called me prophet to the nations (Jer. 1:5), I too call
> thee King of the nations. "[20]

---

[20]Midrash Tehillim, Psalm 93.1 (ed. S. Buber, 1891, repr.
Jerusalem) tr. W. Braude, *Midrash on the Psalms*, New Haven: Yale
University Press, 1959.

Another version of the story occurs in Exodus Rabba 29.9,
a text that discusses the opening words of the Decalogue:

> "I am YHWH your God" (Exod. 20:2): It is written:
> "The lion has roared, who will not fear"? (Amos 3:8).
> This explains what is written: "Who would not fear
> thee, O King of the nations? For this is thy due."
> The prophets said to Jeremiah: "What do you mean by
> saying King of the nations? All the other prophets
> call him King of Israel, and you call him King of
> the nations." He answered them: "I heard him say
> to me: 'I appointed you a prophet to the nations'
> (Jer. 1:5), and I say: 'King of the nations.' If
> he does not spare his own children and his family,
> will he then spare others? As it is said: 'Terrible
> is God in his sanctuary'"etc. (Psalm 68:36; Jer.
> 10:7).

In this version, the point is that God, the king of the Gentile
nations, will also judge them, just as he judges his own people.

Whether they deal with pleonastic or contrasting passages,
all the texts which we have surveyed agree in affirming that God
is the God of all mankind but especially the God of Israel.
Both universalistic and particularistic statements in Scripture
are upheld as valid, and a complete congruence between Scripture
and reality is an axiom beyond discussion. Otherwise, the
explanations are open to some variation. The most common opinion
is that the God of all has given a special distinction to his
people by letting himself be called the God of Israel or by letting
his name rest upon his people. But the explanation can also be
turned the other way round: the preservation of the world is a
consequence of God's special care for Israel. Occasionally, the
conclusion is drawn that the God who judges his own people will
even more judge the other nations. But we have also encountered
the opinion that the particular relationship between God and
Israel exists in this age only; in the age to come he will manifest
his kingship and be the one God of all mankind. Whatever the
variations, there is a general consensus that God is not the God
of Israel only but also the God of the Gentile nations--and
yet there is a distinction.

Rabbinic tradition traces the methodical discussion of
apparently contradictory or pleonastic passages back to Hillel.[21]
The reliability of this tradition may be questionable, but the
name of Hillel remains in any case a symbol for a type of exegetical
research which originated among Jewish sages during the last century
before the destruction of Jerusalem in 70 C.E. The earliest
examples of such discussions do, however, deal with halakic

----

[21]See chapter IX above, pp. 162-164.

antinomies. It would seem that it was only after the reconstruction
of the rabbinic academies after 70 C.E. that the form became
stereotyped and was also used in discussions of haggadic questions,
including problems of theology. Yet, already at the time of Paul,
the problem of God's relationship to mankind in general and to
Israel in particular must have existed, even if the stereotyped
forms for discussing it did not.

A passage from the Mekilta on the Song of Moses may serve
to illustrate that the rabbis could discuss the problem without
referring to any specific passage in support of their universal
monotheism. The passage is a comment on Exod. 15:2:

> "YHWH is my strength and my salvation." Thou art
> a helper and supporter of all who come into the world
> but of me especially. "And my song is YHWH": Thou
> art the subject of song to all who come into the world
> but to me especially. He has proclaimed me of special
> distinction (*' m y r h*) and I have proclaimed him of
> special distinction . . . (Deut. 26:18 and 17). But
> behold, all the nations of the world declare the praise
> of him by whose word the world came into being! Mine,
> however, is more pleasing (*n ' y m*), as it is said:
> "But sweet (*n ' y m*) are the songs of Israel" (2 Sam.
> 23:1).[22]

The impact of Greek philosophy is much less obvious in
rabbinic writings than in Philo and Josephus. Yet, an apologetic
note is discernible in the attempt to show that the concepts of
election and covenant do not contradict universal monotheism.
The rabbis could also defend the impartial justice of God by
other means, e.g. by the concept of the noachic commandments
which the Gentiles have failed to observe.[23] Of special importance
was the idea that God had offered the Torah to all nations but that
only Israel had accepted it.[24]

Whereas Philo and Josephus thought of Moses as the wise
lawgiver who had modeled the constitution (*politeia*) of the Jews
upon that of the universe, the rabbis identified the revealed
Torah with the hypostatized Wisdom of God and thus with the beginning

---

[22]Shirata (or Shirta) 3, Lauterbach II, 23f. See also
translation and comments in J. Goldin, *The Song at the Sea* (New
Haven: Yale University Press, 1971) 109-111. The midrash continues
by quoting other pairs of passages that illustrate the mutual
relationship between God and Israel: Deut. 6:4 and 1 Chron. 17:21;
Exod. 15:11 and Deut. 33:29; Deut. 4:7 and 8; Psalm 89:18 and
Isa. 49:3.

[23]Tos. Abod. Zar. 8:4,6; B. T. Sanh. 56b; Sifre Deut. 343
on Deut. 33:2. Cf. Billerbeck, III, 36-38, 41f.

[24]See e.g. Mek. Bahodesh 5 on Exod. 20:2; Sifre Deut. 343
on Deut. 33:2. Cf. Billerbeck, III, 38-41, and e.g. S. Aalen, *Die
Begriffe 'Licht' und 'Finsternis' im Alten Testament, Spätjudentum
und Rabbinismus* (Oslo: Norske Videnskapsakademi, 1951) 295f.

and principle of creation, with the cosmic world order itself.[25]
When the rabbis stressed that the one God of all was in a special
sense the God of Israel, they did not at all intend to separate
God's saving action from his universal activity as the Creator
and Judge of all mankind.[26] Their idea was, quite to the contrary,
that God had acted as Creator and Judge when he gave the Torah to
Israel, thereby claiming the world for himself, establishing
his kingship and his law and order in the world which he had
created. Accordingly, Israel's acceptance of the Torah was an
event of cosmic significance. The righteous man (the ṣaddî̂k),
who observes the commandments of the Torah, does not only care
for his own salvation; he upholds the world.[27]

It is within this general context that we have to understand the rabbinic statements about the God of Israel who is also
the God of the whole world, including the Gentile nations. Israel
has received a mark of distinction, God being called her God,
because it is by means of the Torah that God vindicates himself
and his salvation, manifesting that he is the Creator and the
Judge of the whole world. Only if we understand the rabbinic
doctrine of God on its own premises does it become clear in what
sense Paul turns against it "with unheard of boldness."[28]

Concluding Comments on Rom. 3:29-30

The series of short questions and answers in Rom. 3:27-31
(and 4:1-3) are typical of what is generally regarded as diatribe
style.[29] A somewhat similar dialogical style also occurs in
rabbinic midrashim, as illustrated by passages quoted earlier in
this chapter, some of which were formal as well as material parallels

---

[25]See e.g. W. D. Davies, *Paul and Rabbinic Judaism*, 165-
172; Aalen, 175-178, 183-195, 262-265, 272-279, 289; J. Jervell,
Imago Dei (Göttingen: Vandenhoeck & Ruprecht, 1960) esp. 114-119.
Cf. also my critical reviews of the books of Aalen and Jervell
in *NovTT* 53 (1952) 61-84, and *NovTT* 61 (1960) esp. 87-90.
[26]Commenting upon the passages from Exod. Rab. 29, Käsemann
writes: "On the basis of the concept of the covenant, the saving
action of God is here separated from the work of the Creator and
Judge, as was indeed later (sic!) the case in Marcion's doctrine"
(*An die Römer*, 96, my translation). This is a distortion.
[27]Cf. e.g. Aalen, 282-289; R. Mach, *Der Zaddik in Talmud
und Midrash* (Leiden: Brill, 1957).
[28]"In unerhörter Kühnheit," *An die Römer*, 96.
[29]The definition of diatribe has proved to cause difficulties.
Stan Stowers, a graduate student at Yale, is preparing a fresh
investigation, with special attention to dialogical style in Romans.

to Rom. 3:28f., with the difference that the rabbinic texts included
explicit quotations from the Bible. Considering the dates of the
sources, we would do better not to assume that Paul made a creative
use of the stereotyped rabbinic pattern. If there is more than a
general similarity of style and content, the Pauline form, without
quotations, is more likely to be an antecedent of the more elaborate
rabbinic form than vice versa.[30]

In our context it is not necessary to pursue the question
of Greek and of possible Jewish affiliations of the dialogical
style in Rom. 3:27ff. It is more important to observe that not
all of the direct questions are of the same nature. Some of them
raise problems or objections (3:27 and 31), possibly attributed
to an imaginary discussion partner (thus 3:31a, cf. 2:17). In
Rom. 3:29, by contrast, Paul uses direct rhetorical questions to
advance his own argument, in order to convince his dialogue partner
and his audience: "Or is God (the God) of the Jews only? Is he
not (the God) of the Gentiles also?" The answers are obvious.
No Jew or Jewish Christian would deny that God, being one, is not
only the God of the Jews but also the God of the Gentiles. The
discussion partners agree in upholding a universal monotheism,
as they also agree that salvation is effectuated by the grace of
God (*sola gratia*).[31] Paul's "unheard of boldness" emerges only in
the appended, attributive relative clause in 3:30: the one God
is the one "who will justify the circumcised on the ground of
their faith (*ek pisteōs*) and the uncircumcised through their
faith (*dia tēs pisteōs*)." This means that, just as with respect
to sin, there is no distinction with respect to salvation (see
Rom. 3:22-23).

Within the context, Paul's reflection upon the oneness of
God serves to support his doctrinal thesis that a human being--Jew
or Greek--is justified by faith apart from works of the Law (Rom.
3:28). Paul has formulated this thesis as a summary of his
interpretation of the gospel concerning Jesus Christ, the Son of
God (see esp. 1:1-6, 16-17, and 3:21-26). His chief warrants he
draws from the Old Testament (see esp. 3:21 and 4:1-25). By
comparison, the argument from the oneness of God adds a secondary,

---

[30] If so, the development of the form would be analogous
to that of enumeration of biblical examples, in which proof-texts
are a "secondary and changeable part of the pattern." See W. S.
Towner, *The Rabbinic "Enumeration of Scriptural Examples,"* (Leiden:
Brill, 1973) 248f. etc.

[31] Cf. Käsemann, *An die Römer*, 23: "Im sola gratia sind
die Gegner sich einig" (the adversaries agree in [justification by]
grace alone).

more general and almost rational support: justification by faith,
without any distinction between Jew and Greek, is in full harmony
with the universal monotheism which the Jew also professes, but
the radical consequence of which he fails to draw.

In drawing the consequence that radical monotheism excludes
any distinction, Paul shows some affinity with Greek philosophical
monotheism, which was universalistic and more or less cosmopolitan.
Since Xenophanes, it could include polemic against religious
particularism. Paul would seem to draw upon this tradition,
whether he was conscious of it or not. Yet, he has given a very
special twist to the ideas of the philosophers. In that respect,
his remarks in Rom. 3:29-30 are similar to earlier passages in
the letter.

In Rom. 1:19ff.; 2:14-15, 25-29 Paul makes use of ideas
concerning a natural knowledge of God and of moral values and
stresses the contrast between appearance and inner reality. Such
ideas can be traced back to Greek philosophy.[32] Probably they
were mediated to Paul by a Hellenized Judaism which used them for
apologetic purposes, in order to prove that Jewish monotheism and
the Jewish way of life were in full harmony with the insights
of the best among the Greeks.[33] Paul reverses the perspective
and uses the ideas polemically, in order to demonstrate that
possession of the Mosaic Law does not make any fundamental
difference.

Something very similar goes on in Rom. 3:29-30. Hellenized
Jews had made an apologetic use of universalistic Greek monotheism,
in order to prove the excellency of the Mosaic legislation and
of the Jewish nation.[34] To the rabbis, the confession of the One,
who alone is God, implied willingness to observe his commandments.
Paul, on the contrary, gives a polemical twist to the monotheistic
confession, turning it against the Jew who relies on the Law and
boasts of his special relation to God. The oneness of God, the
sovereign Creator of all, is demonstrated by the impartiality of
his judgment and of his grace upon Jews and Greeks without any
distinction. In the Pauline perspective, monotheism has become

---

[32]Cf. Käsemann's commentary on the passages, with biblio-
graphies. Esp. G. Bornkamm, "The Revelation of God's Wrath,"
(1935) in *Early Christian Experience* (New York: Harper & Row,
1969, tr. P. L. Hammer), 47-70; A. Fridrichsen, "Der wahre Jude
und sein Lob. Röm. 2,28f.", *Symbolae Arctoae* (*Osloenses*), 1 (1927),
39-49.

[33]See e.g. Bornkamm, 52-53 and my book, *Das Volk Gottes*
(1941, repr. Darmstadt: Wissenschaftliche Buchgesellschaft, 1963),
72-73, 95-104, 109-119.

[34]See e.g. Philo, *Spec. leg.* II 164-166; Josephus, *Against
Apion*, II. 165-192.

a warrant for the doctrine of justification, just as the recognition that all men are sinners, and that righteousness and glory belong to God alone, has become a criterion of genuine faith in the one God.

Ernst Käsemann has for good reasons stressed that Paul's doctrine of justification is a consequence of his Christology, and that Paul maintains the sovereignty of the Creator. But he seems to have failed to break radically with the common but simplistic notion of a contrast between Christian unversalism and Jewish particularism. Jewish monotheism at the time of Paul was universalistic in its own way, and Christian monotheism remained exclusive. The condemnation of idolatry is an evidence of that (see e.g. Rom. 1:18ff.). We would come closer to the truth by saying that both Jewish and Christian monotheism are particular as well as universal, specific as well as general. Paul's objections to the Jewish doctrines of God and of salvation are due to his faith in the crucified Christ. To Paul, it was not by giving the Torah at Sinai but by sending Jesus and raising him from the dead that God proved to be the Creator and Judge who claims the whole world for himself. The shift of the specific focus meant also that the universal aspect of biblical monotheism took on a new character. The universal law and order, embodied in the Torah, has been replaced by the universality of God's judgment, grace, and righteousness, revealed in the gospel for men and women who are all sinners, without any distinction.

The rabbis held that there was a distinction, but would not deny that God is the God of Gentiles also. Paul argues that there is no distinction but does not deny that God has associated himself especially with Israel, the people to whom he gave his promises. But when he elaborates on the privileges which God has granted to Israel, Paul does it in a very special way. Even when he brings salvation to his own people, God acts as he always does, justifying the ungodly and making the dead alive. That is how he is the one God of Jews and Gentiles.

196